SUCCESSFUL SCHOOL EDUCATION

Books by Marlow Ediger and D. Bhaskara Rao Published by Discovery Publishing House

Science Curriculum

Philosophy and Curriculum

Psychology and Curriculum

Elementary Curriculum

Improving School Administration

School Curriculum and Administration

Language Arts Curriculum

Elementary Curriculum Improvement

Relevancy in Elementary Curriculum

Quality School Education

Successful School Education

Successful School Administration

Issues in School Curriculum

Teaching Science Successfully

Teaching Mathematics Successfully

Teaching Social Studies Successfully

Teaching Language Arts Successfully

Teaching English Successfully

Teaching Mathematics in Elementary Schools

Teaching Science in Elementary Schools

SUCCESSFUL
SCHOOL EDUCATIC

By

Dr. Marlow Ediger

Professor Emeritus
Division of Education
Truman State University
P.O. Box 417, 201 W, 22nd St
North Newton KS67117
United States of America

Dr. Digumarti Bhaskara Rao

M.Sc., M.A., M.A., M.Ed., Ph.D.
Reader
R.V.R. College of Education
Srinivasa Nagar Colony
Guntur–522 006
&
Member
Board of Studies in Education
Acharya Nagarjuna University
Nagarjuna Nagar, A.P.
(India)

DISCOVERY PUBLISHING HOUSE
NEW DELHI-110002

First Published - 2006

Reprinted - 2018

ISBN: 978-81-8356-054-2

Successful School Education

Published by:

DISCOVERY PUBLISHING HOUSE PVT. LTD.
4383/4B, Ansari Road, Darya Ganj
New Delhi-110 002 (India)
Phone: +91-11-23279245, 43596064-65
Fax: +91-11-23253475
E-mail: discoverypublishinghouse@gmail.com
sales@discoverypublishinggroup.com
web: www.discoverypublishinggroup.com

Printed at:
Infinity Imaging Systems
Delhi

Dedicated

to

The Doyen of Teacher Education

Prof. Ramesh Ghanta

Dean, Faculty of Education

Kakatiya University

Warangal, Andhra Pradesh

Preface

School education is the crucial component of any nation's education system. It need due encouragement from all concerned for its success. This book on successful school education discusses several aspects of successful school education and is useful to the people and personnel associated with school education.

Author

Contents

Preface

1.	The Administrator as an Instructional Leader	1
2.	School Climate and Learning	8
3.	Objectives, Learning Activities and Assessment	15
4.	Statewide Testing and the Innovative Mind	20
5.	Who Should Determine the Curriculum?	28
6.	Sequence and Scope in the Curriculum	36
7.	Content in the Curriculum	40
8.	Curriculum Changes and Improvement	46
9.	Issues in Organising the Curriculum	57
10.	Subject-Centred Versus an Activity-Centred Curriculum	62
11.	Step by Step Teaching Versus an Open Ended Approach	65
12.	Adjusting the Curriculum to the Learner Versus Adjusting the Learner to the Curriculum	74
13.	The Basics in the Curriculum and Moral Development of Learners	81
14.	Quality in the Multicultural Curriculum Excellence and Equity	86
15.	Reading and Recent Educational Philosophies	94

16. Increasing High School Reading Comprehension 105
17. Read Alouds for Students 112
18. Reading in Health Education 119
19. Analysing the Goals of the National Reading Panel 129
20. Student Motivation in Reading 135
21. Homogeneous and Heterogeneous Grouping in Reading Instruction 143
22. The Middle School 148
23. Increasing Listening Comprehension 154
24. Quality and Quantity in the Mathematics Curriculum 162
25. Recent Trends in the Mathematics Curriculum 170
26. Psychology in Teaching Mathematics 180
27. Science Learning and the Student 187
28. Guidelines for Teaching Science 192
29. Sequence of Learning in the Science Curriculum 201
30. Organising the Social Studies Curriculum 205
31. Challenging All Students in the Social Studies 209
32. Teaching History in the Classroom 217
33. The Psychology of Learning and Adult Education 226
34. Evaluation and the Psychology of Learning 231
35. Promoting Oral Communication Experiences 235
36. Cooperative Learning Versus Competition Which is Better? 244
37. Decision-making on Which Level? 254
38. An Analysis of Teacher Education Online 260
39. Philosophy of Kindergarten Education 269

Additional Reading 278

Index 299

1

The Administrator as an Instructional Leader

School administrators have diverse responsibilities. A major responsibility should be to improve the curriculum. Students need to experience the best in objectives, learning activities, and appraisal procedures. Learners deserve the right to achieve optimally. Human beings have much worth and need to attain in an optimal manner in personal and social development. Each person needs to develop fully as an individual. Individuals need to achieve vital understandings (facts, concepts, and generalisations), skills (listening, speaking, reading, writing, and thinking), and attitudes (values, beliefs, and feelings). Persons also interact with others in society. Developing social skills then also becomes important. Each is a member of the societal arena.

Issues in Instructional Leadership

There are numerous issues involved in the concept of administration and curriculum development. One issues pertains to the extent or scope of administrators working in improving the teaching-learning situations. Thus, the school administrator could play a minor role as compared to a very extensive role in achieving an improved curriculum.

A second issue involving administrators and the school curriculum emphasises which facets need to be diagnosed and remediated or changed. There are numerous curriculum areas. Within a specific curriculum area, there also are many points of intervention and modification. Careful consideration needs to be given in evaluating which area(s) of the curriculum need to be changed from what is to what should be. Quality leadership is needed to modifying the curriculum.

A third issue involves which philosophy or philosophies to emphasise in teaching-learning situations. Experimentalism stresses a problem solving philosophy. The school administrator together with faculty members, need to identify curricular problems. Data must then be gathered in answer to the problem. A hypothesis or answer to the problem(s) should result. The hypothesis is tentative and subject to testing. After being tested the hypothesis is accepted modified or refuted.

Realism, as the philosophy of education, emphasises the use of measurably stated objectives in teaching students. Realists also advocate management by objectives (MBO) for administrators in achieving a quality curriculum.

Idealism advocates an idca centred curriculum. Textbooks, workbooks, and worksheets may provide major learnings for students to attain subject matter. Audio-visual aids, as learning opportunities, are good to the point that students achieve salient vital facts, concepts and generalisations.

Existentialists advocate individuals learn to make personal choices and decisions. Whether it be students, faculty members, or school administrators, decision making skills are needed, according to existentialists. Each person must accept responsibility for decisions made. A learning centre philosophy and/or teacher-student planning is then important in the curriculum.

Each of the four above named philosophies differs much from the other. An issue then remains as to which school of thought administrators need to follow and which curricular decisions are to be made. A fourth issue in school administration pertains to which psychology of learning should be emphasised in the curriculum. Behaviourism, as a psychology of learning, stresses the use of programmed learning. Small amounts of subject matter are learned before students respond to a test item. Feedback is given to students after each response made. Programmed learning can be emphasised in textbook form or software for computer use. Other forms of behaviourism include instructional management systems (IMS) and mastery learning. Each of these methods of teaching stresses the use of precise, measurably stated objectives.

Somewhat toward the other end of the continum is humanism, as a philosophy of learning. Humanists emphasise student input in selecting objectives, learning activities, and evaluation procedures. Teacher-student planning, as well as the utilisation of learning centres, further stresses tenets of humanism. Students then need to learn the art of decision-making.

Additional psychologies of learning include Jean Plaget's developmental psychology and Jerome Bruner's recommendations of using inductive procedures in teaching students. An issue for school administrators then exists pertaining to which psychology or psychologies to emphasise in teaching-learning situations.

A fifth issue for school administrators pertains to how much emphasis should be placed upon staff development of teachers. A comprehensive, systematic approach may be utilised here. A definite scope and sequence is involved in conducting inservice education programmes. Toward the other end of the spectrum, school administrators may place limited emphasis on staff development or delegate responsibilities in this area to other instructional leaders, such as a curriculum director or teacher mentors.

The Role of an Instructional Leader

School administrators as leaders in improving the curriculum must be able to work effectively with faculty members. A domineering leader cannot generally win the support of teachers and other workers in the school setting. Nor can an administrator be effective who avoids problems which need solving in the curriculum. These are two extremes which need to be avoided.

School administrators are models for others to emulate. This model emphasises being highly knowledgeable about trends and issues in the curriculum. Enthusiasm for curriculum development is reflected within teachers. Enthusiastic principals and superintendents desire to discuss and reflect upon ideas in education with teachers.

The model of the school administrator also emphasises definite attitudes of acceptance, respect, and tolerance. Teachers feel free to voice their opinions pertaining to recommendations, issues, and opinions in education. The administrator collaborates with teachers in developing the best of objectives, learning activities, and appraisal procedures. Trust between and among teachers and the principle of superintendent is definitely in evidence. Teachers feel they can come to the school administrator with their problems and anxieties to receive needed understanding and assistance.

The school administrator needs to be skillful in using techniques of inservice education to bring about positive changes in the curriculum. Inservice education programmes too frequently are unsuccessful. Why? Teachers may perceive little or no purpose in their implementation. Topics pursued in these kinds of inservice programmes lack relevance for the classroom teacher. The dynamics and vitality of inservice education are lacking. Principals and superintendents rather need to work in the direction of inservice programmes which promote purpose and meaning. Teachers need to perceive inservice education as a means of becoming better instructors. Utilitarian motives must be perceived by the teachers in attending inservice education programmes. What is learned here can be applied in teaching-learning situations. The role of the instructional leader in inservice education is to assist teachers to perceive value in diverse kinds and programmes of inservice education.

Problems in Teaching-Learning Situations

To improve the curriculum, school administrators need to identify and solve problems pertaining to the classroom/school setting. Which problems then need identification and solutions?

Students achieve poorly in school due to a high absentee rate. Sequence is lacking then in understandings, skills, and attitudes acquired by the student. Teachers and administrators must work with parents to assist the latter to have their offspring attend school regularly. Parents need to be guided to see what happens to the student as a result of absenteeism. Understandings, skills, and attitudes are sequential. Breaks in the sequence accrue with absences by the student. Students who are ill or cannot attend school need homebound instruction. Quality is a key word to emphasise in teaching students in the home setting by qualified teachers.

Tardiness also hinders student progress in school. Tardy students disrupt the classroom when they enter late. Vital tasks and experiences are omitted from the learner's experiences in situations such as these.

High rates of absenteeism and tardiness can make for future dropouts from school. When there is no apparent reason for a student being absent or tardy, problems, no doubt, will increase for these individuals. A potential dropout has little cause to be optimistic about the future.

A student who attends school may not perceive purpose in completing the high school years. Physically, but not emotionally and intellectually, the student is in school. Perhaps, these students are waiting for the day to drop out of school

School administrators need to be leaders to assist in developing a quality curriculum for those who cannot perceive value(s) in school attendance.

Other students who are at risk may achieve at an average and somewhat below average level of attainment, but feel it is important rather to earn money. Income from a job competes with the desire to achieve well in school. Ultimately, with heavy expenses, such as owning a car, the student decides to drop out of school and work full time. School attendance then competes with earning money. The latter ultimately has more purpose for the high school student. These students need identification, prior to dropping out of school. Objectives, learning activities, and appraisal procedures must be selected which aid the potential dropout to perceive schooling as being more important, as compared to earning money.

Pregnant teenage girls are becoming increasingly larger in number. Selected specialists state teenage pregnancy as being epidemic. Secondary school principals and superintendents need to take leadership roles in providing learning opportunities for these students. These activities assist in emphasising the holding power of the school. The holding power, however, must emphasise a relevant curriculum, which assists pregnant teenagers to complete high school diploma requirements. Individual differences need to be provided for. All teenage pregnant girls need to attain as much as possible.

At risk students can include the gifted and talented. Too many of these students are not challenged in the school curriculum. The gifted and talented may then drop out of school. These situations are costly and expensive. A nation and a society lose out when the skills and abilities of the talented and gifted are not utilised. These individuals tend to take the lead in governmental positions, in industry and in the professions. Each school system must identify the gifted and talented. A curriculum for the gifted and talented must be in evidence which assists to achieve optimally.

Students with drug abuse problems need appropriate guidance and counselling services. These students must be referred to specialised services when needed. Critical situations and moments are involved when students involved in drug abuse are left to cope for themselves. Lives, talents, skills and persons are lost when students with drug abuse problems are left alone with little or no assistance given by teachers, administrators, counsellors, and the helping professions. Each person has worth and must be given assistance to achieve as well as possible.

Students who lack status or feel a lack of belonging within a group or class need attention. These students need assistance to work well with others. Carefully selected committees comprised of learners highly accepting of others can be a good starting point for an isolate or one who is on the verge of being an isolate. The student who lacks feelings of status should be asked to provide ideas or materials in which he/she excels. Most students have a skill that can be shared with others. Perhaps, a hobby or interest can be shared with others in the class setting. This is a way for the student to feel status and prestige. Perhaps, at the same time, this same student can develop feelings of belonging to a group or committee.

Certainly, school administrators need to assist teachers to guide each student to achieve well be they handicapped, average achievers, or talented and gifted. Human beings are a nation's most prized entities. Each needs to achieve as much as abilities permit to attain optimally in understandings, skills, and attitudinal goals.

Summary

The school administrator, as an instructional leader, has vital, salient, relevant responsibilities. These responsibilities include:

1. Resolving issues in leadership roles and responsibilities;
2. Revealing appropriate roles to be an effective leader in instructional improvement;
3. Emphasising problem solving skills in curriculum development.

Principals and superintendents need to assist teachers to stress the following in teaching-learning situations:

1. Learning activities should be meaningful to students;
2. Learners need to perceive purpose in ongoing lessons and units;
3. Students should experience interest in the curriculum;
4. Individual differences among learners need adequate provision.

REFERENCES

Knezevich, Stephen J. *Administration of Public Education*. Fourth Edition. New York: Harper & Row, Publishers, 1984.

Krajewski, Robert J., et.al. *The Elementary Principalship*. New York: Holt, Rinehart and Winston, 1983.

Roe, William H., and Thelbert H. Drake. *The Principalship*. Second Edition. New York: Macmillan Publishing Company, 1980.

Snyder, Karolyn J., and Robert H. Anderson. *Managing Productive Schools* London: Academic Press, 1986.

Wood, Charles, et. al. *The Secondary School Principal*. Boston: Allyn and Bacon, Inc., 1979.

2

School Climate and Learning

Teachers and supervisors need to spend a considerable amount of time in providing school climate. With an improved school climate, pupils should learn more than previously. A climate which is conductive to optimising learner achievement is a must! A negative school climate hinders pupils from achieving and may well also develop inappropriate attitudes. The writer has long felt that a negative school environment makes for lower state mandated test scores and all around lower achievement in the classroom.

Classroom Attitudes

The classroom setting and its environment needs to be assessed continuously to identify and weed out that which hinders learner progress. Rudeness, for example, makes for undesirable learning situations. People in society, have known for a long time that rudeness is an inappropriate way of behaving and yet it is frequently observed in checkout lines, restaurants, as well as in churches. Somehow, the message does not get across that politeness in behaviour is a much more pleasant way of human interaction as compared to rudeness. To have to interact with others in school endeavours involving rudeness is indeed very unpleasant and hinders achievement. That might be a salient reason for absenteeism when a polite person is required to do a school project with one or more rude persons in close contact. The polite person may fear to interact with his/her suggestions when the result are rude responses. Teachers may not desire to correct the behaviour of rudeness. The child is the victim in these situations. Attending school then becomes a situation to avoid.

A second kind of negative behaviour is intimidation. The intimidator attempts to get away with frightening another pupil by having friends nearby to support the unpleasant deeds. Perhaps, the only friends the perpetrator has are those involved in helping to intimidate others. It is a very unpleasant situation for the one who experiences the intimidation. The perpetrators may do the unpleasant to a pupil when no one else is nearby. The support system for the pleasant pupil is completely lacking. There may be feelings of no one else being there to turn to for offering some kind of help. The intimidators may enjoy harming of their targets. Too frequently, teachers shy away from those doing the intimidating, fearing that classroom interruptions may occur later if attempted corrections are made involving the intimidators (Ediger and Rao (2003 Chapter Six).

Bullying, a third kind of negative behaviour, tends to occur on the playground largely. The bully desires to lord to over others. The bully may be quite strong physically and is able to force others to do what he/she wants. Pupils tend to fear bullies and give in to what is wanted. Then, too, it is very difficult to get out of the way of bullies. Bullies know which targets are easy to use. Selected bullies may like to obtain hush money from the meek. The bully will harm a child if the latter does not pay money in order to avoid being harmed physically, such as being punched until it hurts. Sometimes, the "marks" become obtrusive when kicking the shins is being emphasised. The shins might become quite blue if pay offs are not received in time.

A pupil's lunch money may be "stolen" if he/she does not make pay offs in due time. If the stealer has a friend or two to assist in the "stealing", he is able to commit the action quicker. A threat is added "not to tell anyone". Children who give the hush money to the perpetrator feel very threatened and at all costs avoid telling his/her parents of what is happening. Dreadful consequences have occurred if a child has told a close friend of what has transpired with the intent of getting hush money perpetrators caught. Some times the chain of events has been stopped in which the perpetrator has been caught and punished. There is a solid base of support here for victims who tell the right people of hush money being obtained, with threats to be given to those who squeal. Sophisticated approaches are used to extract money under duress from vulnerable individuals. The vulnerable individual, even a grown person of seventeen years of age, may fear to tell parents or other responsible persons of the agony of never eating school lunches. The student has been duly warned of not eating home packed lunches!

Additional harmful approaches used by pupils to deal negatively with each other include the following:

- *The put down.* Highly embarrassing means are use to put an individual in his/her "proper place". The taunts used by the offender "cut deep" into the one being offended. The taunts are highly offensive and the receiver does not wish to hear of these offensive statements. Adults who use the put down and are skilled in doing so use highly offensive statements and if the receiver shows any resentment is asked, "Can't you enjoy a good joke?" The put down is used to even make the perpetrator look good.
- *To egg the next person or persons on.* Two boys may have a disagreement. Each side is egged on to throw the first punch. By this time, a small crowd has gathered and no teacher or supervisor is there to stop the fighting. The blows can become quite vicious. Neither boy is likely to back down from fighting. Both have become victims to the shouts off encouragement of the bystanders. Bruises and cuts began to be seen on one or both of the fighters. The involved boys are the victims in this embarrassing event from which no one wins but both lose, and may lose heavily. The cheering crowd has egged the two boys on to do foolish things which are harmful to both. The next engagement may be easier to encourage. "Cowards" tend not to be liked. A wise peacemaker is difficult to locate within the crowd. Hopefully, an adult will come very soon to break up the fighting or the combatants will pretend to be brave and merely fake wanting to fight.

There are definite things which may be emphasised to minimise rudeness, intimidation, bullying, the put down, and the egg on. A charismatic teacher may be able to demonstrate the detrimental effects of using these approaches to in dealing with others. He/she might also be able to model correct behaviour in dealing with others in a positive manner. A quality learning environment is needed for pupils to do well academically and socially. Something needs to be in the offing to take the place of rudeness as well as curb intimidating behaviours. Objectives, too, need to be decided upon to minimise the "put down" and the "egg on". Within each lesson and unit of study taught, clearly stated objectives need continual emphasis to curtail undesirable behaviours. Teachers need to search for an review the educational literature pertaining to the identified forms of pupil misbehaviour. A professional library for teachers in the school setting as well a university teacher education library should provide needed information in solving identified problems. The research done provides learning opportunities for teachers and for pupils to achieve objectives. Materials for pupils need to be adapted to their own unique levels of achievement. Additional learning opportunities to achieve objectives include films, filmstrips, slides, video tapes, video disks, DVDs. These assist learners in attaining objectives. Objectives should emphasise knowledge, skills, and attitudes ends on rudeness, intimidation, bullying, the put down, and the egg on (Ediger and Rao, 2003, Chapter Eight).

In utilising materials of instruction, the teacher needs to make learnings interesting, purposeful, and meaningful so that it makes sense to learners. Additional standards of teaching to use in implementing the curriculum include:

- Providing for individual differences so that all may benefit optimally from the curriculum;
- Emphasising reasons for learning so that wholehearted involvement by learners is possible;
- Maximise pupil active involvement in learning, not passive receptivity.

Evaluation to Measure Achievement

Videos may be made to ascertain if rudeness is present during a discussion. The point of rudeness in the playback need to be pinpoint and the statements made by the perpetrator need to be corrected to eliminate the undesirable. Proper ways of saying things may be stressed to replace the undesirable. Recording of discussions may be made rather continuously to notice deficiencies of rudeness and remediation made. Different ways need to be shown on intimidating others. Sometimes, the pupil does not realise he/she intimidates others. Selected dramatisations may make this clear. Intimidating is a subtle way of embarrassing and making others do what the perpetrator wants him/her to do.

Bullying is an overt way of forcing a person to do that which the perpetrator wants him/her to do. The language used, the force demonstrated, and the verbal/non-verbal cues used make bullying relatively easy to identify.

The egg on is easy to emphasise in drama form. For example, several boys may disagree on a path of action. The disagreement gets louder until the fists are to be used. The role play should indicate this with the onlookers encouraging the using of fists. The boys are called cowards if they do not show their bravery. The situation should be life like and real, but involve a perfectly safe atmosphere.

In the classroom and school lunchroom, pupils may assist in helping to determine when a put down occurs. Appropriate ways of saying things may be emphasised in place of the put down. Individuals need to be careful in refraining from put down use due to its embarrassing intentions. There should be discussions on how the person feels who received the put down. It is harmful to both—the one putting someone else down as well as the victim of the put down. The former may lack friends in many cases and is one to be avoided. The victim develops feelings of revenge and hostility even though he/she may fear to retaliate. The egg on needs to notice the damage that may accrue from getting others to join in on the fight. When both sides are eagerly involved due to the cheering, the results may be emotionally and physically damaging.

For each of the five cases in being the victim discussed above, it is appropriate for the perpetrator to know how extreme the feelings of insecurity are on the part of the victim. The victim then has:

- fears of being alone with no help available;
- fears of being harmed physically;
- fears of not living down the embarrassment and ugly perceptions held by the onlookers;
- fears of having no friends;
- fears of having to face the taunts and injustices of others continuously;
- fears of disliking the self for not being able to defend the self;
- fears of being left *alone* with no one to assist or protect the self.

There are problems inherent in democratic living as well as when participating in society. Thus, there will be reservations in interacting with others in the societal arena for the good of society. A democratic society encourages:

- each person to participate in decision making responsibilities;
- each person to have a wholesome attitude toward the thinking of others;
- each person to take part in identifying and solving problems;
- each person to be accepting of others;
- each person to have his/her ideas accepted by others;
- each person to do his/her share of work in society.

A democratic society does not emphasise letting a few people make the decisions and do all the work to improve society. All are to be involved.

"The kids at a suburban St. Louis school used to tease each other and keep students out of their exclusive cliques, but now that can be seen chatting at breakfast and helping other with their homework.

Principal Karen Smith credits character education with making the difference. The practice which involves kids getting kids to care more about their school and each other, seems to be working—and not only at Smith's Mark Twain Elementary School in Brentwood.

A study of school based character education programmes across the nation indicates the effort can work to improve attitudes toward elders while reducing violence, drug use, and risky sexual behaviour. What's more, the programmes can help pupils get better grades...The study found some of the most effective techniques included peer interaction and training directed at a specific skill, such as anger management and conflict resolution. The programmes are also more effective when teachers and staff receive training, according to the study (Latze, 2003).

REFERENCES

Ediger, Marlow and D. Bhaskara Rao (2003) *The Elementary Curriculum*. New Delhi, India: Discovery Publishing House, Chapter Six.

—(2003), *Philosophy and the Curriculum*, New Delhi, India: Discovery Publishing House, Chapter Eight.

Latze, Jeff (2003), *Study Suggests Character Education*, Boosts Academics, Too", Kirksville, Missouri Daily Express, p. 2.

3

Objectives, Learning Activities, and Assessment

Which is most important in teaching—objectives, learning activities, or assessment procedures? Perhaps, the reader will say they all are important, and they definitely are. There is an interrelationship between the objectives and learning activities. The learning activities are there for students to achieve the stated objectives. The assessment procedures have as their role to evaluate if the objectives have been achieved. But, the writer feels that major attention in educational manuscripts and speeches at conventions is focused on assessment. Thus, state mandated assessment and the National Assessment of Educational Progress focuses upon test scores and results. With state mandated testing, the emphasis is upon:

1. testing students in grades three through eight and grade ten;
2. the number of schools which will be in the "needs improvement" category;
3. the number of students who fail the graded standards;
4. the number of students from "needs improvement" school who will be able to transfer to satisfactory schools which have met state standards;
5. the elimination of social promotion.

Should more attention be paid to the objectives of state mandated tests and/or learning activities?

State Mandated Objectives

Much attention should be given to the quality of state mandated objectives. Each objective needs careful consideration in having much worth. This is a highly salient task. Many terms have been given to salient objectives such as being relevant, important, significant, and being meaningful. When an entire state chooses its final objectives, careful consideration needs to be given to the overall importance of its goals for all school districts within its borders. Presently, only reading and mathematics are being tested in terms of student achievement. In 2007, science will be added as an academic area for student testing. The areas covered in a state mandated test will, no doubt, receive the most instructional time. Many educational articles have been written lamenting the excessive instructional time spent on what will be tested and that being reading and mathematics. Is this adequate when considering the scope of the curriculum?

Objectives for mandation should cover the scope of what is taught in the public schools within a state. This should then cover content in basal texts used in teaching, different syllabi for a grade level being taught in diverse schools, and recommended psychologies of instruction in reading and in mathematics. Scrutiny of objectives needs to be continuous and ongoing. Emphasis must be placed upon relevancy of subject matter in objectives for student attainment.

The final set of objectives for reading and for mathematics should be readily accessible to teachers and administrators. The objectives need to be:

1. clearly stated so that teachers understand what students are to learn;
2. stated as precisely as possible so that little interpretation is involved as to their meaning. Vague objectives need to be rewritten;
3. broad in scope to cover vital goals in reading and mathematics;

4. challenging but achievable. This is a difficult situation when all students in a grade level are to achieve these objectives. This means that the gifted and talented as well as special education students should achieve the same objectives as measured by the same test.

Learning Activities to Achieve Objectives

Learning activities for students has received much less attention in the educational literature as compared to the objectives, and *much* less as compared to the testing facet of the curriculum. And yet, it is the learning activities which propel achievement. Subject matter and skills taught are actually an integral part of the curriculum, but need to be treated separately to indicate their importance. Learning activities chosen by the teacher should provide for individual differences among students in the classroom. With twenty to twenty five students per classroom, the teacher indeed has a difficult task in selecting and implementing learning activities. Ability and interest differences among students truly do present problems in making adequate provision for individual differences. There are a plethora of learning activities available such as concrete, semi-concrete, and abstract experiences. These activities should:

1. engage students fully in learning;
2. assist students to perceive purpose or reasons for learning;
3. help students to become motivated individuals. Preferably, intrinsic motivation should be emphasised;
4. develop interest for learning;
5. be used to scaffold learnings for students when needed;
6. guide students to perceive meaning and understanding;
7. permit students to choose, periodically, if individual or committee endeavours are desired as methods of learning;
8. use learning stations to enrich student experiences;
9. have students engage in self selected activities as well as those stressing teacher direction;

10. emphasise student self assessment as well as teacher directed assessment of learner progress.

Learning activities are actually the heart of the curriculum since the objectives provide direction as to what students are to learn and the assessment portion stresses the determination of what each student has learned. It is the learning activities which energies accomplishment. Students are actually doing things in order to achieve. Thus, students are involved in:

1. listening, speaking, reading, and writing to achieve objectives;
2. interacting with concrete, semi-concrete, and abstract learning opportunities;
3. inferring, predicting, generalising, summarising, and concluding;
4. thinking critically and creatively, as well as engaging in problem solving;
5. meeting to large groups, small groups, and in doing individual tasks;
6. learning by doing as well as learning from print materials;
7. using one or multiple intelligences;
8. choosing sequential tasks to complete at different learning stations as well as working on assigned activities;
9. stressing inductive as well as deductive learning;
10. assisting others to achieve and developing a caring, humane feeling toward others.

There are multiple learning activities for students. Computer use has further increased the number of activities available for students such as using the internet, web site, word processor. CDs and DVDs. Computer work may also involve doing spread sheets, painting, drawing, presentations, and data base use.

Assessment Procedures

State mandated testing has placed major emphasis upon evaluation rather than the objectives, and learning activities in the curriculum. Test results of students then predominate in importance, increased concern then should be shown toward the quality of tests. All state mandated tests need to be pilot tested to take out kinks such as weak, vague test items. Tests also need to assess validly. Thus, they need to cover what has been taught. This goes back to the statements of objectives in that they are clear and in the hands of all teachers to use as guidelines for teaching. The tests when administered should.

REFERENCES

Aiken, Adel G., and Lisa Bayer (2002), *"They Love Words"*, The Reading Teacher, 56 (1), 68-75.

Astleitner, Harman (2002), *"Teaching Critical Thinking Online"*, Journal of Instructional Psychology, 29 (2), 53-76.

Chappuis, Stephen, and Richard J. Stiggins (2002), *"Classroom Assessment for Learning"*, Educational Leadership, 60 (1), 40-41.

Ediger, Marlow and D. Bhaskara Rao (2000), *Teaching Reading Successfully*. New Delhi, India: Discovery Publishing House, Chapter Eight.

Ediger, Marlow (2002), *"Developing a Reading Community"*, Edutracks, 1 (4), 16-19.

Ediger, Marlow (2002), *"Social Studies and the Guidance Counselor"*, Experiments in Education, 30 (9), 176-181.

Ediger, Marlow (2002), "Improving Spelling", Reading Improvement, 39 (2), 69-70.

Gardner, Howard (1983), *Frames of Mind: The Theory of Multiple Intelligences*. New York: Basic Books.

Maslow, A.H. (1954), *Motivation and Personality*. New York: Harper and Row.

Meyer, Richard J. (2002), *"Captives of the Script: Killing Us Softly with Phonics"*, The Reading Teacher, 79 (6), 452-461.

Searson, Robert and Rita Dunn (2001), *"The Learning Styles Teaching Model"*, Science and Children, 38 (5), 22-36.

4

Statewide Testing and the Innovative Mind

There have been a plethora of recommended innovations which have been advocated and/or implemented. These innovative ideas come from within the school district, the school, and/or the teacher. State mandated testing stresses innovation from without or from personnel external to the local school system as compared to those which are more closely home based including those innovative ideas which may come from the individual teacher. The question which arises here is the following: How do external rules and regulations such as state mandated testing influence local development of the curriculum?

Characteristics of State Mandated Testing

State mandated testing emphasises selected philosophical beliefs which differ from locally determined efforts in working toward curriculum improvement. Thus, state mandated objectives stress the following:

- objectives developed and written on the state level make for a core of learnings which all pupils are to achieve in their states and on their respective grade levels;
- salient subject matter can be measured and reported in the numerical terms;
- comparisons can be made among states, schools and teachers when reporting pupil achievement;

- report cards may be included in the media to indicate measured comparisons among states, school districts, and schools;
- failing schools may be identified which did not meet average yearly progress (ayp) standards;
- pupils may transfer to a different school if their school is determined to be failing two years in a row, as determined by measurable state mandated test results;
- reading and mathematics are the two leading curriculum areas in which pupils need to be tested. These two curriculum areas represent the basics for learner mastery;
- pupils are to be tested in grades three through eight; a pupil may be held back from promotion if he/she does not pass a grade level state mandated test.

State mandated tests are standardised in that the time limits for test taking are the same for all pupils regardless of ability levels or handicaps involved. The test items, too, are the same for all test takers. When test results are reported, separate categories are shown for majority groups as well as minority students be they African Americans, Hispanics, Native Americans, and English as a Second Language students. The purpose here is to narrow or eliminate achievement gaps among all categories. This indeed is a worthy goal!

- reading and mathematics are the only two academic areas in which students take state mandated tests. This tends to minimise other academic areas such as science, social studies, and the fine arts. Those areas tested do receive major attention in the school curriculum. What is to be tested is what will be taught;
- much time is spent by teachers in drilling pupils on possible content on the state mandated test. Drill is rote learning and de-emphasises higher levels of cognition such as critical and creative thinking as well as problem solving;

- considerable time is taken in classroom instruction for students to learn the art of test taking. Students then are taught skills to take multiple choice test items, adhere to time limits in test taking, and use the same format as is stressed on state mandated tests. Test taking is not a life long skill;
- a single test score determines pupil achievement and promotion.

Innovations in the Curriculum

There are specific curricular plans which have received much attention in educational journal articles as well as in oral presentations given at state and national teacher education conventions. These will be mentioned briefly and how each does not fit into a state mandated curriculum.

- local efforts to improve the curriculum. The locally developed curriculum may not harmonise with state mandated testing. Thus if creativity is stressed locally, state mandated tests stress conformity of pupils to drill in memorising subject matter which might be on a test;
- multiage instruction whereby younger and older pupils are taught together in purposeful lessons and units of study. State mandated tests stress learnings for separate grade levels such as grades three through eight;
- multicultural instruction. This is not emphasised in mandated tests. The separate subjects of reading and mathematics, presently, receive priority and are tested upon only. Multicultural education is a social science discipline largely and at the present time, social studies has not been discussed for inclusion, at this point in time, for state mandated testing;
- portfolio development as an alternative or supplement to testing. Portfolios stress each pupil collecting a random selection of daily classroom work which indicates progress of pupil products; state mandated testing ignores every day work of each learner, completely. Rather, a single test score indicates pupil achievement;

- community service projects do not count in determining pupil achievement since this does not involve academic course work such as in reading and mathematics. It is true that reading and mathematics may be used in degrees in community service, but they do not zero in on these two curriculum areas. However, a good citizen does assist in community service;
- drug abuse education is not inherent in state mandates testing. Unless there is time for drug abuse education, reading and mathematics, as basics in the curriculum, will be focused upon largely by teachers. Drug abuse is rampant in the societal arena and is a major concern in terms of health of individuals and related crimes committed to support the negative habit;
- the fine arts of music, drama, and art education are important in a well rounded personality. There is, however, no thinking about testing in these three curriculum areas;
- social development is not measured in state mandated tests. However, social development in getting along well with others is of utmost importance to all, in the here and the now;
- moral education certainly is a worthy area of concern for educators. Immortality can be very costly for the individual and for society. Each person needs to have a clear vision of moral standards in every day living. Moral education could be taught as a separate unit of study or woven in to each curriculum area. Modelling proper moral standards, also, is indeed salient;
- peer mediation gives pupils opportunities to be actively involved in governing the self. It takes time for individuals to be proficient in peer meditation. Here, pupils involved need to be good listeners to both sides in a disagreement and then come up with a solution which is fair to the opponents. State mandated objectives has no room for peer mediated instruction and does not test pupils in this area. And yet, it is important for pupils to be able to govern themselves;

- citizenship education is completely omitted in state mandated objectives and testing. The role of the individual in a lawful society needs adequate attention. To be a contributing societal member is relevant where there is rampant or considerable crime in society. Citizenship education is vital for all in society and be contributing members in state or nation. It is very costly to society for any individual to be a prison inmate.

Recommendations for Improving Assessment Procedures

There arc numerous ways to change assessment practices from what is to what should be. First, state mandated tests need to be tried out in pilot studies more so than what has been done. It does not make sense for 25 per cent or more of high school graduates to fail the high stakes test and not receive a diploma. Item analysis needs to be done to sort out good from bad test items which are vague and hazy. Clearly written test items need to be in the offing. Test items need to be valid and cover what pupils have had chances to learn. Thus, objectives should be available to all teachers and these objectives need to provide guidance as to what should be taught. The objectives should possess clarity to teachers so that benchmarks are available as to what needs to be taught. Adequate time needs to be spent on writing relevant objectives which truly reflect worthwhile subject matter for pupil acquisition. Validity and reliability data on state mandated tests need to be available to schools. This information, in part, will say something about the quality of the state mandated tests. Test sores should be used to analyse difficulties faced by pupils and remediate that which is unacceptable.

Second, a single test should not be used, solely, to determine if a pupil passes or fails the state's standard for promotion. A good second evaluation device might well be the portfolio whereby a pupil may indicate how well he/she did in the classroom on a daily basis. With a portfolio of randomised selection of a pupil's products may be assessed with a quality rubric. Here, the evaluator of the rubric may actually see work completed by the pupil. This is quite difficult than looking at a single test score which is to tell it all about a pupil's achievement.

Third, development of tests to appraise learner achievement and objectives for teachers to use in teaching takes much time and effort. The entire process of state mandated testing needs to be thought through carefully. It seems as if state mandated testing has been rushed through the senate and the house and signed by the governor. When may are failing because of low test scores, is that the way to go? What happens to the learner's self concept in the process? Is it a good procedure to set the bar so high that many fail the state mandated test in grades three though eight as well as on the exit exam for high school graduation? Before NCLB, there were a plethora of articles written on the harmful affects of flunking students on any grade level. Research was then quoted on how detrimental this practice was on pupils. Presently then, there are attempts to flunk a certain number of pupils through state mandated testing.

Fourth, results from state mandated tests should provide information to teachers on which test items a pupil missed and what is recommended to assist these pupils to achieve more optimally. Helpful information is needed, not punitive results for pupils. The No Child Left Behind (NCLB) Act of 2001 punishes schools for not meeting annual yearly progress (ayp) goals. The ayp was established by each state in the union and is merely an estimate, not an absolute of what pupils should achieve yearly. When pupils lack ayp standards in a school for two consecutive school years, they may opt out and attend a different school. The poorly performing schools generally are in low income areas. Research does substantiate this with no exceptions. Perhaps it would be better to improve services within the "poorly" performing schools with the following assistance:

- an adequate number of good tutors to work one on one with selected pupils who need individual assistance;
- ample materials of instruction to use in assisting each pupil to achieve optimally;
- qualified teacher aides to help the regular classroom teacher to meet needs of learners in a classroom;
- have enough of manipulative materials for pupil use in learning;

- use of adequate audio-visual materials to guide pupils to understand learnings stressed in ongoing lessons and units of study;
- state of the art computer services for all pupils in school.

Fifth, positive approaches should be emphasised in assisting pupil achievement. The NCLB stresses punitive procedures such as the following which need to be eliminated:

- report cards in the media which make comparisons among states, schools, and school districts of pupil achievement based on state mandated test scores;
- pupils opting out of a school due to two consecutive school years of that school not having met annual yearly progress scores;
- failing of pupils due to not having passed a state mandated test;
- passing of an exit test in order to receive a high school diploma. More evidence of failure is needed than the single test only.

Quality Criteria Needed in Instruction

The classroom teacher needs to experience inservice education which helps pupils to achieve optimally. He/she needs to use criteria from educational psychology in teaching and learning situations. First, the teacher needs to capture pupil attention when teaching. Thus, this teaching strategy involves obtaining the interests of learners. Otherwise pupils will not be attending to what is being taught. Interest is a powerful factor in learning. After the teacher has taught a given set of pupils for a period of time, he/she will know what it is that captures pupil attention. Relating the subject matter taught to the pupil's very own experiences will generally help to secure pupil interest.

Second, assisting the pupil to attach meaning to and in ongoing experiences will help learner achievement. Meaningful learning is at the heart of optimal pupil achievement. If pupils do not understand that which is being taught, the chances are subject matter being acquired will soon be forgotten. Before reading the subject matter, pupils need to have background information which relates directly to the ongoing lesson. This will assist pupils to integrate the new with the familiar knowledge. What is learned must make sense.

Third, pupils need to perceive purpose in learning. Sensing purpose assists pupils to strengthen felt needs to learn new subject matter. There is a reason then from learning. It takes a short amount of time for the teacher to state a purpose for pupils to acquire new subject matter. The purpose must have inherent the reason or reasons for achieving the new facts, concepts, and generalisations. If a new skill is to be acquired by pupils, the teacher may say the skill or ability when stating the purpose or reasons for learning.

Fourth, the goals of instruction always need to be kept in mind by the teacher in teaching and learning situations. These goals or objectives help to maintain a vision for what needs to accomplished by pupils and keeps learning on track.

5

Who Should Determine the Curriculum?

There are a plethora of ideas on who should make curricular decisions. Each has a rationale for its determination. Diversity of philosophies need to be analysed. After analysing each school of thought, decisions may be made on which plan or combination thereof should be adopted in the school setting.

Student Centred Views

Student centred views generally put the learner at the centre of instructional decision making. The student then should be heavily involved in determining what to learn with teacher guidance. Student/teacher planning of the objectives, learning opportunities, and assessment procedures might then be in the offing. This takes time to plan a quality curriculum, but a student centred curriculum also stresses the importance of cooperative decision making. Making choices, from among alternatives, is highly significant in school and in society. There are always choices to be made in almost every aspect of life. Student/teacher planning may take several forms among the following:

1. students choosing, from among alternative tasks, at different learning stations. At each station in an ongoing unit of study, students may choose which task to work on and which to omit, and still stay optimally busy;

2. students may select sequential library books to read in an individualised reading programme. There must be

ample genres as well as reading levels of books when students make choices. A conference with the teacher may be conducted following the library book reading. The conference is an informal evaluation of student needs and progress. The Drop Everything and Read (DEAR) plan of student choices of reading materials, during a special segment of the school day, does not have an evaluation session, but otherwise is closely related to the individualised reading programme;

3. student chooses a project to complete for an ongoing unit of study. The project then involves student's individually or committee wise in developing a purpose for the project. Planning needs to be thorough to achieve the goal in doing the project. Carrying out the plan and then evaluating the quality of the project using desired criteria and musts.

Teacher Centred Plans of Instruction

In moving away from a student centred curriculum, the teacher, in a more hierarchical approach, may determine the curriculum. Here, the teacher selects the objectives, learning activities, and appraisal techniques in teaching situations. This may be indicated with the following scenarios:

1. the teacher selecting basal textbooks for the class;
2. the teacher assigning lessons to students;
3. the teacher selecting questions for discussion to check student comprehension and progress on a daily basis;
4. the teacher asking questions, during summative evaluation sessions. These tend to require right responses from students;
5. the teacher testing student achievement frequently, using different kinds of teacher written test items.

District Wide Determination of the Curriculum

School districts may determine the curriculum in selected ways. District wide tests to ascertain student achievement may well emphasise that decision making has gone beyond that of the students and the classroom teacher. The school district then has selected objectives for the teacher to attain in teaching students. District wide curricular decisions centralise decision making to the central office. The thinking here is that:

1. better curricular decisions can be made at the apex of the school district than at lower levels in the hierarchy;
2. the school district is to set up to deal with the curriculum directly such as the offices of assistant superintendent in charge of the curriculum, the system wide curriculum director, and other capable personnel;
3. the central office has the advisors and secretarial help necessary to further efforts in the improvement of the curriculum. Leadership then may come from the central office in working toward the best curriculum possible for students.

The State Level in Affecting Instructional Endeavours

The state level has had much influence over educational decision making. State mandated objectives, as the name indicates, are developed by each state in the union. These objectives have been written to indicate the basics which students are to learn. Ideally, they have been pilot tested to secure validity and reliability. Kinks need to be taken out of any assessment device written and used. Worthwhile knowledge and skills need to be measured, not trivia. There are issues which need to be addressed pertaining to state mandated objectives:

1. Which types of test items should be used to assess student achievement? Multiple choice test items are generally used since, among other reasons, they are easy to score with computerised services;
2. What should be the scope of items on the test? Reading and mathematics are two required areas. Selected states have gone beyond this to incorporate science and social studies;
3. How should test items be sequenced?

The Federal Level

The federal level and the Secretary of Education are heavily involved in decision making within the curriculum. The federal level has determined that the former Elementary and Secondary Education Act (ESEA) should incorporate the features of the No Child Left Behind Act (NCLB) to include the following in order to receive federal moneys:

1. required testing of students in grades three through eight for promotion purposes. Required testing of students in grade ten is required to indicate proficiency to receive a high school diploma;
2. a school meeting adequate yearly progress (AYP) as determined by each state. If a school/school district has not met AYP for two years in a row, they are categorised as "needing improvement". With five years of Needing improvement, the state may step in to redo that school/school system.

Methods of Teaching

There are selected methods of teaching which need to be implemented in order that students achieve desired objectives. The teacher needs to engage learners in teaching and learning situations. Students need this engagement if they are to attend carefully to the ongoing lesson or unit of study. Wasted teacher and student time will lower the efficiency rate of learning. Interesting procedures of instruction, as well as materials of instruction, will assist in optimising learning. Instructional procedures used in an art whereby creativity is involved to encourage student learning.

Purpose must be emphaised in student learning. With purpose involved, the student will perceive reasons for achieving. Perceiving purpose will guide the learner to achieve that which is worthwhile. If the objectives to be achieved are considered to be menial in value, the student may fail to put forth effort in achieving. Purpose within students for learning may be developed through the teacher stating reasons for the value of the subject matter to be learned. This is a deductive approach. The teacher may also use induction to assist student achievement. A questioning procedure is then used to help students accept purpose for achieving.

Meaning theory must be used in the instructional arena. If meaning is omitted, the student will not make sense out of the knowledge and skills to be encountered. With meaning, students understand that which is taught. Too frequently, students, if coerced to learn, might memorise content for a test if meaningless materials are being emphasised.

Individual differences need adequate provision in the classroom. One size does not fit all in teaching and learning situations. Each student is unique and desires to have his/her needs met. Using a variety of teaching materials in order that individual needs are met is important. The teacher may need to diagnose student achievement of objectives in order that weaknesses may be uncovered and remedied.

Learners posses multiple intelligences in the curriculum. These intelligences include:

1. verbal intelligence. Students possessing verbal intelligence prefer reading and writing activities in the curriculum, above others;
2. logical reasoning which is common to mathematics, but is valuable in any curriculum area. The ability to reason logically provides a salient effort to think things through;
3. objective thought, as used in science, is extremely valuable in coming up with truth;
4. musical/rhythmical as in setting words to music, and/or dance activities;
5. intrapersonal in which the student achieves more optimally an individual basis;
6. interpersonal emphasising committee or group work in which the student achieves well;
7. bodily/kinesthetic whereby the student does best in hands on approaches in learning (See Gardner).

The preferred intelligence of the student needs to be sought and emphasised in teaching and learning situations. It is important to use the talents of a learner. Student performance should increase in the curriculum when possessed intelligence are being identified and implemented.

Personal Needs of the Student

Each student has personal needs which should be met, if at all possible. Proper fitting, appropriate clothes need to be worn by students. Shabby, unclean clothes will not do. To feel well about the self, the student must have clothing which harmonises with the present temperature readings of the reason. The clothing should be neat and free from obnoxious odors.

The school environment must be free from human made annoyances. Bullying is not good for the bully, nor for the one being bullied. Generally, one or more bullies will gang up on a student who is vulnerable to something. That student may be ridiculed due to speech habits and patterns. He/she may also be bullied due to the kind of clothing worn, religious beliefs, physical appearance, and/or behaviour. It is very uncomfortable to be bullied and hinders social interaction with others as well as in academic achievement. Teachers and principals must work with students and have strict guidelines to prevent bullying.

Ample, nutritious food should be available for each student. Hungry students can not achieve well in school. Three meals a day, seven days a week must be served to each student or the learner may achieve at a very low level.

A safe, school environment is needed for all learners as well as for adults involved in the educational process in school. Murders of individuals in school has been written about in detail such as in Columbine High School in Littleton, Colorado in the 1990s. These are extreme cases, and do breed fear in schools far away from Littleton. Selected school buildings are old and susceptible to provoking injuries to students, such as slate shingles from a roof sliding down en mass from the roof or plaster falling from the classroom or hallway ceiling. Mold and mildew circulating through the furnace has made for illnesses and even hospitalisation of students. Bad odors and things which do not work need repairs, such as toilets which do not flush properly. Certainly, students required to attend school should have a safe place to be in teaching and learning situations. States and school districts need to budget adequate moneys to pay for upkeep and repairs as well as build new building as needed.

Psychological needs of students must be met. Each student desires to be accepted and belong to a group. Shunning and ridiculing need to be eliminated from a teacher's reportoire. Students need to be taught to respect each other and learn to live harmoniously, students should learn to offer assistance to each other as circular needs demand. A democratic atmosphere needs to be in the offing.

Esteem needs of each learner must be met. Students individually are important and should be recognised for achievements made. Every student then has opportunities to be recognised for contributions made. Belittling and talking down to a student should be omitted from the curriculum.

The student needs to be able to optimise achievement with teacher guidance. No one should be left behind from achieving optimally!

REFERENCES

Cuddeback, Meghan, and Maria A. Ceprano (2002), *"The Use of Accelerated Reader with Emergent Readers"*, Reading Improvement, 39 (2), 89-95.

Ediger, Marlow, and D. Bhaskara Rao (2003), *Improving School Administration*. New Delhi, India: Discovery Publishing House, 141 and 142.

Ediger, Marlow, and D. Bhaskara Rao (2003), *Language Arts Curriculum*. New Delhi, India: Discovery Publishing House, Chapter Thirteen.

Ediger, Marlow (1988), *The Elementary Curriculum*, 2nd Edition. Kirksville, Missouri: Simpson Publishing Company, Chapter Seven.

Epstein, Joyce (1995), *"School/Family/Community Partnerships"*, Phi Delta Kappan, 76: 704.

Gardner, Howard (1993), *Multiple Intelligences: Theory into Practice*. New York; Basic Books.

Friedrich, L.E. (1983), *"The School Budgeting Cycle"*, Winneconne, Wisconsin.

Paris, Scott (2002), *"Centre for Improvement of Early Reading Achievement"*, Reading Teacher, 55 (2), 170.

Richard, Alan (September 4, 2002), *"Florida Sees Surge in Use of Vouchers,"* Education Week, 1, 34.

Risko, Virginia J., et. al. (2002), *"Preparing Teachers for Reflective Practice: Intentions, Considerations and Possibilities"*, Language Arts, 82 (2), 134-144.

Tyler, Ralph (1949), *Basic Principles of Curriculum Construction*. Chicago: University of Chicago Press.

6

Sequence and Scope in the Curriculum

Students need to experience quality sequence to attain well in the school setting. How much any student will achieve may well depend upon a curriculum that permits continuous progress with objectives that are challenging and yet achievable. Objectives that are to difficult to attain make for feelings of failure whereas experiences and activities that are excessively easy may well make for boredom. The teacher's task then is to determine the present achievement level of student's individually and guide each to learn as much as possible. This is indeed a complex responsibility.

How Should Sequence be Determined?

Diverse procedures are available to ascertain the present level of a student's achievement and assist each to attain continuous progress. Measurement Driven Instruction (MDI) advocates using precise objectives written prior to instruction in teaching-learning situations. These carefully selected objectives provide a basis for writing test items, generally multiple choice in nature, to measure learner progress. The test items must harmonise with the objectives in proper alignment so that validity is in evidence.

Students then can be pretested to determine which objectives have or have not been attained. Those objectives not attained provide a starting point for instruction. Objectives for learner attainment can be announced prior to teaching students. Thus students can be rather certain as to what is expected of them in terms of content to be obtained from a lesson presentation. Once learners have attained planned objectives, the teacher adds new goals for sequential achievement. If objectives have not been achieved by students, a new teaching strategy must be used so that learners develop feelings of success. Pretesting before a new unit of study lesson plan is implemented provides guidance to the teacher as to what should come next in terms of learning activities for students. MDI advocates believe strongly that students must reveal mastery of sequential objectives prior to emphasising more challenging ends taught in ascending order of complexity. The teacher arranges the order of objectives logically. Thus a logical curriculum is in evidence as determined by the teacher.

A second procedure to emphasise in determining sequence in the curriculum is teacher-student planning. The teacher may present background information in a lesson to learners using a variety of activities. He/she encourages student questions within the framework of these leaning opportunities. The questions raised can be recorded on the chalkboard. After the questions have been selected, students choose which problem area they would desire to solve. Sequence to a large extent here is determined by learners. Students chose the problem areas and then decided upon the committee to serve on for the problem solving activity. Students with teacher guidance may also select references to use in the problem solving experience. Further situations involving students in sequencing experiences would be to guide learners to appraise their solutions to problem areas. A psychological curriculum is in evidence when learners are heavily involved in sequencing their very own activities.

A third approach in sequencing objectives is to advocate a subject centred approach in instruction. The teacher here has to major role in ordering experiences for learners, but without the use of measurably stated objectives. Mental development of students becomes the major aim of instruction. Mind is real and needs development. The teacher must be highly academically inclined to stress a subject centred curriculum. Objectives emphasising leaner attainment of subject matter need to be important for student achievement. Trivia must always be weeded out when selecting subject matter for learner achievement. There is much subject matter for any student to attain; thus what is emphasised in teaching-learning situations must pass the test of being relevant. With a subject matter emphasis in the curriculum, learners may achieve vital facts, concepts, and generalisations. Higher levels of cognition in the stated objectives reflect critical and creative thinking.

Teachers choose the subject matter for learners to achieve. Students must be motivated to participate in discussing subject matter. Subject matter learner could be used in problem solving, but could also be acquired for its own sake. A demanding curriculum should be in emphasis for all students.

Attitudinal objectives should be stressed as they guide learners to achieve knowledge goals (facts, concepts, and generalisations) as well as skills (critical and creative thinking). With positive attitudes, learners have a desire to learn subject matter.

Scope in the Curriculum

Scope in the curriculum answer the question of what should be taught whereas sequence answers the questions of when should diverse objectives and learning activities be emphasised. There are numerous means of determining scope. Thus the breadth of content for student attainment may be selected on the state level with its mandated objectives. These objectives are stated with precision; students either do or do not achieve these ends as a result of instruction. The total number of objectives determined on the state level then emphasise what will be taught or the scope of the curriculum. On the state level, mandated objectives are selected for each curriculum area. These objectives are available to teachers who in return choose learning opportunities for student interaction so the latter may attain the precise objectives. Evaluation is always done in terms of the precise objectives and emphasises the use of criterion referenced tests. Results from students when having taken the test are stated in quantitative terms.

A second approach in determining scope is to have teachers, supervisors, and administrators in a planned series of meetings identify what students are to learn. Each curriculum area and its scope can be determined by these school professionals. Content and skills to be covered in ongoing lessons and units of study may then be identified. The totality of what is identified becomes the scope of the curriculum.

A third procedure is to place heavy emphasis upon the basal textbooks used in each curriculum area to provide the framework in determining scope. Basal texts have always been used in educational history in teaching-learning situations. They possess a body of subject matter which specialists have selected for learners to attain. Much time, effort, and money has gone in to writing each textbook. The manual section of a basal contains references sources for the teacher to use in the instructional arena.

A fourth method in ascertaining sequence is to use a learning centres approach. The centres may be developed by the teacher alone, or through teacher—pupil planning. More tasks should be available at the diverse centres than what any one student can complete so that choice is involved as to what to learn and what to omit. Decision making here is left up to the student. Thus the student chooses content and skills to learn and to omit. If a student perceives more purpose in activities other than those contained at the learning centres, he/she may discuss this with the teacher and thus pursue alternative activities and experiences. Scope here emphasises the total experiences chosen by the learner with teacher guidance.

Summary

Quality sequence must be in evidence so that each learner may attain more optimally. Appropriate sequence guides students to relate new objectives to be achieved with those already acquired. Objectives that are not excessively complex nor too easy for student achievement should be in the offing. Appropriate scope emphasises the breadth of content to be achieved by learners. The scope can be either too broad or excessively narrow. Careful consideration must be give to "what should be emphasised within each lesson and unit of study. Relevant content, skills, and attitudes must be stressed within each lesson and unit of study in order that excellence in scope is in evidence. Students individually must achieve as much as possible within the framework of a quality designed curriculum involving sequence and scope.

7

Content in the Curriculum

A frequent question that arises pertains to *what* should be taught in terms of content in the curriculum. This is a problem that pertains to scope and sequence. Johann Frederich Herbart (1776-1841) felt that literature and history were the most important curriculum areas in the schools. These curriculum areas might then aid students in developing good moral character. Jean Jacques Rousseau (1712-1778) believed that science (the natural environment) should provide major learnings for pupils. Johann Hienrich Pastalozzi (1746-1827) felt that actual objects and the real environment should be the major source of learnings for pupils.

Certainty of Content to be Learned

There are selected educators who are fairly certain pertaining to content that should be learned by pupils. The essentials under the leadership of William Chandler Bagley (1874-1946) believed that learnings could be identified which all pupils were to develop. The three R's (reading writing, arithmetic) history, English as well as discipline and obedience, may then provide basic content for all learners. Thus, a core of content exists which pupils need to learn and master.

Advocates of behaviourally stated objectives feel that content generally can be identified which pupils are to master. Behaviourally stated objectives generally are written prior to teaching a given set of learners. These objectives are written with much precision. Thus, after instruction, it can be observed and measured if these kinds of objectives have been achieved. Notice the following measurable objectives:

1. The pupil will list in writing the names of all continents on the planet earth.
2. The pupil will write a fifty-word paragraph on how climate affects agricultural crops grown.
3. The pupil will read a one hundred-word essay on global peace and state two facts and two opinions contained in the writing.

Behaviourally stated objectives can be written on the *recall* of information level or on complex levels of thinking. Each of the above objectives indicates that after teaching a given set of learners, it can be measured if the objectives have or have not been achieved. Prior to teaching then, the teacher generally selects what learners are to learn. Thus, certainty exists in the mind of the teacher as to *what* pupils are to learn. The teacher then selects content which pupils are to master.

Humanistic Objectives in Education

Humanistic education emphasises the development of the attitudinal dimension of individuals. Thus, pupils must have a chance to engage in decision making as to *what* is to be learned as well as the media to use in learning. To be sure, the teacher should be adequate opportunities to structure the learning environment in a flexible direction. However, within that structure, pupils have opportunities to determine objectives and learning activities. They also have opportunities to assess their own achievement.

According to humanists, learners need to be assisted in developing well socially and emotionally in that concern for others is an important objective to achieve. Thus, the effective, attitudinal, or feeling dimension becomes important in developing. Developing the self concept of the learner becomes vital. The learner basically selects tasks that are of interest and can be completed successfully. Joy in learning must be in evidence. The learning activities are selected on what appears to be relevant to the learner. Interest, relevancy, and success in learning are viewed from the child's unique perception. Thus, in selecting content to be learned in humanistic approaches to learning, the child is a major determiner when decisions are made. There is considerable less certainty as to which content pupils are to learn when stressing humanistic education as compared to the use of behaviourally stated objectives.

Content and Programmed Learning

In programmed learning, the programmer decides upon what pupils are to learn. The sequence or order of these learnings is also determined by the programmer. Thus, once the learner is ready for utilising selected programmed materials, he/she might participate in the following sequentially:

1. Read selected content and view the related picture or pictures;
2. Respond to an item, such as a completion item;
3. Check the personal given response against that provided by the programmer;
4. Correct answers given by students may be its own reward and provides for reinforcement;
5. If responses given were incorrect, the learner now knows the correct answer, and is also ready for the next sequential programmed item.

The above named steps may be followed again and again in programmed learning. In determining content to be learned, the programmer in developing programmed materials determining what pupils are to learn and in what order. There seems to be considerable certainty in terms of what pupils are to learn as perceived by the programmer.

Content and the Structure of Knowledge

Selected educators strongly emphasise that pupils inductively develop structural ideas as identified by academicians. For example, social scientists from colleges and universities may identify major generalisations from their academic areas of speciality. Thus, key structural ideas are identified by historians, geographers, political scientists, sociologists, anthropologists, and economists. Learners in the school curriculum may realise these ideas inductively on their own understanding level. Pupils should understand these ideas on a more complex level, continuously, as they progress through their respective years of schooling. Learners might also use the methods of acquiring and assessing information as emphasised by these academic specialists in the social sciences. Thus, if pupils worked as historians, an ample number of primary sources among other learning experiences, might be utilised in gathering data. Or, pupils working as geographers, should utilise as well as make maps and globes, among other sources, in gathering and recording data.

The structure of knowledge approach in providing content for learning emphasises degrees of certainty as to content which pupils are to learn. College and university professors then need to identify and agree upon as to what the structure of knowledge is in each of the identified disciplines of content.

Problem Solving in the Curriculum

All individuals face major as well as minor problems in life. Problems in society can be identified. Questions arise when considering and observing the natural and social environment. From these problems and questions, related information may be gathered in terms of solutions. Hypotheses or answers are then obtained in relation to the problem or question. Ultimately the hypotheses are accepted, modified, or refuted. These steps would generally represent a framework for describing problem solving situations in learning. John Dewey (1859-1952) was a leading advocate in emphasising problem solving situations in the curriculum. Problem solving indicates the need for information from any and all academic disciplines and curriculum areas as long as it is relevant in realising solutions. Thus, subject matter is used in solving problems. Disciplines or academic areas used in solving problems have their importance as they aid in working toward solutions. Knowledge then is selected on the basis of being instrumental in solving problems. Thus, content is important in terms of problem solving activities in the school setting as well as the curriculum of life. Content cannot be selected in terms of what will be relevant prior to identification of relevant problems areas. Once problem areas have been identified, subject matter becomes important in terms of realising desired solutions.

Content and the Learner

It is important for pupils to develop relevant understandings, skills, and attitudes. The question arises as to what is relevant for pupils to learn. There certainly are disagreements in thinking when educators attempt to answer this question. It is important to be able to solve personal problems as well as problems that exist in society. Only then can individuals improve their lot as productive members in society. Content used in problem solving is relevant to the problem being pursued. Thus, in problem solving activities, it cannot be determined with certainty as to *what* content is relevant for all learners in the school setting or in life.

Learners' interests vary from individual to individual. It appears that ample opportunities should be given to learners in making decisions pertaining to *what* to learn. Since learning styles differ from pupil to pupil, it would be sound to have learners engage in decision making as to how desired learnings are to be achieved.

Academicians on the college and university level can make tremendous contributions in terms of identifying content pupils are to learn. Their recommendations might also pertain to pupils utilising methods of gaining knowledge that specialists in the diverse disciplines use. Pupils might select tasks in learning where these structural ideas are developed inductively using procedures recommended by academicians.

Learners have diverse learning styles. It may be of benefit to selected learners to utilise programmed materials in achieving relevant understandings, skills, and attitude objectives.

Summary

The history of education states which curriculum areas or skills were perceived to be of utmost in learning as determined by selected famous educators. Certain educators emphasised which discipline or curriculum area was most important for learners. Herbart, for example, felt that literature and history were the most relevant curriculum areas for learners.

More recent approaches in determining relevant content for learners pertain to the following:

1. The teacher, as well as principals or supervisors, determining prior to teaching what pupils are to learn.
2. Pupils deciding what to learn as well as the media of learning within a flexible framework largely determined by the teacher.
3. Programmers determining what pupils are to learn and in which sequence these learnings are to be obtained.
4. Academicians identifying key structural ideas for pupils to achieve utilising methods of procedures recommended by specialists in the diverse disciplines.
5. Pupils with teacher guidance identifying relevant problems or questions from a stimulating environment, thus working in the direction of obtaining possible solutions.

8

Curriculum Changes and Improvement

Society changes and incorporates the concept of change into the curriculum. During the course of history, changes in society have made for changes in the curriculum. The curriculum in school might also take the lead in changing society.

The writer will elaborate on a changing society which has made for changes in the school curriculum. A study of the history of education provides data for the concept of change.

The Middle Ages

During the Middle Ages (approximately 500 to 1400 A.D.) much emphasis was placed upon Scholastic methods of learning. Scholasticism stressed disputations between opposing sides. Thus, each side would present as much information as possible on the thinking and writings of selected Church Fathers. Critical thinking of the ideas of these Church Fathers was not permitted. Rather, each side in the disputation presented as much content as possible favouring a particular point of view as stated by well known leaders in the Christian religion of its day. The disputations did not lead in any direction toward goal attainment. Presentation of ideas of Church Fathers was made to merely show written information to substantiate or refute a point of view.

The logic of Aristotle (384-322 B.C.) was prized highly during the Middle Ages. Thus, a major premise was given, followed by a minor premise. The end result was to reach a conclusion. The methods of logic advocated by Aristotle of ancient Athens was judged to be deficient by reformers. The conclusion did into achieve any worthwhile results. This was due to the major premise already stating a generalisation or fact. If the major premise was "All men are mortal", a fact had already been stated. If the minor premise was "Socrates was a man", a fact also had been stated. The conclusion merely attempted to harmonise the major and minor premise, such as "Therefore Socrates is mortal".

Reformers in education believed that scholasticism amounted to hitting a ball back and forth, with no other purpose(s) being achieved, or even possible. Using syllogistic reasoning of Aristotle did not move in the direction of attaining new knowledge. The major and minor premises in both cases already stated factual knowledge. One group of reformers emphasised that students study the classic of ancient Greece and Rome. This was the age of the Renaissance. There were other philosophies of education stressed during the Renaissance (rebirth) era.

Classical Humanism and the Renaissance

Erasmus (1466-1536) was a leading advocate of students studying the classics and moving away rather completely from Scholasticism. Erasmus believed that literature from ancient Greece and Rome was much superior to that of the Middle Ages. Erasmus attacked Scholasticism in his book *In Praise of Folly*. He was an academic scholar and writer who criticised monks in monasteries for their incompetent use of Latin. Erasmus was a highly capable writer in the Latin language. He had nothing good to say about the syllogistic method of reasoning. Monastic life had nothing of intellectual value to offer. Abuse and corruption by monks in monasteries was criticised heavily by Erasmus.

With a study of classical literature. Erasmus believed that moral standards of students would develop positively. Thus, with a study of the writings of Plato, Quintilian, Plutarch, Horace, Livy, and Cicero, the student would learn worthwhile subject matter and become a moral being. Erasmus placed strong emphasis upon students learning content from classical literature to become better persons. An excess amount of faith was placed upon what the classics could do for people. Ultimately, a change in the curriculum was needed. The results did not bear out that a study of the classics developed moral persons.

Classical humanists emphasised:

1. a curriculum for upper class individuals. Persons of more limited capacities could in general not benefit from studying the complex writings of authors from ancient Greece and Rome;
2. a liberal arts curriculum. Persons of wealth and leisure could enjoy the great literature of the past;
3. non-vocational pursuits in the curriculum. The liberal arts had little or no room for a curriculum which emphasised earning or making a living. Most needed a course of study which emphasised the practical and the utilitarian;
4. abstract learnings for students. Those who learned from concrete situations were at a great disadvantage. In studying the classics, students needed to be proficient readers of symbolic materials. The ability to discuss what had been read emphasised high levels of cognition.

Dr. Mortimer Adler emphasised a Great Books philosophy of instruction. Dr. Adler believes that literature has worth as it has endured in time and space. Recently written literature may not survive in importance. Thus, the classics need to go back in time. They also need to remain important as the centuries progress. Mortimer Adler is very strong in advocating a non-vocational curriculum for students. Rather, students need to study classical literature which provides a common core of subject matter for all students. The classics represent relevant ideas for all students to attain. Later, the student needs to select a vocation which emphasises earning a living. But first, a liberal arts education needs to be emphasised. The liberal arts, consisting of the classics, represents the best subject matter possible for student acquisition, according to Dr. Adler.

Social Humanism and the Renaissance

During the Renaissance era, Michael of Montaigne (1533-1592) emphasised the philosophy of social humanism. He opposed a study of classical literature or the humanities. Rather, Motaigne emphasised travel for students as means of learning. The world itself, rather than books, provided what was needed for students to experience. With travel to view and learn about diverse cultures, students realise likenesses and differences among people. Students need to realise that vital content can be learned from the many diverse cultures. Montaigne, as a young boy, realised that cultures have many common traits. To feel that one culture is superior to another misses major goals of education.

In Montaigne's youth, schools were oppressive places with teachers beating students to motivate the latter to learn. The cries and pains heard in school from students was common in Montaigne's day. Licking and learning went hand in hand. Textbooks were worthless, according to Montaigne.

Michael of Montaigne then was a strong exponent of excursions for students to study society first hand. Learning from books did not provide accurate life-like experiences. Concrete activities, rather than the abstract, were to be preferred. Studying society first hand made for accurate learning. What is in society made for useful learnings for students.

Social humanism emphasised:

1. reality in experiences, rather than the abstract for students;
2. a study of society as being necessary and enjoyable for learners;
3. curriculum revision from a textbook centred to a societal centred approach;
4. a direct study of people and cultures in the natural environment.

Presently, many educators emphasise excursions as a part of the curriculum. Few would advocate using excursions only or largely, to develop the curriculum. Any methods textbook for teacher education in science and in the social studies emphasises the importance of excursions or field trips for students. These direct methods of learning are advocate presently for students, along with textbooks, diverse kinds of audio-visual aids, library books, encyclopaedias and other printed materials, as well as utilising the services of resource persons.

John Dewey (1859-1952), late professor from Columbia University, strongly emphasised not separating school from society. In his book *The School and Society*, published by Chicago University Press in 1900, Dr. Dewey emphasised there is a social and psychological side to students. The social side emphasised students adapting to and solving problems in the societal arena. The psychological side stressed that learners need to perceive interest, purpose, and meaning in ongoing lessons and units. Dewey believed that interest in learning makes for effort. Effort put forth by a student is minimised when the student fails to perceive interest in ongoing activities.

In Dr. Dewey's book *How We Think*, published by D.C. Heath and Company in 1910, he emphasised the complete act of thought when individuals engage in problems solving experiences. These flexible steps of problem solving to use are:

1. identify and delimit a life-like problem;
2. gather data from various sources to solve the problem;
3. develop a hypothesis. The hypothesis is tentative and not absolute;
4. test the hypothesis;
5. revise the hypothesis, if necessary.

Scientific Thinking and the Renaissance

Among others, Francis Bacon (1561-1626) was opposed to Scholasticism of Medieval times. He felt that Scholasticism did not lead to any conclusions. Rather, it merely lead to opposing sides gathering information from the writings of Church Fathers to support their contentions.

Francis Bacon advocated that matter be studied which could be seen, felt, tasted, touched, and/or listened to. The use of the five senses in learning was predominate in the thinking of Francis Bacon. Bacon did much experimenting with matter and nature. Along with his experimentations, Bacon stressed an inductive approach to learning. From the utilisation of the five senses, one perceives specifics. The specifics ultimately lead to generalisations. From the specific to the general, or inductive procedures of acquiring information, was advocated by Bacon. To be sure, Roger Bacon (1214-1294) during Medieval days had recommended the use of induction, rather than deduction as proposed by the scholastics. However, his call for change was not heeded. It took more time, such as the days of Francis Bacon, to have people accept the call to increasingly deal with the here and the now in nature to improve society.

Francis Bacon wrote *The New Atlantis*. In this book, he discussed a new nation whereby its inhabitants believed strongly in science and its methods of objectivity to secure knowledge. Sharing of information in the New Atlantis made for a more prosperous nation. People through medical science enjoyed better health. Productivity in agriculture increased to the point where inhabitants were fed adequately. By sharing scientific knowledge, the inhabitants of the New Atlantis lived healthier lives.

Scientific thinking of Francis Bacon advocated:

1. moving away from disputations of abstract ideas of the scholastics;
2. using concrete materials to learn about the natural world and its phenomena;
3. utilising what had been learned from natural world to improve the human condition;
4. using inductive or methods of discovery to acquire new knowledge.

In the school curriculum of today, science is important for all students. No educator and, perhaps, no lay person would deny this. To train teachers, university schools of education require all students to take classes and course work in the natural sciences. Among others, these classes include biology, botany, zoology, astronomy, physics, chemistry, geology, and environmental science.

Prospective high school and junior high school teachers in science student teach learners in the public schools for a specific interval of time. There are many excellent journals to help preservice and inservice teachers improve in the area of teaching science. Numerous teacher education textbooks for undergraduate and graduate science courses are available to assist teachers to improve their skills in teaching.

Change in Education

From the writings of classical humanism, social humanism and scientific thinking, all in the Renaissance period of time, the reader may notice changes that occurred in education. These changes may be contrasted with scholasticism of Medieval times. And yet, complete breaks between Medieval and Renaissance times were not in evidence in a true dichotomy. During the Middle Ages, there were educators who emphasised the seeds of or actual critical thinking. An example was the brilliant Peter Abelard (1079-1142).

Abelard had a large following of students. At one time he was an instructor at the University of Paris, the leading institution of higher education for its day. Wherever he taught, Abelard had many students who were inspired by his teaching. He wrote *Sic et Nun* meaning "yes" and "no". Answers to questions were not clear cut, according to Abelard, but had shades of gray. In discussing with his students if God knew evil and was the author of evil. Abelard believed in critical thinking. With understandings developed through analysing subject matter. Abelard believed he would come out as a better person with strong faith in God. This philosophy was opposite of those who believed faith and beliefs in God should not be questioned. Thus, in the Middle Ages era, Abelard along with others, questioned and identified problems in life which lead to analyzation of subject matter and critical thinking.

Presently, changes in American education are rampant. Quite rapid changes have been made during the 1980's. Each change represents an issue. Too frequently, changes made in education are called reforms. Modifications of what existed previously in education and changes in evidence presently, include the following issues:

1. state mandated objectives and testing versus decision-making by the classroom teacher of objectives, learning opportunities, and appraisal procedures;
2. statewide testing of tenured teachers to determine their future employment in teaching;
3. career ladders to differentiate pay among teachers;
4. lengthening the school day as well as the school year;
5. requiring high school students to take more courses in english, mathematics, science and the social studies;
6. requiring more inservice education of teachers;
7. requiring principals to appraise teachers more frequently. This may involve evaluating tenured and non-tenured teachers once a year, as a minimum, as required by state law;
8. national certification of teachers to teach in the public schools;
9. alternative routes to certify teachers. Individuals with a baccalaureate degree and no teacher education course work may then teach in the public schools;
10. a five year teacher education programme being recommended. A four year baccalaureate degree in liberal arts plus a fifth year in teacher education would be required for all, prior to teaching in the public schools. The first year of actual teaching in the public schools would be supervised by a teacher having demonstrated outstanding abilities to teach.

There, no doubt, will be many changes in American education as the years go by. The writer recommends the following reforms:

1. local decision making emphasised thoroughly. Thus, a well trained teacher would select objectives, learning activities, and appraisal procedures for a given set of students. These decisions should assist public school students to achieve more optimally. State mandated changes should be greatly minimised. The state is too far removed to help each student learn as much as possible on an individual basis;

2. statewide testing of non-tenured and tenured teachers should be abolished. These tests are costly and cannot undo what a teacher has worked for in completing a four year baccalaureate or five year master's degree. Competency tests, instead should be given on the undergraduate level of preservice education. The competency tests should be valid and reliable to measure vital knowledge of subject matter;
3. career ladders need to emphasise quality, vital criteria. Politics, favouritism, and other negative approaches must not be used by administrators to appraise teaching performance;
4. research needs to be done on the effects of a longer school year and day to determine if students achieve more optimally therein. Merely adding hours and days to a school year may have negative consequences on students. An improved curriculum is also needed.
5. requiring high school students to make more required classes in English, mathematics, science, and social studies in and of itself has no merit whatsoever. What is important about increasing the number of required classes is to meet needs of students. A vocationally orientated student may be hindered in achievement by being required to take more of the above named academic courses. Then too, qualified faculty members are not available if a state quickly requires students to take more classes. There has long been a battle between those educators who advocate an increased number of required classes as compared to those stressing more elective classes for students;
6. Inservice education of teachers is good if there are definite needs and goals. Writers who verbalise more inservice education of teachers is needed may not say and many do not say what the goals of inservice education for teachers should be. Too frequently, inservice education becomes a slogan. Goals in inservice education should rather reflect and pinpoint specifics,

when attained, would assist students to attain at a higher level in the public schools;

7. requiring principals to appraise teachers can be good if the criteria being emphasised are relevant and vital. Then too, principals need to be knowledgeable about quality philosophies of instruction. Evaluation by principals needs to stress honesty and integrity.

8. national certification of teachers in and of itself may not be beneficial. The standards to be implemented need to reflect that which emphasises quality in teaching and learning situations. The criteria used by the national certification board for teachers should not reflect the acquisition of subject matter in a liberal arts degree per se. Rather, certificates issued should emphasise needed skills to assist each student/pupil to achieve as much as possible;

9. there should be no routes to certification unless teachers demonstrate needed skills to be used in teaching students in a classroom setting. A liberal arts degree is not adequate to teach students in the public schools. Teachers must teach and teach well. Merely having acquired much subject matter is not adequate. There is more to teaching than possessing a liberal arts degree;

10. there should be a five year teacher education degree in colleges and universities if this assists teachers to do a better job of teaching. A fifth year degree should not exist for the sake of having one, but the five year preservice programme is to assist teachers to guide each student to learn as much as possible.

The curriculum needs to change as society changes. This was true in a study of the history of education in the days of the Renaissance. The same is true today.

REFERENCES

Cruickshank, Donald R. *Teaching is Tough*. Englewood Cliffs, New Jersey: Prentice-Hall, Inc., 1980.

Henson, Kenneth T. *Secondary Teaching Methods*. Lexington, Massachusetts: D.C. Health and Company, 1981.

Joyce, Bruce, and Marsha Weil. *Models of Teaching*. Third Edition, Englewood Cliffs, New Jersey: Prentice-Hall, Inc., 1986.

Joyce, Bruce, et. al. *The Structure of School Improvement*. New York: Longmans, 1983.

National Society for the Study of Education. *Staff Development*, Part II. Chicago, Illinois: The Society, 1983.

National Society for the Study of Education. *The Humanities in Precollegiate Education*, Part II. Chicago, Illinois: The Society, 1984.

National Society for the Study of Education, *Becoming Readers in a Complex Society*, Part I. Chicago, Illinois: The Society, 1984.

National Society for the Study of Education. *Education in School and Non-school Settings*, Part I. Chicago, Illinois: The Society, 1985.

National Society for the Study of Education. *The Ecology of School Renewal*, Part I. Chicago, Illinois: The Society, 1987.

National Society for the Study of Education. *Society as Education in an Age of Transition*, Part II. Chicago, Illinois: The Society, 1987.

9

Issues in Organising the Curriculum

There is considerable debate among educators pertaining to means of organising subject matter for pupils to acquire. One may perceive the school/class setting as emphasising the separate subjects curriculum. In the separate subjects curriculum, for example, the teacher may teach separate units pertaining to history only. Or, entire units of study may emphasise the social science discipline of geography. In attempting to relate content in the social studies, a teacher may teach diverse units of study correlating history and geography. Thus, historical events occurring in specific geographical regions is then being emphasised in teaching-learning situations. One may also perceive curriculum organisation as emphasising fusion of content. Thus, each social studies unit emphasises related content from the social science disciplines of history, geography, political science, economics, anthropology, and sociology. To emphasise an integrated curriculum, further relationship of subject matter is needed. Thus, content acquired by pupils has lost its specific identifiable academic boundaries.

There are inherent assumptions in emphasising each specific plan of curricular organisation. These diverse plans in organising the curriculum will be discussed in the balance of this chapter.

The Separate Subjects Curriculum

To emphasise a separate subjects curriculum, the teacher may select educational objectives pertaining to one academic discipline for learners to attain. Thus, for example, in a selected historical unit of study, the teacher may write and emphasise the following goals for learners to attain:

1. The pupil will list in writing five causes of World War I;
2. The pupil will write a 100 word paper on the effects of World War I.

Each of these objectives largely emphasises content from the social science discipline of history. For learners to attain these goals, the teacher needs to select learning activities which contain historical content. Ultimately, the teacher may appraise if involved learners have acquired what is stated in the measurable objective.

There are numerous assumptions inherent in utilising the separate subjects curriculum. Among others, these assumptions include:

1. a separate subjects curriculum may truly reflect depth, rather than survey means of teaching and learning. If the teacher focuses largely upon one academic discipline in the instructional process, pupils may master specific content sequentially and in a comprehensive manner. Each academic discipline contains its own body of structural content for pupils to acquire. A watered-down curriculum occurs when teachers attempt to teach subject matter from several academic disciplines as being related. No single academic discipline receives adequate attention in the curriculum if subject matter from several academic areas is perceived by learners as being related;
2. each academic discipline contains, its own unique sequence. In historical units of study, for example, pupils with teacher guidance may experience chronologically ordered events in space and time. Thus, in a study of history, pupils experience a selected order of vital happenings and events.

The Correlated Curriculum

The correlated curriculum emphasises an initial approach in relating subject matter disciplines. Thus, for example, two academic disciplines may be presented by the teacher as being related. The following objectives, measurably stated might well illustrate correlation of content:

1. The pupil will list in writing five influences that geographical features had on battles fought during World War I. The social science discipline of geography is then correlated with history.
2. The pupil will write a 100 word paper on how productivity in five major nations, actively involved in battle during World War I, affected ultimate outcomes in this conflict. The social science disciplines of economics and history may then provide related subjects for pupils to acquire.

Advantages given for emphasising the correlated curriculum in teaching-learning situations include the following:

1. There are fewer separate subjects to emphasise in ongoing units of study when correlation as a concept is emphasised as compared to the separate subjects plan of curriculum organisation;
2. Individuals in society generally do not compartmentalise knowledge. Academicians tend to isolate/separate subject matter into component parts.

The Fused Curriculum

The fused curriculum as compared to correlated methods, increasingly relate from diverse academic disciplines. Thus, each subject matter area in the social sciences can provide content for ongoing social studies units of instruction. The following pertain to specific goals involving fusion of content:

1. The pupil will write a two hundred word paper pertaining to seven causes, as a minimum, of World War II incorporating historical, geographical, political, economic, and cultural factors;
2. The pupil will list in writing five consequences of World War II. Consequences to be incorporated must relate to at least four social science disciplines.

There are selected positive marks given for stressing fused means in organising the curriculum.

1. Specialists in academic areas separate content into component parts. In society and life itself, individuals tend to synthesise content in order to solve problems.
2. Knowledge perceived as being related generally is retained for a longer period of time as compared to subject matter taught as being isolated or fragmented.
3. Borders, and boundaries between/among subject matter areas are not distinct but rather overlap. To divide the social sciences into component separate disciplines then becomes artificial rather than reality based.

The Integrated Curriculum

The integrated curriculum emphasises problem solving experiences for pupils in the school/class setting. To solve problems, related context is utilised as diverse academic disciplines and life's experiences demand. Needed subject matter then loses its boundaries and boarders with the framework of attempting to solve problem areas. Content from the social sciences, as well as from mathematics, science, language arts, music, art, and physical education are utilised as needed to achieve synthesis in problem solving.

Life in society demands that a person be able to solve personal and social problems. Thus, content must be perceived as being related by the problem solver. Problems need to be determined and the best solutions possible need seeking.

Gestalt psychologists believes that individuals initially perceived the whole of something rather than specific parts. It appears then that a viewer tends to perceive subject matter as being related rather than in terms of separate academic disciplines or fragmented knowledge. After introductory perceptions have been made, learners may then separate content as necessary to think critically and creatively. Selected academic disciplines might well be chosen to solve identified problems. This, of course, is pursued after wholeness (gestalt) has been perceived in subject matter.

Summary

There are selected questions which need answers pertaining to diverse means of orgainising the curriculum. One may perceive the problem in terms of points on a continuum. Toward either end, a point may represent the separate subjects curriculum. At the other end of the continuum, a point may represent an integrated concept of curriculum development in which subject matter loses its boundaries and borders within a problem solving framework. In between points on the line may represent the thinking of the correlated and fused curriculum. There are selected questions which need answering when resolving the inherent controversies.

1. Which specific curriculum area (e.g. social studies, language arts, mathematics, or science, among others) should emphasise (a) separate subjects, (b) correlation, (c) fusion, or (d) integrated means in organising content from the academic world? Adequate rationale needs to be given to justify reasons given for organising content in each curriculum area in the school/class setting.
2. Which plan/plans of curriculum organisation might assist each learner to achieve optimally in intellectual emotional, physical, and social achievement?

10

Subject-Centred Versus an Activity-Centred Curriculum

There are selected educators and many lay people advocating a subject centred school curriculum. Textbooks, workbooks, worksheets, as well as oral and written reports, might then be heavily emphasised in ongoing units of study. A few audio-visual aids may also be used as learning activities to clarify meanings and vary the kinds of experiences provided for learners. The teacher needs to choose vital, relevant subject matter for pupil attainment. Otherwise, pupils might learn irrelevant facts, concepts, and generalisations.

Advantages given for advocating a subject centred curriculum include the following:

1. Pupils need to acquire vital subject matter in the curriculum to prepare themselves to be effective members in society;
2. Learners develop feelings of self-discipline in acquiring significant subject matter. Effort must be put forth to learn vital content;
3. There is much subject matter available in society. Only a small part can be learned. It behooves each learner to attain as much subject matter as possible in an era of knowledge explosion;

4. Society tends to prize individuals possessing adequate subject matter knowledge. Thus, content mastery may assist individuals to be accepted more highly by other.

Subject matter selected to be taught to pupils must be (1) interesting, (2) meaningful as well as understandable, (3) purposeful and acceptable, (4) attainable to each involved pupil.

An Activity-Centred Curriculum

There are numerous educators emphasisng the implementation of an activity centred curriculum. A variety of methods of materials might then be utilised in ongoing units of study. Learning by doing must be a key ingredient in the curriculum. Dramatic activities, art projects, creative writing, music and dance experiences, construction work, and research activities may well provide vehicles to achieve understandings, skills, and attitudinal goals being emphasised in ongoing units of study.

Advantages given for emphasising an activity centred curriculum include the following:

1. Pupils are active, not passive individuals. Thus, an action centred curriculum needs to be emphasised;
2. Activity centred methods of teaching harmonise more with child growth and development characteristics. Each pupil generally desires to be an active participant in learning;
3. Learning experiences need to be interesting to pupils. Diverse projects and activities may well provide situations to develop learner interest in the curriculum;
4. Pupil involvement in planning, developing, and evaluating each project may guide in learners perceiving purpose or reasons for active participation in the curriculum.

Synthesis of Subject Matter and Action

Teachers and supervisors may think of and implement a synthesis of content and activity centred methods of teaching. The following are presented as examples on integration:

1. Pupils, with teacher guidance, reading and acquiring subject matter learnings. What has been read might then be dramatised.
2. What has been read may well be presented in art form. Art products might include murals, dioramas, and pencil sketching, among others.
3. Follow-up activities to reading might involve diverse purposes in creative writing. The purposes may include writing poetry, plays, biographies, autobiographies, myths, legends, mysteries, and adventure stories.

11

Step by Step Teaching Versus an Open Ended Approach

Step by step teaching approaches has numerous advocates in the profession of education as well as by members in society. With a step by step approach, a predetermined curriculum is in evidence for students. The sequential objectives, learning activities, and appraisal procedures have been decided upon prior to the student being involved in the curriculum.

Toward the other end of the continuum, a more flexible curriculum is in evidence. Preplanning of goals, learning opportunities, and evaluation procedures, in degrees, has been done for students. However, open-endedness is much in evidence in ongoing lessons and units.

B.F. Skinner and Programmed Learning

B.F. Skinner advocates a step by step curriculum predetermined for students. Dr. Skinner believes in students acquiring a small bit or amount of subject matter. The student then responds, perhaps, to a multiple choice item covering the content. If correct, the student experiences reinforcement. If incorrect, he/she sees the right answer and is also ready for the next sequential linear item. Read, respond, and check are stressed over and over again in programmed learning.

B.F. Skinner believes in:

(a) programmers determining subject matter for students to acquire;

(b) ordered or sequential content being arranged for the student to attain;

(c) each step of learning is specific and identifiable;

(d) precise, measurable results are obtained from each student for each step of learning;

(e) reinforcement is provided the learner for correct responses made;

(f) immediate feedback is given to students pertaining to each response made.

Students in programmed books or software and computer use learn items in small sequential steps. Testing to determine if each step has been learned is important.

James Popham and the Use of Behaviourally Stated Objectives

James Popham advocates utilising behaviourally stated objectives in ongoing lessons and units. The teacher is in the best position to write these precise ends for student attainment. The measurably stated objectives might even be arranged in ascending order of complexity for students to achieve. If a student does not achieve an objective, a different teaching strategy should be used by the teacher. It is always measurably and observable if a learner has or has not achieved an objective. Objectivity in measurement here is important.

Prior to initiating a unit, James Popham advocates pretesting students based on the predetermined behaviourally stated objectives. Those objectives students have attained in the pretest should not be emphasised in a lesson or unit. As a result of the pretest, the objectives may be augmented or lowered in complexity depending upon pretest results.

To assist students to perceive purpose in learning, extrinsic motivational devices should be utilised. For extrinsic motivation, prizes and privileges may be given to students, providing they attain the predetermined level of achievement, an announced by the classroom teacher. Achieving the prize and/or privilege is a reward for students attaining a definite number of behaviourally stated objectives.

To achieve sequential objectives in the Popham plan, the content acquired by students in each step of learning is broader in scope, as compared to B.F. Skinner's programmed learning approach of instruction.

James Popham stresses that students should clearly understand the objective(s) of each lesson prior to instruction. These ends should be announced to learners so the latter knows what is to be learned as a result of instruction. Measurement of student achievement is against each objective emphasised in teaching-learning situations. Criterion referenced tests (CRTs), not norm referenced tests, should be utilised to determined student progress.

Madeline Hunter and Specific Steps in Teaching

Madeline Hunter developed a definite sequence in instructing students. The first step to emphasise in teaching is to establish set within students. The student here is aided to develop interest in the ongoing lesson. The teacher should state clearly to student precise objectives to achieve in the lesson. He/she must also assist students to perceive purpose in learning or reasons for achieving an objective. The second step in teaching, according to Madeline Hunter, is to teach major concepts. Clear explanations, drawings, models, and demonstrations are needed to clarify the concepts. Thirdly, Hunter advocates appraising what students presently know. Students reveal what has been learned by holding thumbs up or thumbs down, depending upon a statement being true or false, as presented by the teacher. Hunter's fourth step in teaching emphasises guided practice. Here, students answer questions and receive feedback to responses made. Questions, worksheets, and workbook exercises provide guided practice for learners. Teachers must provide feedback to students in terms of the quality of work completed. Evaluation is measured against the stated behavioural objectives. Fifthly, students are given independent practice to solidify previously acquired learnings.

The above named five sequential steps of teaching need to be followed in any curriculum area, according to Madeline Hunter.

Johann Friedrich Herbart and Sequential Steps in Teaching

Step by step approaches in teaching had a fascinating history. Johann Friedrich Herbart (1776-1841) advocated the use of five sequential steps in teaching. In developing his psychology of instruction, Herbart stressed the preparation and utilisation of lesson plans to teach students. The first step of teaching, according to Herbart, was preparation. Preparation emphasised teachers helping students to review what had been taught previously. The second step in teaching stressed the concept of presentation. Here, new subject matter is presented to students. Step 3 emphasised association by students of new subject matter presented (step of presentation) with previous content learned (step of preparation). Step number four in developing lesson plans, stressed students achieving generalisations or broad ideas, after associating the new and the previously acquired subject matter. The last step in Herbart's plan for teaching is *use*. Students should be assisted to utilise what had been learned. The concept of use is emphasised to prevent forgetting on the part of the student.

John Friedrich Herbert was a pioneer in the field of educational psychology. He emphasised five sequential steps for teachers to follow in writing and implementing daily lesson plans. Many educational historians believe these five steps had become more formalised than what Herbert had wanted.

Herbert in the 1800's as well as B.F. Skinner, James Popham, and Madeline Hunter today, advocate a sequential step by step procedure in teaching students.

Open Ended Procedures in Curriculum Development

With state mandated objectives and Instructional Management Systems (IMS) in vogue, there are selected educators strongly advocating an opposite and open-ended procedure in selecting objectives, learning activities, and appraisal procedures.

Theodore Sizer and Curriculum Development

Theodore Sizer, formerly headmaster of Phillips Academy (Andover, Massachusetts) and Dean of the Graduate School at Harvard University, established the Coalition of Essential Schools comprising 11 core and 34 associate schools. In these high schools, the thinking of Theodore Sizer is emphasised.

Dr. Sizer is opposed to the rigidity and formality of most secondary schools. Fifty-five minute class sessions and rote learning by high school students in traditional settings hinder student achievement, according to Sizer. Sizer's "Study of High Schools", a book written based on a six year study provides necessary background information in developing the Coalition of Essential Schools. Sizer's second book *Horace's Compromise: The Dilemma of the American High School* emphasises the importance of teachers on the local level making curricular decisions. In this book, Horace Smith, the name of a fictitious teacher, faces difficult decisions as an English Teacher. Horace is dedicated to his profession and possesses much ability. His school is a common bureaucracy. Tradeoffs are made with students. If students behave passively, Horace will not expect much achievement from them. Dr. Sizer believes that Horace Smith represents a typical teacher in high schools. Sacrificing academic achievement for docile students must be changed. He advocates that high schools narrow the scope of what is taught to include an achievable range of subject matter and skills. The goals of education would be the same for each student in that the essentials need to be acquired. Individual differences among students would need to be provided for. The curriculum would then be adjusted to each student, rather than adjusting the latter to the curriculum. Diplomas would be awarded on the basis of mastery of knowledge and skills, instead of the amount of time a student spent in the classroom.

Decision-making for teaching, according to Sizer, must be in the hands of teachers and administrators. He would oppose state mandated objectives or local instructional management systems (IMS). Class size needs to be reduced so that teachers may work with smaller numbers of students. The latter would need to assume increased responsibilities for learning. Local school autonomy is advocated by Theodore Sizer. This is quite opposite of reforms in education being emphasised by many states. Student-centred teaching is stressed by Dr. Sizer.

A step by step prescribed way of teaching is definitely not advocated by Sizer. Teachers and administrators are responsible for their own endeavours in teaching students.

John Goodlad and Curriculum Development

John Goodlad wrote *A Place Called School: Prospects for the Future* (New York: McGraw Hill Book Company, 1984). This book represents a major study made about American schools. A representative sampling of schools was used and the resulting data analysed in depth. Goodlad believes that the individual school is the basis for improving instruction. This again is quite opposite of having stated mandated objectives and district-wide development of instructional management systems (IMS).

Dr. Goodlad advocates that more time in a classroom be spent on instruction. High levels of cognition need to be emphasised, rather than factual knowledge. Too frequently, the entire class is taught as a unit, rather than teachers working with students individually and within committees. The teacher is at the centre of the stage in instruction. Goodlad believes that students should receive the major focus in teaching-learning situations.

Dr. Goodlad also believes that students receive too little feedback pertaining to their successes and errors. Students tend to be passive in a routine, boring environment. The teacher lectures, explains, and assigns, whereas students listen passively to requirements demanded. Goodlad believes that students should be actively involved in learning with much teacher-student interaction. In studies made for the book *A Place Called School*, Goodlad and his associates saw little of what has been called progressive education in the classroom and yet progressivism has been blamed for much of the school's ills. A variety of activities such as excursions, audio-visual aids, and reading materials should be utilised to provide for individual differences. Again, higher levels of cognition are important to emphasise, according to Goodlad.

Ralph Tyler and Curriculum Development

Ralph Tyler published his paperback *Basic Principles of Curriculum and Instruction* in 1950. This paperback continues to be popular in educational literature. It receives little or no attention in today's emphasis upon reforms instituted by the state with its required objectives, Instructional Management Systems (IMS), and career ladders/merit pay.

Dr. Tayler raises for questions which provide guidance in developing the curriculum. These are broad, open ended questions:

1. What educational purposes should the school seek to attain?
2. What educational experiences can be provided that are likely to attain these purposes?
3. How can these educational experiences be effectively organised?
4. How can we determine whether these purposes are being attained?

Tyler has been called the father of the behaviourally stated objectives movement. However, the above four named questions indicate flexibility and openness in developing the curriculum. The questions can be answered by individual teachers or by groups of teachers as the curriculum is being planned. Dr. Tyler's above named book provides a framework in curriculum development. There is much leeway and flexibility in lesson and unit development here. The four questions raised by Tyler indicate:

1. what teachers should aim toward in the instructional arena (goals);
2. how goals are to be achieved by students (learning opportunities);
3. the degree to which subject matter should be related (separate subjects, correlated, fused, or integrated approaches);
4. the necessity of appraising student progress with the use of appropriate evaluation procedures.

Tyler emphasised three sources from which objectives should come. These are from a study of society, a study of the learner, and from recommendations of subject matter specialists or academicians.

John Dewey and the Curriculum

John Dewey (1859-1952) was a rather early advocate of open ended approaches in teaching. Dewey believed strongly that school and society should not be separated from each other. What is salient and worthy in society should definitely become an important facet of the school curriculum. Change is a key concept in the school and society related entity. With change, problems arise and need identification. Dr. Dewey emphasised flexible steps in problem solving. Students with teacher assistance need to identify problems. The problems are life-like and real. Subject matter is acquired and is instrumental to securing answers to the problem. A hypothesis results. The hypothesis is tentative (not absolute) and subject to testing. The hypothesis may need to be revised as a result of testing.

When developing a hypothesis, one must look at alternatives and consequences of each choice. In problem solving, effort in learning comes from the interests of students. Interests and effort are not separate, but integrated entities. Problems solving emphasises a complete act of thought.

Summary

Presently, much structure in the curriculum is in evidence. Diverse states have precise objectives that public school pupils are to achieve. State mandated testes are based on these objectives. Selected educators, past and present, emphasising a tightly structured curriculum include B.F. Skinner, James Popham, Madeline Hunter, and Johann Friedrich Herbart. Toward the other end of the curriculum, those educators stressing a more open ended curriculum include Theodore Sizer, John Goodlad, Ralph Tyler, and the late John Dewey.

Predetermined, sequential objectives for students to attain emphasise a logical curriculum. The curriculum then is developed logically by educators prior to teaching students. No input from students has accrued in terms of selecting objectives, learning activities, and appraisal procedures.

Toward the other end of the spectrum, those emphasising a more open ended curriculum believe in increased student input and local teacher involvement in developing ongoing lessons and units. The tendency then is to develop a psychological, rather than a logical curriculum.

The writer believes strongly in stressing a curriculum which in broad outline emphasises:

1. the interests of students;
2. meaningful content for each learner;
3. purpose on the part of students in achieving goals and objectives;
4. adequate input from students into each curriculum area. Inputs from learners include teacher-student planning, use of learning centres, as well as questions and problems identified by pupils in ongoing lessons and units.

12

Adjusting the Curriculum to the Learner Versus Adjusting the Learner to the Curriculum

Two opposing philosophies of teaching are in evidence in the educational arena. One philosophy emphasises the adjustment of the curriculum to meet readiness factors possessed by the student. Thus, the curriculum must meet the personal needs, interests, and abilities of students. An opposite philosophy stresses a preplanned curriculum in which the learner needs to possess the background understanding and have the necessary attitudes to attain the stated objectives. Both philosophies will be examined and attempted resolutions made.

Adjusting the Curriculum to the Learner

Each student possesses a unique capacity, ability, and purpose for learning, different from other learners. The teacher needs to determine where each student is achieving presently. Instruction starts with where the student is presently in achievement. If content taught is too easy for the student, boredom and a lack of challenge to learn can be an end result. Toward the other end of the continuum, should the subject matter be too complex, the student will experience failure in school. A middle ground is for the teacher to ascertain where the learner is presently in subject matter achievement and assist the learner to make continuous progress.

David Ausubel, a leading psychologist, states that the most important responsibility of any classroom teacher is to find out which level the student is achieving at presently. The classroom teacher then needs to provide learning opportunities which will guide students to achieve new content and yet be successful as learners.

The teacher when adjusting the curriculum to the student does not perceive subject matter to be an absolute to attain. Rather, what is to be learned by students is flexible and subject to change. There are several models to emphasise when the goals of learning for any set of students are tentative and subject to change. Behaviourism as one psychology, tends to stress the utilisation of measurable stated objectives. These are written prior to instruction. State mandated objectives and tests, as well as Instructional Management Systems (IMS) emphasise the implementation of measurably written ends in teaching-learning situations. The measurably stated objectives and their use stress a rather formal curriculum. Students have no input into writing and selecting these kinds of objectives. A logical curriculum is then in evidence. Thus, prior to instruction, the measurably stated objectives have been predetermined for learner achievement.

Behaviourally stated objectives can stress adjusting the curriculum to the learner. This would tend to be the case if students are pretested on the precise ends prior to instruction. Based on pretest results, the teacher adjusts the curriculum to where each student is presently achieving. If the objectives in the pretest were too complex for learner attainment, the ends are revised to a lower level of difficulty. Conversely, if students attained exceptionally well on the pretest, more complex objectives may then be selected for teaching students.

A second method of adjusting the curriculum to the student involves the use of humanism as a psychology of learning. Humanists believe in heavy input from students in sequencing their own experiences. A psychological curriculum is then in evidence, as compared to a logical organisation in which learners attain prespecified objectives, such as behaviourally stated ends.

A learning centre's philosophy emphasises a psychological curriculum. With an adequate number of centres and enough tasks at each centre, the student may select which tasks to complete and which to omit. Sequence resides within the students in a psychological curriculum.

Teacher-student planing of objectives, learning activities, and appraisal, procedures further represents humanism as a psychology of learning. There needs to be heavy student involvement in developing the curriculum. The teacher here, as was true of the learning centres philosophy, is a stimulator and guide to motivate student learning.

A contract system also stresses humanism, as a psychology of learning. Within a contract the student involved needs to determine what should go into the agreement. These learning opportunities in the contract should be spelled out clearly. The teacher motivates, encourages, and suggests, but does not dictate what the student is to complete within the contract. Again, sequence or order of learning opportunities to be completed resides within the student. Sequence does not exist within textbooks, workbooks, or audio-visual aids. Only the student can sequence his/her own experiences.

With humanism, as a psychology of learning, the student chooses and makes decisions in terms of tasks of pursue. Thus, the curriculum is adjusted to the present achievement level of the involved student.

Adjusting the Student to the Curriculum

There are selected assumptions made by educators and the lay public when adjusting the student to the curriculum. First of all, an assumption is made that a definite body of knowledge exists for all students to attain. A further assumption is made that the body of knowledge to be acquired prepares the student to function well in the future in society. All students must achieve the subject matter knowledge regardless of capacity levels. Slow learners may well need more assistance through drill and practice than fast learners to acquire the subject matter. Time then is the variable to consider in that pupils who achieve at a lower level need additional assistance to attain the same/similar subject matter as compared to fast learners. Selected educators have even advocated that the same subject matter should be learned by all students, regardless of readiness levels of individual students. Perhaps, the same subject matter learned by all students represents democracy in action to these educators.

With a core body of subject matter to be taught to students, each learner needs to reach out to learn. The subject matter may be stated in terms of behavioural objectives. Teachers then select learning activities for students to attain the needed ends. No adjustments are made as to the behaviourally stated objectives being too easy or too difficult for students, prior to instruction. Each student needs to achieve a standardised set of objectives.

Further examples of absolute standards that students need to achieve in the curriculum include the following:

1. students should be held to high expectations. The teacher needs to have high standards for each learner to attain;
2. students need to attain much in an era of knowledge explosion. Learners must achieve more than ever before to realise a nation's competitive needs among other countries around the world;
3. students nationally score lower on international tests than to learners of other industrial nations;
4. students must will to learn and stay on task regardless of inherent interests, purposes, and needs.

Recommendations to Improve the Curriculum

An excess amount of attention is given in society to how well students do on tests, be they norm referenced or criterion referenced. There are additional philosophies to emphasise in teaching, other than the measurement school of thought.

Experimentalism, as a philosophy, advocates students with teacher guidance engage in problem solving activities. Flexible steps to stress in problem solving activities include:

1. clarity in identification of problems. Relevancy in problem selection is vital. Trivia is to be avoided;
2. gather data or information to solve the problem;
3. develop a hypothesis. The hypothesis developed is based on the data gathered. Each hypothesis is tentative and not absolute. The consequences of each hypothesis need to be evaluated;
4. test of hypothesis in a life-like situation;
5. revise, refute, on accept the hypothesis.

Experimentalists believe that students should solve life-like problems. Life-like problems in mathematics exist in society. Story problems in textbooks and workbooks lack reality and realness. The true test of a student's achievement in mathematics rests with his/her ability to solve problems in society. School and society should be one and not separate entities.

Students with teacher guidance identifying problems should make for effort in learning. Interest in the mathematics problem and effort in learning become one. The student is not separated from the mathematics curriculum. Knowledge becomes a means to an end and that end being the solving of problems. In comparison to experimentalism, the measurement movement emphasises mathematics teachers teaching toward ends. These ends are behaviourally stated objectives in criterion referenced tests (CRT) or the ends of doing well on a norm referenced test.

A second philosophy in teaching mathematics which needs much emphasis is existentialism. Existentialists believe strongly in each individual choosing and making decisions. Each student must assume responsibilities for choices and decisions made. No one else can set objectives for the student. If others do set predetermined ends for the learner, the latter ceases to be human.

Existentialists advocate the following concepts in the curriculum:

1. learners selecting tasks to complete from among alternatives. An adequate number of tasks need to be available so that those lacking purpose and meaning

for the student do not need to be completed. A learning centre's philosophy might then be emphasised;

2. student-teacher planning of the mathematics curriculum. The learner needs to have input into developing the objectives, learning opportunities, and appraisal procedures.

In contrast to existentialism, the measurement movement emphasises predetermined objectives for student attainment. The student becomes a passive being to absorb, hold, and contain information. The learner then has no input into the mathematics curriculum.

The writer strongly recommends the following pertaining to the utilisation of measurement movement philosophies of education:

1. students be pretested in a new unit of study based on behaviourally stated objectives involved. Based on pretest results, the curriculum is adjusted to the present achievement level of each student;
2. students exhibit readiness for learning new concepts and generalisations. Failure to achieve situations for students must be avoided;
3. students must experience additional philosophies of teaching and learning. Thus, experimentalism and existentialism should be emphasised. Students may then be active learners in the curriculum rather than passive recipients of knowledge.

REFERENCES

Cruickshank, Donald R. *Teaching is Tough*. Englewood Cliffs, New Jersey: Prentice-Hall, Inc., 1980.

Henson, Kenneth T. *Secondary Teaching Methods*. Lexington, Massachusetts: D.C. Heath and Company, 1981.

Joyce, Bruce, and Marsha Weil. *Models of Teaching*. Third Edition. Englewood Cliffs, New Jersey: Prentice-Hall, Inc., 1986.

Joyce, Bruce, et. al. *The Structure of School Improvement*. New York: Longmans, 1983.

National Society for the Study of Education. *Staff Development*, Part II. Chicago, Illinois: The Society, 1983.

National Society for the Study of Education. *The Humanities in Precollegiate Education*, Part II. Chicago, Illinois: The Society, 1984.

National Society for the Study of Education. *Becoming Readers in a Complex Society*, Part I. Chicago, Illinois: The Society, 1984.

National Society for the Study of Education. *Education in School and Non-school Settings*, Part I. Chicago, Illinois: The Society, 1985.

National Society for the Study of Education. *The Ecology of School Renewal*, Part I. Chicago, Illinois: The Society, 1987.

National Society for the Study of Education. *Society As Education in an Age of Transition*, Part II. Chicago, Illinois: The Society, 1987.

13

The Basics in the Curriculum and Moral Development of Learners

Much is being communicated orally and in writing pertaining to the significance of the basics in the curriculum. Generally, the 3r's (reading, writing and arithmetic) have been perceived to comprise these basics in the school curriculum. Statewide testing programmes have been implemented to appraise pupil's competencies in the 3r's, along with other selected subject matter areas, such as history and geography. A few states in competency based testing programmes have stressed practical situations. In appraising learner achievement including the writing of business and friendly letters, completing job application forms, utilising the telephone directory, and maintaining chequebook balances. Thus, numerous questions have arisen in terms of which understandings and skills should pupils acquire in teaching-learning situations in a kindergarten through grade twelve sequence. Understandings and skills may be appraised through the utilisation of paper-pencil tests in competency based testing situations. A third category of objectives—the attitudinal development of pupils—may well be reflected within the framework of an individuals' score on competency based tests. An area of attitudinal proficiency important for pupil achievement is moral development. Moral standards and principles give direction to deeds and acts performed. It would appear that the development may have significant implications as a basic in the school curriculum.

The Basics Arena

There are numerous questions which need identifying and resolving pertaining to the concept *the basics in the school curriculum*.

1. Has adequate dialog occurred between educators and lay citizens to truly determine which subject matter areas comprise the basics?
2. Which understandings, skills, and attitudes do pupils need, to participate optimally in society?
3. Which criteria need to be followed to determine basic learnings which are necessary for all pupils in the school-class setting, as well as in society?
4. Should measurable behaviourally stated objectives alone be utilised in teaching-learning situations? If so, what implications does this have for learning experiences devoted to moral development of human beings?
5. Who is accountable for emphasising moral development of pupils? Possible answers to this question would include all or part of the following institutions or groups—the home, the church or the associated religious body, the school, social agencies, as well as diverse clubs and organisations;
6. Which method or methods of emphasising moral development should be stressed within the framework of the school curriculum, institutions in society, or social group?
7. Who should be involved in choosing objectives, experiences, and appraisal techniques in the moral development arena?
8. Is it possible to determine a quality scope and sequence curriculum when determining units, partial units, or incidental learnings in moral developmental?

Thus it is quite apparent that there are numerous problems and needed solutions in the moral development arena as a basic in the curriculum.

Methods of Emphasising Moral Development

Several methods have been presented by educators in guiding pupils to achieve well in the moral development arena. These means differ considerably from each other to achieve desired objectives.

1. A traditional approach still utilised by many teachers pertains to indoctrinating learners with selected values. These teachers feel that a core of tested values exist which *all* must adopt. The expressed values have stood the test of time and are not subject to revision. Among others, specific values pertaining to the work ethic, love and marriage, self sufficiency in life, misuse of tobacco and alcohol, church attendance, wise use of leisure time, and proper relations with other human beings have been advocated;
2. The telling approach to moral development emphasises the teacher dictating to pupils what to do in situations where values adhered to guide decisions made in life. The teacher then expects pupils to follow through with specific kinds of responses given by the former to problematic situations involving values.
3. Values clarification approaches emphasise that pupils possess clear concepts and generalisations pertaining to values presently possessed. Values clarification approaches definitely do not recommend teachers indoctrinating or dictating ideals to pupils. Rather, values adhered to by learners are clarified objectivity. Thus, for example, learners in a values clarification session may list ten things they like to do best. This may be followed by pupils placing a dollar sign in front of listed items costing five dollars or more. Pupils, among other learnings, gain insight into what is prized most highly and costs attached. Other designations may also be marked pertaining to the ten cherished activities listed by pupils, such as the frequency of participation within a given activity. Sidney Simon and his associate (Simon, Sidney B., et.al.) have been leading advocates

of utilising values clarification approaches in guiding moral development within learners.

4. Modelling by the teacher and parents or guardians has been utilised much (consciously or unconsciously) to provide direction for pupil emulation. Thus, for example, the teacher sets an example for learners to follow by being honest, preparing adequately for teaching, showing concern for others, possessing feeling of empathy, and accepting others as human beings having much worth. Hopefully, pupils will pattern their own behaviour in terms of desired models presented.

5. Rewarding desired moral behaviour of pupils may be a powerful method of guiding pupils to reveal proper standards of mortality. The teacher or another rewarder would, of course, determine which behaviours adhere to criteria of mortality. If a learner is truthful, helps others in need, respects others, shows increased concern for the welfare of others, and evaluates his/her own behaviour in terms of desirable standards, the teacher may reward desired behaviours with acceptable verbal and non-verbal means of communication.

6. A day in school may be spent in giving the desirable activities and experiences to girls in a class. Boys then would be asked to perform the less desirable tasks. Ultimately, the boys would feel what it means to be discriminated against due to the sex of the individual. These feelings can become quite pronounced toward the middle and end of a school day. The roles of boys and girls may be reversed for the next school day. Adequate time must be given here for pupils to truly reflect upon the meaning or meaning of the concept *discrimination*.

7. Lawrence Kohlberg from Harvard University has done much work in the moral development arena for pupils. Dr. Kohlberg has emphasised the moral dilemmas approach in guiding pupils to realise higher levels of morality. Thus, dilemma situations are provided for

pupil consideration. Learners are to respond in terms of what they would do within the framework of the dilemma producing situation.

Conclusion

There are numerous methods to utilise in teaching-learning situations to guide pupils in the moral dilemma arena. Moral standards provide guidance and direction to deeds and acts in society. Thus, the question arises as to which curriculum areas should comprise the basics in the school-class setting. It certainly becomes apparent that it is indeed complex to determine that which constitutes the basics in the curriculum. Could moral development of learners be conceived of as a basic in the curriculum?

REFERENCES

Ediger, Marlow, *Relevancy in Elementary Curriculum*. Kirksville, Missouri: Simpson Publishing Company, 1975.

Ediger, Marlow, *"Values and the Curriculum"*, New Frontiers in Education, July-September, 1982.

Ediger, Marlow, *"Values Clarification and Biblical Literature"* Virginia English Bulletin, Winter, 1986.

Moore, W. Ediger, et. al. *Creative and Critical Thinking*. Second Edition. Boston: Houghton Mifflin Company, 1985.

Morris, Van Cleve, and Young Pal. *Philosophy and the American School*. Second Edition. Geneva, Illinois: Houghton Mifflin Company, 1976.

Rippa, S. Alexander, *Education in a Free Society*, New York: Longman, 1980.

Simon, Sidney, et.al. *Values Clarification*, New York: Hart Publishing Company, Inc., 1972.

14

Quality in the Multicultural Curriculum Excellence and Equity

It is vital to have quality in the multicultural curriculum. Excellence and equity are also necessary ingredients. To have the concepts of quality, excellence, and equity, there are vital components to emphasise in curriculum development. The curriculum needs to be planned thoughtfully and carefully with each learner achieving as much as possible. The objectives section is of prime importance. There needs to be rational balance among knowledge, skills, and affective ends. Knowledge objectives need carefully consideration in that they contain salient structural ideas. These ideas when achieved by students provide major generalisations for student use in relating new ideas thereto. The generalisations need to be accurate and provide much information on diverse cultures. Subordinate contain achieved might then be related to the main ideas.

Skills objectives emphasise students applying knowledge in useful situations. Thus, students should use information on many cultures when working together with others of diverse races and creeds. There are a plethora of useful skills to stress by students when working harmoniously together. Acceptance, critical and creative thinking, problem solving, and hands on approaches in learning are vital.

Attitudinal objectives emphasise feelings that one person has toward others and is exemplified with empathy, helpfulness, wanting to learn from others, kindness, and thoughtfulness (Ediger, 2002, 7-10).

Learning Opportunities to Achieve Objectives

A variety of learning opportunities need to be used to assist students to achieve objectives in multicultural education. These learning opportunities need to be developmental and provide for individual differences. Students and the teacher need to discuss proper attitudes toward others of diverse racial groups. These standards should be listed and posted in the classroom. Referring to these standards is a must to notice classroom climate and individual achievement in attitudes.

Reading experiences are highly significant to emphasise. Books need to be available on a variety of topics dealing with diverse cultures. Also, they must be on the reading level of the involved reader. The student might choose which book(s) to read sequentially. He/she may also select the assessment procedure used to ascertain progress. Many, will wish to have a conference with the classroom teacher to discuss ideas read. There are diverse ways for student use to show achievement from having read a book. The teacher may discuss discussion possibilities with pupils. Adequate stress should be placed upon a set of readers having read the same paper back on current issues in racism. The teacher will want to assess student achievement on attitudes toward people of other races. Hopefully, continual improvement will be shown. The ideal is to accept others as equals in all situations. Books for students to read might include the following:

- Clements, Andrew (2002), The Jacket. New York: Simon and Schuster for Young Readers.
- Green, Jan (2000), Talking About Racism. Austin, Texas: Steck—Vaughn Company.
- Katz, Karen (1999). The colours of us. New York: Henry Holt and Company.
- Mitchell, Lori (1999), Different Just Like Me, Watertown, Massachusetts: Charlesbridge Publishing Company.
- Monk, Isabell (1999), Hope. Minneapolis: Caroirhoda Books.
- Parks, Rosa (1992), Rosa Parks, My Story. New York: Dial Books.

- Torres, Leyla (1993), Subway Sparrow. New York: Farrar, Straus, and Giroux.
- Wyeth, Sharon (1998), Tomboy Trouble. New York: Random House.

A special section in the library should house reference books for teachers to use in teaching about racism and multicultural education.

Daily newspaper and weekly news magazines may be used to read articles and discuss problems in equity in society, be it in jobs, housing, education, wages, and salaries. Inequities need identification and issues discussed freely. Here is where respect for each student and his/her ideas are important. A fair, open place for each committee's discussion must be in the offing. Biases need to be addressed and solutions sought through problem solving. Minority groups, in particular, must feel that they are being listened to and accepted. Criteria, listed on the chart, for treating each person fairly need to be referred to periodically. Students need guidance fo assess the self in emphasising growth toward being accepted of individuals and groups of diverse racial groups.

Students need to study units dealing with other cultural groups in the nation. For example, committees may be formed to develop indepth studies of the Old Order Amish whose value system is quite different from other subcultures in the United States. Each committee then may choose to inquire about a certain facet of Old Order Amish culture, such as in the following categories:

- means of transportation. The use of horse and buggy or carriage is emphasised instead of the modern automobile.
- means of earning a living. Amish formerly farmed, but due to scarcity of farm land, many go into other kinds of work. These kinds of work include carpentering; construction work; carpet laying; as well as weaving beautiful blankets, place mats, rugs, and carpets using scrap materials only or largely.

- cottage industries are salient. Making carriages, harnesses, and horse collars; sewing aesthetically pleasing blankets for selling; baking cakes, roles, cookies, bread, and dough nuts; making candy, for example, one Amish owned candy factory employs eight women of their own faith making 500 pounds of peanut clusters, 800 pounds of bon bons, and 500 pounds of peanut brittle each day. A truck hauls the candy each day to places of selling.
- farming is done with draft horses which pull plows for plowing the fields, disks for disking the farm land, and a drill for seeding the crops. These scenes may be compared with those of modern farming operations (Ediger, 2001, 743-751). Internet sources are excellent for obtaining information on the Old Order Amish.

Students need to develop interest in and be accepting of other cultures. These cultures may be highly unique such as the Old Order Amish. All people need respect, acceptance, and a realisation of how needs are alike of all peoples such food, clothing and shelter. How needs are met may vary from culture to culture.

Different patterns of grouping may be used in teaching students of diverse racial groups. It is good to have in each groups students of diverse racial groups. This presents excellent opportunities to learn from each other and practice desirable behaviours of acceptance toward others. Homogeneous grouping emphasises uniformity of achievement in what to is be studied. Heterogeneous grouping stresses students being of mixed achievement levels. Both may be emphasised in ongoing units of instruction. A major goal here is to have students learn from each other as well as develop positive attitudes. Satisfying experiences among racial groups are musts! Sometimes, each student may work on an individual project or activity. With different learning styles inherent among students some may prefer to work by the self at times. At other times, small groups and collaborative experiences may be preferred. Individual differences and needs must be met in a harmonious manner among students of different racial groups. Approaches in grouping practices must be kept flexible.

A variety of activities assists students to achieve as optimally as possible. Construction projects, art experiences, and dramatic activities emphasise a hands on approach to learning whereas reading and writing stress abstract experiences. Multiple intelligences theory stresses that there are a plethora of intelligences possessed by students and one size does not fit all. These intelligences possessed may be stronger in one area individually and include the following:

- verbal/linguistic with emphasis upon reading and writing. Each student needs opportunities to read subject matter on famous leaders, past and present, involving those from different racial groups;
- visual/space with art products and processes showing student achievement in learning about people from diverse cultures;
- logical/mathematics in which learners may reason and think logically about solving problems between/among selected racial groups;
- musical/rhythmical whereby students learn to sing and compose music pertaining to specific racial groups. Dance activities are also salient in the rhythmic realm;
- intrapersonal in which a student pursues tasks individually as compared to interpersonal intelligence whereby learners desire to work collaboratively on a group project;
- bodily/kinesthetic involve experiences pertaining to physical prowess as in quality athletic and game skills. Here, learners may achieve in learning to play games and sports endeavours of other cultures;
- scientific which emphasises objectivity and develops skills in objective thinking as in science activities (See Gardner, 1993).

In each of the above named multiple intelligence learning opportunities, students need to grow in working harmoniously with individuals of diverse racial groups. Showing respect toward other learners is of utmost importance. Being members of heterogeneous racial groups with stress placed on goal attainment must be emphasised. There are a plethora of learning opportunities stressing multiple intelligences.

Journal writing harmonises well with multiple intelligences theory of learning as well as in providing for individual differences. Each student is owner of personal journal writing being stressed. The contents of a journal may contain personal impressions of what was learned in a given lesson or unit of study. Thus, in a news clipping discussed in class, the student may write about discrimination in salaries between men and women paid in the work place as well as among diverse racial groups. By writing content in the journal, the student has a better chance to assess involved problems. Directly related to journal writing is a slightly more structured approach such as writing diary entries. The diary entries are dated and a student may record on a daily basis what was learned, for example, about Rosa Parks and Martin Luther King, Jr., which was not known before.

Port folio development by a student with teacher guidance may supplement information from state mandated tests to reveal learner achievement. In the port, folio, the following products and processes, selected at random, may be filed by a student:

- book report written, such as on Caesar Chavez, a leader in obtaining migrant worker rights;
- diorama made on Mexican workers coming into the United States and doing impoverished kinds of low paying work. Considerable research needs to be done in planning for the diorama. If the product is too large for containment in a port folio, a related snapshot may substitute;
- a mural may be made of crowded older building in a slum area and being replaced with modern updated structures;
- use of software and computer assistance having simulation content on racism involving minority students problems in choosing a profession, finishing requirements, and then looking for a work place position (Ediger, 1997).

Evaluation of Achievement

There should be a variety of means used to appraise student achievement. Teacher observation with the use of recommended criteria needs adequate emphasis. The teacher may observe rather continuously how each learner is improving in attitudes toward other races and cultures. The observational results may be used to improve sequence in learning, remedy deficiencies in knowledge and skills obtained, and as well as objectives to be stressed in teaching.

Teacher self evaluation is salient to use. Approximately ten criteria may be listed with the teacher responding to each using a five point Lickert Scale. Items to be listed for the self evaluation might well include the following:

- I try to understand each student's cultural needs.
- I try to treat each student fairly and equitably.
- I try to learn as much as possible about racial injustices.
- I try to be a model of students in class in revealing respect for all peoples.

Essay test items may be used to appraise learner achievement. Results from the essay test should be used to improve student knowledge, skills, and attitudes in accepting individuals of other racial groups. Essay test items need to be written clearly so students understand what is wanted. There needs to be definite objectives which the teacher wishes to assess pertaining to learner achievement in improved racial attitudes.

Classroom discussions may be used to appraise student participation. Within the discussion, students may reveal understandings, skills and attitudes pertaining to subject matter learned, feelings generated, and eagerness to learn about issues and problems pertaining to race in society.

Committee endeavours may be appraised in terms of effort put forth by participants, acceptance of peers, and democratic procedures used. The committees need to work in the direction of having good human relations.

Construction and art projects may be assessed in terms of neatness, understanding of inherent ideas, and uses made of the completed products. The quality of interaction among committee members is very important to assess.

Problem solving may be appraised in terms of relevancy of identified problems, motivation in working toward solutions, and cooperation shown in working with peers.

Critical thinking may be assessed in terms of indepth perception of ideas, as well as relating ideas gleaned and applied to other thought situations. Appreciation of obtaining carefully thought through ideas should improve attitudes among the races.

Creative thinking may be assessed in terms of growth in this area of the student's total development. An increase in novel, unique, and originality of ideas need to be forthcoming.

REFERENCES

Ediger, Marlow (2001), "*Studying the Old Order Amish*", Education, 121 (4), 743-751.

——(2002), "*Measurement Theory Versus Constructivism*. Journal of Research in Education, 1 (1), 7-10.

——(1997), *Teaching Reading and the Language Arts*, Kirksville, Missouri: Simpson Publishing Company.

Gardner, Howard (1993), *Multiple Intelligences: Theory into Practice*. New York: Basic Books.

15

Reading and Recent Educational Philosophies

The curriculum needs to be developed thoughtfully and carefully. The considerations of student interests, purposes, and talents need ample study in order to develop the implemented curriculum. Students differ from each other in a plethora of ways. These need ample consideration in achieving a quality curriculum. Parental assistance need also to be incorporated into curriculum development. Proper methods and philosophies of instruction also might well help pupils to achieve, develop, and grow.

Essentials in the Curriculum

There is a school of thought which emphasises that pupils attain essential, not learner chosen knowledge. The thinking is that the basics need identification and implemented in teaching and learning situations. Necessary knowledge for now and in the future must be emphasised in teaching and learning situations. There are selected knowledge and skills which then need identification and implementation in the classroom. The identified essential knowledge is to be taught to all pupils. Knowledge and skills identified are taught to develop the educated individual who can apply what has been learned for the personal self and for the future job, occupation, and vocation selected. Major emphasis should be placed upon expository kinds of reading. Reading in the different subject matter areas should assist pupils to acquire knowledge, useful now and at the future work place.

Grammar and writing need to emphasise a core of spelling words which research has shown to be salient for all learners. These words are used frequently by pupils in writing and stress utilitarian goals. Grammar needs to emphasise those learnings which guide pupils to write more clearly and more meaningful in the communication arena. Grammar is to be studied not for its own sake but for purposes of conveying ideas to others. The parts of speech and how words are to be used in sentences must be stressed. There is a structure to the English language consisting of sentence patterns, and diverse kinds of dependent clauses. Proper sequence in writing sentences helps the reader to attach sequence in what is being read.

Oral communication provides the basis for writing. What is said aloud can also be written down. Oral communication skills should emphasise clarity in pronunciation. Thus words need to be clearly enunciated. Appropriate stress, (saying individual words louder or quieter) breaks and monotony of saying each succeeding word within sentences. Stress in oral communication is like a crescendo in music.

Words should be pitched higher or lower depending upon what makes for good communication. Proper pitch should be stressed in oral communication. Thus words need to be pitched higher or lower, depending upon what is needed for effective oral communication. A monotone voice is difficult to listen to for even a very short period of time. Musical scores contain notes on a scale to show the different levels of pitch in signing a note or playing it on a musical instrument. Linguists generally identify four levels of pitch from highest to lowest in oral communication. Juncture or pauses should be stressed adequately within a word, or within a sentence, as well as within sequential paragraphs. Too frequently, pupils do not pause adequately, as needed, and thus words and sentences are joined together needlessly, whereas there needs to be adequate juncture or pause(s). Pupils need much assistance in oral communication since practical skills are necessary to convey ideas effectively, now as well in the future.

Reading is certainly a basic and should stress a demanding curriculum of understanding content read. Phonics instruction will assist the pupil to unlock unknown words. Phonics is to be separated from whole language approaches. With phonics instruction, the learner can become an independent reader. If a word is not identified in reading print, use of phonics will help pupils to read, and read more fluently. There are a core of words which pupils need to master. These words are met up with again and again in reading. The core words in reading are to be considered as basics. All kinds of information can then be read independently with a quality programme of the basics.

A quality mathematics curriculum can well provide for a basics programme of instruction. Addition, subtraction, multiplication, and division objectives can be determined whereby pupils learn what is essential. Frills and fads need to be eliminated. The scope and sequence of mathematics then may emphasise the four basic operations on number. Pertaining to essentialism, the founder William Chandler Bagley (1938) advocated the following:

1. strong discipline in the classroom with appropriate standards for pupils to achieve;
2. a separate subjects curriculum. Opposite of the separate subjects curriculum would be to relate mathematics with other academic areas such as social studies;
3. student interest should be played down and a more demanding mathematics curriculum be stressed.
4. a stable mathematics curriculum, rather than one of continuous modification and change;
5. vital subject matter taught using basal textbooks rather than an activity centred curriculum;
6. a teacher determined curriculum rather than using pupil-teacher planning in curriculum design.

Bagley opposed the following trends in education:

1. The complete abandonment in many school systems of rigorous standards of academic achievement;
2. The disparagement of system and sequence in learning and a dogmatic denial of any value in, even any possibility of learning through, the logical,

chronological, and causal relationship of learning materials;

3. The wide vogue of the so called "activity movement";
4. The discrediting of the exact and the exacting studies;
5. An increasingly heavy emphasis upon the "social studies";
6. Using the lower schools to establish a new social order;
7. The "curriculum revision" movement and its vagaries.

Essentialist then advocated a school setting whereby, in the discipline arena, teachers teach and pupils learn. They stressed, too, that pupils study subject matter systematically rather than pupils engaging in an activity centred curriculum. Each academic discipline should be taught separately, not stressing integration of subject matter. The curriculum should be stable and not emphasise curriculum revision continuously. Life in society changes rather rapidly and schools need to provide stability in the curriculum. Life is demanding and cannot stress only or largely that which is of interest.

Science and social studies should also emphasise clarity in stated subject matter objectives. The scope and sequence in subject matter should be clearly spelled out. A no nonsense approach should be stressed in teaching and learning. There are exact standards, which pupils need to achieve, regardless of interest involved. Pupils need to achieve subject matter knowledge in school and not experience entertainment only or largely. A stable curriculum is to be emphasised rather than one with continuous change.

An Activity Centred Curricula

Activity centred advocates, in developing the curriculum, tend to de-emphasise using basal textbooks for teaching and learning situations. They advocate using a variety of learning opportunities to provide for individual differences. Thus, an activity centred curriculum may stress construction activities for pupils to show what is being learned. A learning by doing approach is emphasised. In a construction activity, for example, pupils may make models pertaining to what has been or is being taught. Additional items to construct dealing with related units of study might include the following:

1. anemometers and wind vanes pertaining to a science unit titled, "The Weather and How It Affects Us".
2. a Contestoga wagon in a social studies unit on "The Westward Movement". The latter may be used in creatively dramatising what settlers did as they moved to California.

It is important to notice in the above two named activities active involvement by pupils in learning is being emphasised. They do not learn only from a basal textbook, but from a variety of reference sources to make anemometers, wind vanes, and the Contestoga wagon. The basal text is used as a resource, as are other development materials of instruction. Learning by doing stresses the following:

1. doing art projects relating to an ongoing activity;
2. dramatising concepts and generalisations acquired;
3. problem solving involving a dilemma situation;
4. movement, interaction of learners and motion in learning become purposeful and paramount.

Within each project, pupils need to have a purpose or reason(s) for participation. They need to carry out the purpose, followed by assessing the final product or process. William Heard Kilpatrick (1871-1964), late professor of Columbia University in New York City, was a leading advocate of the project method. He emphasised pupils do the following flexible steps (Wahlquist, 1942):

1. pupil purposing or having one or more reasons for doing the project;
2. pupil planning of how to do the project;
3. pupil execution in caring out the plans;
4. pupils judging of the final product in terms of desired criteria.

Pupils may work individually or preferable collectively in working on the project. Intellectually, skills are developed in doing the project. Intellectually, pupils need to read background information on the project so that adequate knowledge is present. They need to write summaries, outlines, diary entries on a day to day basis while working on the project, do summaries of articles read, and keep a log to summarise the diary entries. Good attitudes are an outcome of a positively developed project. Social abilities might well be achieved as a result of working with others. Holism is stressed as pupils work together on a project which stresses an integrated curriculum.

The Measurement Movement

The measurement movement stresses the importance of teachers being able to document what pupils have learned. To measure a distance, for example, where, accuracy is involved, a measuring tape may be used. Depending upon the accuracy needed, the readings from the tape should provide quite accurate measurements. There will be small amounts of error from one measurement to the next when repeated measurements of the same distance are involved. But the sequential measurements will be very close as compared to estimating the distance.

Toward the early 1900s, Edward Lee Thorndike and his colleagues applied the measurement concept to measuring pupil achievement in spelling, handwriting, arithmetic, and other academic subject matter areas. Presently, there are standardised tests, criterion referenced tests, and state mandated tests devised to measure pupil achievement in all academic areas. All states in the union by the school year 2005-2006 are to have state mandated tests in place to measure learner achievement and progress. If a pupil fails the state mandated test, he/she might not receive a high school diploma. This indeed would be quite a penalty for any pupil in the early 21st century.

To achieve satisfactorily on the state mandated test, the teacher needs to teach pupils to achieve well on each test. The curriculum then needs to be aligned carefully with each test item. Pupils do better on a test if the curriculum is aligned with the state mandated test. Why are measurably stated objectives to be used in teaching and learning situations?

1. the accountability of teachers can best be determined with measurably stated objectives, resulting in a precise score from pupils such as percentile, to notice how well a pupil has done under a teacher's teaching. Teachers are to be held accountable for pupil achievement;
2. percentiles are relatively easy for a teacher or parent to understand;
3. with percentiles, pupil comparisons with each other may easily be made;
4. failing schools may be sorted from those doing well in pupil achievement;
5. remedial work may be stressed with those pupils not achieving on a satisfactory level, based on state mandated test results.

The Feeling Dimension in Learning

The feeling or attitudinal dimension is very important to evaluate. Existentialism is a philosophy which is very closely related to feelings taught and developed/possessed of/by the pupil. It is very difficult to measure pupil achievement of inherent feelings. The author when being a doctoral student in Curriculum and Instruction, as his major, used the California Test of Personality (CTP) to measure if public schools pupils did better academically and socially in the classroom with or without the assistance of university student teachers. The CTP, as does any personality test, have a high standard of error in test results. Thus, the actual score received on a CTP test can vary much from one measurement taken to the next on the same or alternative form of the test. This variation can make for considerable fluctuation in interpreting the results of a pupil's test results. Then too, generally, there are few test items on a personality test, making for problems in reliability.

Existentialism stresses the importance of feelings possessed by a pupil, but does not recommend testing to ascertain these feelings. In fact, existentialism is a very open ended curriculum with much pupil freedom in the making of choices an decisions as to what to learn.

Existentialists emphasise that a person first exists and then must find his/her essence or purposes in life. These purposes are not given to the person, but must be found. To find these purposes, there may be dread, anxiety, fear, alienation, and loneliness. Each person is "thrown" into the world and then needs to find reasons for life and living. Feelings are subjective as well as knowledge is subjective. The objectivity of science is not found in existentialism. What then might make up the major part of the existentialist curriculum?

1. literature which deals with the human condition;
2. history which stresses the consequences of decision making.

Pupils with teacher assistance need to study about the human condition in literature and history to locate problems in the making of decisions. They need to think of alternatives to the decision which were made. Feelings in the making of decisions must be noted. Choices of reading materials should be left to the individual pupil. In discussion groups, each pupil needs to feel free in the making of choices to alternative decisions than those made. Hindering the flow of discussion on ideas discussed, relating to the topic, is to be discouraged. Authentic decisions must be made. Responsibilities for choices made, vicariously or real, rests with the learner.

The Classics Curriculum

A classical curriculum emphasises the importance of pupils studying content which has survived in importance, in time and in place. This is an attempt at identifying core knowledge for pupils to acquire. Other names for a classics curriculum are perenialism, and The Great Books philosophy of education. Recently written literature read might not be important or even be forgotten after a short duration of time, perhaps after a few years or even months. Literary writings, for example, of Robert Louis Stevenson, Henry Wadsworth Longfellow, Mark Twain, William Shakespeare, Nathaniel Hawthorne, among others, have endured in importance and provided excellent literature in terms of style, content, and meaning. The content might well have positive values as well as standards of morality for pupils to learn. Advocates of the Classics believe strongly that:

1. good literature reveals its importance and quality as it is judged to be good with its enduring merit;
2. good literature does not out live its usefulness;
3. good literature is read by scholarly people as the years keep showing its relevance and beauty in language use;
4. good literature, such as the classics, has its utilitarian values today;
5. good literature possesses needed standards of characterisation, setting, plot, sequence and novel use of language.

Great minds of the past have ideas which reveal worth and merit today, such as Plato's *Republic*. In his ideal nation, Plato divided the worker population into there categories—rulers, soldiers, and artisans. The very highest of citizens in terms of ability and talent were the rulers or governmental officials of the ideal republic. These population had attended school for the longest period of time of any in the republic. The rulers were to see that the best rules, laws, and regulations were in the offing for citizens. Below that of being in the ruler's category were the warriors. The warriors were guardians of the *Republic*. They were the soldiers and policemen in guarding the ideal state from enemies, foreign and domestic. The lowest group in Platonic society were the artisans who provided for the physiological needs of all people such as food, clothing, and shelter. These were considered as being menial tasks by Plato. From a discussion on the contents on the *Republic*, pupils may debate the following as an example:

1. can people in society be divided into three categories, only, as Plato indicated?
2. how can pupils be educated so that they can indicate their talents in a tripartite division?
3. what do you believe would make for an ideal republic or nation?

Implications from the Classics in curriculum development are the following:

1. liberal arts curriculum assists a learner to explore knowledge and, perhaps, find his/her niche in life;

2. vital content is acquired which has been evaluated in space and time. The unimportant is then weeded out in the process;
3. clear communication with others is then possible when all college students have a two to four year programme of liberal arts instruction with a common body of classical knowledge;
4. general education, like the classics, needs to be obtained prior to choosing a vocation, job, or profession. General education provides the necessary prerequisites in pursuing studies for a job, occupation, or professional;
5. a common body of knowledge for all college students occurs when a core curriculum is being emphasised such as the Great Books of the Western World;
6. the mind or mental facets of a pupil need to be developed with imbibing the thinking of the great minds of the past who have demonstrated achievements and accomplishments;
7. what is deemed to be important for pupil learning has been developed by advocates of core knowledge for all to acquire.

Accordingly, educational intellectualism tends to be past orientated and the emphasise stability—the continuity of the great enduring, enduring ideas, over time. In general, the eternal ideas, are best represented in the abiding masterworks of the world's greatest of the world's greatest minds as these are conveyed thorough the cultural heritage of mankind. The overall goal of education is to identify, preserve, and transmit essential Truth (that is the essential principles that govern the underlying meaning and significance of life). More specifically the intermediate role of the school as a particular social institution is to teach students how to think (that is, how to reason) and transmit the best thought (the enduring wisdom) of the past.

In contemporary education, philosophical conservatism expresses itself primarily as educational intellectualism and theological, intellectualism, Philosophical intellectualism is best represented in America today by such individuals as Robert Maynard Hutchins and Mortimer Adler, who are both primarily concerned with metaphysical wisdom in the traditional Aristotelian sense and who both tend to place great emphasis upon on traditional liberal arts education in the spirit of the "Great Books" (O' Neil, William F., 1981).

REFERENCES

Bagley, William Chandler (1938), *"An Essentialists Platform in the Advancement of American Education"*, Educational Administration and Supervision, 24: 241-256.

O' Neil, William F. (1981), *Educational Ideologies*. Santa Monica, California, p. 168.

Wahlquist, John T. (1943), *Philosophy of American Education*. New York: The Ronald Press Company, 223-224.

16

Increasing High School Reading Comprehension

It is indeed difficult for high school teachers to provide for individual differences among students when the gap in reading achievement is large in a classroom. With 25 students in a high school sophomore class, there may be a range of student reading achievement from a low of third grade reading level to a high of grade fourteen. The teacher then must attempt to meet achievement levels of all students in this classroom. How is this to be done? The teacher may print legibly the now words in the next lesson on the chalkboard. The teacher may then pronounce each word clearly as the student looks at it carefully. The textbook meaning needs to be provided for each new word. It is good to use the related illustrations as each new word is being defined or used contextually. Good readers may be reading other subject matter rather than following the proceding plan of providing readiness for reading for the next day's lesson (See Beach, 1993).

Understanding Indepth What Has Been Read

Quality comprehension of what has been read by the student needs to be stressed by the teacher. Too often, shallow thinking has been an end result of student reading. Instead, there are a variety of comprehension skills which need to be emphasised.

Students may need considerable assistance in reading factual information. Every fact read need not be remembered. In reality, it is impossible to do so. There needs to be a yardstick for student use to ascertain which are salient and which facts are of lesser value. These needs to be taught to students. By looking at the topical heading, the student may determine which facts are of major value to retain. The important facts will relate directly to the topical heading and thus increase their meaning. Students need direct practice to analyse which are major and which are minor facts. Then too, finding specific details which answer a question may well provide more security as to the worthwhileness of some as compared to other facts.

Reading for a sequence of ideas does aid in providing meaning to subject matter read. Sometimes, the content does not possess the best order and thus hinders student understanding. When writing is connected to reading, students may fail to communicate well in written work due to inappropriate sequence written by the author. The author must present a model to students. When communicated orally during a discussion what an author said, the student may well be a more effective communicator when providing ideas which are sequential.

History, as an academic discipline, emphasises chronological order of information. If the chronology is incorrect, the subject matter is erroneous. Adequate time needs to be spent in assisting students to read, write and speak in a sequential manner (See Durkin, 1993).

As students mature in the language arts and as it cuts across the curriculum, they will meet up with two or more points of view in a reading selection. In contrasting the multiple points of view, the student needs to comprehend each thoroughly. Meaning theory is very important. He/she needs to draw upon background experiences in order to achieve richer and fuller understandings. Liberal and figurative language needs to be weighed in terms of involved meanings. Vocabulary terms used also change meanings, since a synonym may make for shades of difference in understanding the author's purpose. The author's purposes when making these comparisons need to be adjudicated to ascertain when the intended learnings are.

Alalysing also becomes an important interpretation skill. When analysing, the student thinks, critically in terms of indicating if a statement is accurate versus inaccurate, fact or fiction, and/or realistic versus fantasy. Reflection by the student is salient here in that the learner needs to think upon thinking. Thus, the learner needs to determine what is known and what is left to know. Then too, the student must determine how something is known. Sometimes analytic thinking is called critical thinking.

Students need to experience making contrasts and comparisons. In contrasting, one notices how two or more ideas are alike. Careful thinking is necessary here. There may be very slight differences. At other times, the differences are more obvious (See Norton, 1992).

Logical thought is involved in making the contrasts. Mathematics makes heavy use of logical thinking. For example, if "a" is greater than "b", and "b" is greater than "c", then "a" is greater than "c". In much of life, logical thinking is done such as — if this worked in that situation, then it also should work here in the new situation; this is done frequently in ongoing activities. In making comparisons, the student wants to know the differences between two or more ideas. For example, how is the formula for finding the area of a square different from that of finding the area of a rectangle?

The student needs to determine how the subject matter read relates to his/her own life. A student may perceive very little or no relationship of what was read *to* his/her own personal life. Subject matter becomes more meaningful if the student relates what is read *to* his/her personal life. This is something which must be taught and be reflected upon. Ideas becomes more useful if they become a part of the personal self. Frequently with the development of background information, the reader tends to be able to integrate the self with the contents read. Familiarity with the subject matter contents assists the reader to integrate the self with the script more thoroughly. Thinking abilities and skills also assist the student to develop indepth, learning and increase the fund of ideas to be used.

Cause and effect thinking skills are highly useful. Too frequently, the student fails to realise there are reasons for a certain happening. It is easy to think of the cause for eating and that is one is usually hungry. However, the writer has noticed frequently that students do not think of historical events being caused. It seems that events to many persons seem to occur in a vacuum. There may be multiple causes for events such as for a conflict, e.g. World War Two. In the natural sciences, students may think of natural disasters, including earthquakes, to seemingly have just happened. Rather, indepth study depending upon the developmental level of the student, requires serious intensity study be given to the many causes of this and other natural phenomena of mudslides, avalanches, erosion, volcanic eruptions, among others. Explanations are indeed complex for indepth reading!

To read and study intelligently, the reader needs to be able to make predictions. This is true not only in word recognition but also in terms of what might happen in a narrative account. A good recogniser of words uses the context to ascertain what the next words will be and thus read more rapidly than otherwise would be the case. A fluent reader who reads at an understanding optimal rate of speed tends to comprehend much better than those who read more slowly. A slow reader is definitely handicapped in grasping sequential ideas. He/she struggles much over word identification and then loses out on comprehension and higher levels of thinking. High school students need to develop word recognition and comprehension skills which in return permit diverse kinds of complex thinking. When making predictions of future events in a novel, the student needs to be a good predictor of ideas to be read. As he/she reads, checking on the accuracy of the original prediction is made. The prediction may well be modified if need be. Being able to predict well is salient in society, also. Very frequently, an individual makes predictions or speculators on the near future or even on events may occur in space and time. By making predictions, the individual attempts to orientate himself/herself better in terms of what will be read. As the act of reading continues, the reader makes needed adjustments in ideas adhered to, with modifications forthcoming (Ediger, 1998).

Drawing conclusions is a highly worthwhile skill for students to develop. Not only must the student relate ideas to draw conclusions but also read between the lines. In other words, the conclusions contain what was read literally figuratively, and inferentially. Literal interpretation contains content the way ideas are written. The reader then attempts to obtain a duplicate of written subject matter. Realism as a philosophy of education emphasises that the observer may secure reality as it truly is. One then can know what is real in its entirety. Here, the reader obtains subject matter as it is written with no alterations. A minimum of creative ideas are added as possible in securing subject matter read in a literal manner. Figurative interpretation stresses the use of words in a creative manner and novel interpretations made by the reader. The following phrases cannot be taken literally:

- He/she finished the work in a blink of the eye;
- He/she rolled up the sleeves and used elbow grease to get the work done;
- They discussed the topic until it was like beating a dead horse;
- He saw the handwriting on the wall;
- I felt like walking on water when giving my report;
- She was a good Samaritan;
- It will take a loaves and fishes miracle to earn enough money;
- That person had the patience of job;
- She was a Dorcas.

In comparison, inferential reading emphasises reading between the lines and intelligent guessing about ideas. With inferential reading, not everything is said by the author in the printed script. Something is left unsaid, but can be gleaned in creatively in meaning. Creativity is necessary on the part of the student to read inferentially.

Thus, to draw conclusions, there is a fusion of ideas such as in combining literal, figurative, and inferential interpretations. Summarising ideas is sometimes confused with drawing conclusions. However, in a summary, the major ideas read are joined together in a main idea. The summary is broad and contains specific ideas joined together to form a whole (See Rosenblatt, 1993).

Reading and thinking may indeed be quite complex when mental operations are involved. High levels of cognition are involved in thinking. Thinking skills are always useful, presently as well as in the future. Many people have made decisions based on inadequate information and have made minimum or little progress in life. This is regretful! It behooves the teacher to assist students to do well in diverse kinds of thinking skills. Students, too, need to put forth much effort to become the quality of person desired. Motivation is required. Reading is involved when thinking skills are developed. It becomes complex in the thinking arena when word recognition and comprehension of script are also inherent (Ediger and Rao, 2003).

Life in Society

Life is society continually becomes increasingly complex. With a complex society, much information is available for everyone. More media are there to bombard the person with information. This means, among other things, that each person needs to be able to deal adequately with the mass amount of information. Each person then needs the ability to read effectively with quality comprehension. In addition to reading, each individual needs to be able to listen carefully and accurately to content presented. Beyond that, every person must become a good thinker. There are a variety of kinds of thinking, possible such as assessing factual information obtained. Selected facts are then more salient to retain as compared to others. Much more complex levels of thought would involve developing a conclusion from a mass amount of information gleaned. The conclusion needs to hold water with considerable information therein. One would be very limited indeed when knowing only a few facts from the mass number available. Some order needs to be developed from these many important facts. When information is needed, one needs to know where to secure the essential knowledge with the many reference sources available. Prior to that, the individual needs to know what to look for. A problem needs to be identified. Thus, problem solving becomes important. The problem needs to be relevant to the self. A perplexing situation is involved in that a lack of clarity exists on what to do. The dilemma, among other things, involves identifying a relevant problem. There needs to be clarity in stating the problem so that it may be tentatively solved. To solve a problem, information needs to be gathered. The information may come from a variety of reference sources be it concrete or semiconcrete. Concrete sources include the real environment, realia, samples, collections of reality, excursions, among others. The semiconcrete include illustrations, films, filmstrips, slides, video tapes, CDs, DVDs, single concept film loops, student made teaching models, reading materials, and reference persons, among others.

From the information gathered, the student may organise the content to be used in problem solving. The credible information gleaned becomes a tentative hypothesis to be tested in a life like situation. The hypotheses then may be accepted, refuted, or modified as needed.

There are problems which are simpler and those which are much more complex to solve. Selected problems can be solved quickly, but others defy solving for some time. Problem solving is a highly kind of thinking for all students presently and later at the work place.

REFERENCES

Beach, R. (1993), *A Teacher's Introduction to Reader Response Theories*. Urbana, Illinois: National Council Teachers of English (NCTE).

Durkin, Deloris (1993), *Teaching Them to Read*, Sixth Edition, Boston: Allyn and Bacon.

Ediger, Marlow (1998), *Reading and the Language Arts in the Elementary School*. Kirksville, Missouri: Simpson Publishing Company.

Ediger, Marlow and D. Bhaskara Rao (2003), *Teaching Language Arts Successfully*. New Delhi: Discovery Publishing House.

Norton, D. (1992), *The Impact of Literature Based Reading*. New York: Merrill Publishing Company.

Rosenblatt, Louise (1983), *Literature As Exploration*, Fourth Edition. New York: Modern Language Association.

17

Read Alouds for Students

There are a plethora of reasons for emphasising reading aloud for students. It is enjoyable for most students to read orally. Embarrassment should be eliminated for all oral reading experiences. Students should not minimise others with put downs, rude statements, or non-verbal communication pertaining to anyone reading aloud. Definite developmental objectives need to be in the offing. Learning opportunities need to relate to the objectives. A quality programme of assessment of student achievement should indicate how well students are doing in oral communication. This writer will discuss different oral reading activities in this chapter.

Reader's Theatre

All students should ample opportunities to participate in reader's theatre. This is an activity which requires cooperation among participants. Each student has a definite part to read in reader's theatre. The part may be a person, object, or to present background information. The theatre presentation may be purchased commercially or learners might use an appropriate selection from a basal textbook and revise it to make for reading parts aloud. Students need to practice reading aloud their very own part until fluency is involved. Reader's theatre requires that each reader use voice inflection and intonation, propertly. Generally, students are seated in a circle and face the audience as much as possible when reading. No props or background scenery is needed. The selection read aloud needs to attract listener attention. Other classrooms of students may be invited to hear the reader's theatre presentation. Educational opportunities given for a classroom reader's theatre presentation are the following:

1. it provides all students in a classroom a chance to perform in front of others. Social competence is important;
2. it provides a purpose for practicing reading alouds to others;
3. it involves improving voice quality;
4. it makes working together an important goal;
5. it develops respect for others in the group setting.

Round Robin Reading

Round Robin reading has been criticised by some, but does have considerable merit if emphasised properly. Every student likes to read aloud to others and the basal reader provides this opportunity. Generally, five or six are taught in a small group. Readiness is developed for oral reading of the selection. Questions are raised and answered by students covering content read orally. The teacher then has students read aloud in sequence. Here, the teacher, in an atmosphere of respect, may notice difficulties students individually have in reading. These problems may be recorded and then stressed as objectives of instruction. Each student has a chance to read aloud. Students generally like to read aloud and will indicate if they have been omitted from doing oral reading in the round robin approach. Reading within enthusiasm and having proper pitch, voice inflection, and pleasantness may be worked upon in future sessions involving oral reading.

Choral reading is enjoyable to many students as an oral reading activity. Generally, the teacher or another student reads a main part, followed by students, collectively, reading the refrain. Here, voices need to be blended with clarity of enunciation. There can be solo parts, small groups, and the class as a whole being actively involved in choral reading, Wanda Gag's trade book *Millions of Cats* is a good example of the teacher, or student, reading aloud a main section, followed by students joining in the refrain. Or, students together with teacher guidance may read an entire selection together as a choral reading activity. A humorous writing, a rope jumping chant, or repetition within a poem, may well, provide content for the choral reading activity. Iris M. Tiedt in her book *The Language Arts Handbook*, wrote the following poem for choral reading which contains repetition:

Sing Out!
Sing, sing, sing
Racing to the swing.

Hum, hum, hum:
Spring at last has come!
Call, call, call;

The grass is growing tall.
Shout, shout, shout;
School will soon be out!

It is relatively easy to provide the above poem into a solo part (lines one and two), a duet part (lines three and four), and the total class joining in for the remaining lines. Different arrangements may be tried out to notice the effectiveness of each in choral reading.

Reading Poetry Aloud

Poetry needs to be read aloud for enjoyment purposes. A variety of poems need to be read and some of these may be chosen for choral reading experiences. Poetry deals with many subject matter areas such as science, social studies, mathematics, health, and literature. There are poems which are classified as being classical. These poems were written some time ago and yet have stood the test in remaining relevant. Robert Louis Stevenson's *A Child's Garden of Verse* was written in the 1800's and is still enjoyed by many today. To gain optimally from reading, it is good to make connections with writing. When students write, they need to think about content, word choice, syntax, grammar, vocabulary, and the mechanics of written work. Thus, reading can be extended through written work.

Poems are written in different styles. Rhymed verse fascinates some students. Thus, couplets (two lines with ending words rhyming) triplets (three lines with ending words rhyming), quatrains (four lines with ending words rhyming) and limericks (lines one, two, and five rhyme as well as lines three and four rhyming) may be written. Models for each of these kinds of rhymed verse should be seen and experienced by learners. The teacher must read aloud to students each of the rhymed types of poetry. The model for each should be printed on the chalkboard for students to notice likenesses and differences. Perhaps, one kind of poem, the couplet, should be taught separately from the others. Individual differences among learners need to be provided for when developmentally appropriate poems are taught.

Additional kinds of poetry to teach include free verse which may have no rhyme and is open ended in terms of poem length. Haikus and tankas have a certain number of syllables per poem. Haikus have five, seven, five syllables for each of three lines in a poem. Add an additional two lines, each having seven syllables, and the result is a tanka.

The author recommends, when readiness is in evidence, for students to write of poem and voluntarily read it aloud to listeners. Poetry is to be enjoyable and shared.

Formal Dramatisations

Formal dramatisations provide opportunities for reading play parts to others in the classroom. Formal plays may be purchased relating to social studies, science, mathematics, and literature units of study. They may also be written by students with teacher guidance. In social studies, for example, students may be studying a unit on Colonial America. From the basal textbook, students may write play parts. Each person is assigned or volunteers for a part and then practices rehearsing its contents to be read aloud, along with the others involved in the play. The formal dramatisation is practised a few times, but is not to become a highly polished performance. Rather it has educational values with students learning much about colonial America. Learners also practice good habits of orally reading their respective parts well. Gestures, facial expressions, and needed background scenery may be made. Formal dramas also provide students with facility to perform in front of others.

Singing Activities

Singing together provides students opportunities to learn about the lyrics and also the music. Music teachers are generally very cooperative in working with students and the regular teacher in singing activities related to a social studies unit being studied. Much history, for example, may be learned from the lyrics contained in the music. Songs were written in different periods of time and reveal the feelings people had at the time of their writing. Thus, there are songs written during each historical period of time such as Colonial America, the Civil War, the Reconstruction Time, the Depression, World Wars One and Two, among others. When supervising student teachers in the public schools, the author noticed a few students, over the years, who wrote poetry and set the words to music from their respective poem. With the assistance of the music teacher, a few of these resulting songs were sung in the classroom.

The music teacher will emphasise blending of voices, pitch, stress, and juncture. Oral communication is then being furthered as a necessary skill.

Oral Book Reports

Oral book reports provide opportunities for public speaking when using narrative, subject matter, or creative content. The student may wish to read aloud a few direct quotes as the oral book report progresses. The student needs to show the library book being reported upon to listeners. With young learners, the illustrations contained in the library book may be shown as the report progresses. The book report may be given with accompanying notes used as reference points. Forgetting is less likely to occur when the student has notes to refer to when giving the oral report. What should a student focus upon when giving the report?

1. details of the character;
2. important ideas pertaining to the setting of the story;
3. sequential content involving the plot;
4. what the student liked about the library book;
5. an evaluation of the entire book.

If there are time limits for reporting, these need to be adhered to. Clarity of content presented is vital to secure listener attention. The rate of speaking needs to harmonise with what a student can reasonably comprehend.

Additional Oral Reading Experiences

There are many additional oral reading activities for students. The teacher needs to be creative in developing these experiences as they relate to different curriculum areas. The following are very worthwhile activities:

1. joining and dialog journaling;
2. writing diary entries of what was learned daily in a curriculum area. These may be shared with other students;
3. reading directions for doing a construction project for a science unit of study;
4. reading aloud to the class the summary of a concluded chapter from the basal textbook;
5. writing and proofing an article for the local newspaper telling about what has been accomplished in the classroom.

REFERENCES

Anderson, T.H., and B.B. Armbruster (1984), *Studying*. In Pearson, Barr, Kamil, and Mosenthal (Eds.), Handbook of Reading Research (pp. 657-659). New York: Longman.

Ediger, Marlow, and D. Bhaskara Rao (2000), *Teaching Reading Successfully*. New Delhi, India: Discovery Publishing House, Chapter Eight.

Ediger, Marlow (1997), *Teaching Reading and the Language Arts in the Elementary School*, Chapter Twelve.

Ediger, Marlow (1998), *The Holy Land*. Kirksville, Missouri: Simpson Publishing Company, 53-59.

Ediger, Marlow, and D. Bhaskara Rao (2001), *Teaching Social Studies Successfully*. New Delhi, India: Discovery Publishing House, 114-115.

Gardner, Howard (1993), *Frames of Mind: The Theory of Multiple Intelligences*. New York: Basic Books, Inc.

Gerke, P. (1996), *Multicultural Plays for Children*, Lyme, New Hampshire: Smith and Kraus.

Gunning, Thomas G. (2000), *Creating Literacy Instruction for All Children*, Third Edition. Boston: Allyn and Bacon, 366-372.

Murray, D.M. (1989), *Expecting the Unexpected: Teaching Myself—and Others—to Read and Write*. Portsmouth, New Hampshire: Boynton/Cook.

Searson, Robert, and Rita Dunn (2001), *"The Learning Styles Teaching Model"*, Science and Children, 38 (5), 22-36.

Tiedt, Iris M. (1983), *The Language Arts Handbook*. Prentice-Hall Inc., Chapter Thirteen.

18

Reading in Health Education

There is much the teacher can do to assist pupils to achieve more optimally in reading subject matter in ongoing lessons and units in health education. The teacher needs to motivate pupils to comprehend ideas and not hope for print materials to do the job alone. There are definite strategies to encourage reading comprehension which might be used by the teacher. What then might the teacher do to assist pupils in reading comprehension in the health curriculum?

Reading to Understand

The teacher needs to develop background experiences for pupils prior to reading. The background information may be called "advanced organisers". Here, the teacher tells pupils in a few, meaningful sentences what is to be comprehended. By facing pupils and having appropriate eye contact, the teacher need to use proper stress, pitch, and enunciation in providing the advance organiser. Along with the advance organiser, the teacher may have pupils look carefully at the pictures inherent in the content to be read. Each picture may provide for an excellent discussion to clarify ideas. In interactions during the discussion, pupils might well experience the concept of scaffolding. With scaffolding, pupils experience the filling in of knowledge between where they are presently in achievement and where they should be, according to the subject matter to be read. Scaffolding provides pupils the opportunity to understand what will be read (Ediger, 1997, Chapter Two).

While discussing the related illustrating pertaining to what will be read, the teacher should bring to the attention of pupils new words to the encountered in reading. With previous observations made of pupils, the teacher may develop expertise in ascertaining which words might cause difficulties in pupil reading. Identification of new words in print is salient in becoming a good reader. These new words may be printed in neat manuscript style on the chalkboard for all pupils in class to see. Pupils need to look at each word carefully and practice their identification. Meaning for each new word should be developed within a sentence. By this time, learners will have identified questions which they would like to have answered. The above named experiences should have obtained pupil readiness for reading the new subject matter on health education. Depending upon the topic to be read, the following questions are given as examples:

1. where and how does digestion begin in the human being?
2. what happens when cancerous cells invade an organ, such as the esophagus?
3. what are enzymes and how do they aid in digestion?
4. how do the large intestine and the small intestine differ in function?
5. why do selected people suffer from indigestion? (Ediger, 2000, Chapter Nine).

Pupils might then read to secure information in answer to the questions. Teachers need to have a model available to guide instruction in a satisfactory manner. The model is substantiated by recommended principles of learning and carefully follows tenets of educational psychology. A carefully devised sequence of experiences for pupils is needed so that each learner may achieve as optimally as possible from reading activities in the health curriculum.

After pupils have completed the reading activity, they might be guided by the teacher in a variety of experiences as a follow up. The following are appropriate:

1. discuss answers to questions, such as the five enumerated above as an example;
2. have a committee develop a mural covering subject matter read;
3. conduct a panel discussion involving content read. A chair person and three panel members with each presenting subject matter as panel topics dictate;
4. assist pupils in writing journal entries pertaining to impressions gained from the ongoing lesson or unit of study;
5. make a list of key ideas gained from reading;
6. write an outline in proper form containing the main and subordinate ideas as well as details of subject matter read;
7. develop drawings pertaining to content read;
8. draw a web of major and subordinate ideas gleaned from reading;
9. construct paper mache' models of organs in the human body, as contained in the reading selection;
10. put together a college directly related to what was read (see Douillard).

Guidelines for Teaching Pupils

There are selected guidelines which teachers need to use in ongoing reading activities. Interest is a powerful factor in learning. Thus, when presenting background information as advanced organisers for reading a given selection, the teacher needs to observe pupils, carefully, in order to notice which experiences secure learner attention. Fascinating experiences need to be provided so that continuous pupil attention is in the offing. Without interest, the chances are pupils will not achieve as optimally as possible.

Second, the teacher needs to be certain that pupils attach meaning to ongoing experiences in reading. For example, when new words are introduced to pupils prior to reading, pupils need to understand meanings of new words either as definitions or in contextual sentences. If pupils do not understand that which has been presented, the reading task, no doubt, will be rather meaningless.

Third, pupils need to perceive purpose in reading. The questions pupils raise prior to reading will assist to perceive reasons for reading. The reading task then provides purpose for reading when securing information in answer to the questions. A high degree of purpose provides impetus for learning and achievement.

Fourth, individual differences among pupils need adequate recognition. Each is a human being with unique qualities which need identification and cherished to help pupils to achieve as optimally as possible. Acceptance for and of each pupil is a necessity to provide a classroom climate of caring among learners. The classroom becomes a more pleasant place to live in when acceptance and caring are in the offing.

Fifth, motivation is a key concept in teaching. Learning needs to be energised. The learning opportunities available together with the teacher's teaching needs to stress quality so that pupils achieve viable objectives in reading health information. To stay healthy and fit, the learner needs to be a life long reader and user of information to live a productive life. Good health should help pupils to be motivated readers. In the media, there are a plethora of sources from which health information may be obtained. Reading is a quality way of securing information on improved health practices. The level of application is important in using what has been read and learned in the health arena (See Cassel).

The health curriculum needs to focus upon pupils and tenets from educational psychology. Integrating the learner and the curriculum is necessary. To separate the two invites for a lack of pupil interest, meaning, purpose, acceptance, and motivation. Thus, the psychologies of learning needs to be implemented in teaching and learning situations in order that pupils may achieve optimally in reading health information.

Comprehension of Subject Matter

To comprehend well, pupils do need to be able to identify words correctly while reading. The teacher needs to assist pupils in word recognition by using recommended procedures. The following approaches may be used when a pupil cannot identify a word:

1. context clues. Thus if a word is not recognised in print, the pupil should be encouraged to try a word which makes sense within the sentence. This is an attempt to engage in meaningful reading;
2. if the attempted word makes sense, but is incorrect, the pupil needs to look at the initial consonant. Initial consonants tend to be quite consistent between symbol (grapheme) and sound (phoneme). Generally the unknown word is then identified. If not, the ending letter needs to be sounded out of the still unknown word;
3. primary grade pupils may view pictures on the same page as the printed script to identify unknown words while reading. Generally, in health education literature, there are a good supply of illustrations on the same page as the content. Thus, by looking at a picture, the child may identify a word which is unknown. It is good also for all learners to look at pictures carefully so that the printed script may make more sense;
4. selected pupils have learned to recognise unknown while reading by looking at the length of the word as well as the tallness or shortness of the letters. Each word has a unique appearance and might be recognised through these configuration clues;
5. sometimes, a pupil identifies an unknown word by dividing it into syllables. There are common syllable which are contained in words. By analysing a word, the pupil may readily recognised the unknown word. A very common syllable is "un" as in "unlike". The "un" of course means "not", and among other commonly used syllables might well make it possible to recognise an otherwise unknown word (See Brown).

Word recognised is not equal to comprehension of subject matter read. It is important, however, when becoming an independent reader to be able to identify unknown words and read fluently to improve the quality of understanding that which has been read. Which comprehension goals then are important for the reader? Certainly, there are relevant facts to remember from reading subject matter. Facts are the building blocks to use in thinking about what has been read. Thus, using what has been recalled is salient so that the student applies knowledge in school and in society. But before it is applied, subject matter must be analysed in terms of being accurate versus inaccurate, important versus unimportant, and reality based versus fantasy. Thus, what has been read might be unimportant to the reader or highly important depending upon the present situation. A pupil then facing diverse kinds of allergies may be highly interested in reading about this topic. Others might be interested and perceive purpose in reading about other health topics. There are selected learners who need to be motivated in desiring to comprehend information on topics pertaining to health. Analysing what has been read is highly important when a multiplicity of information is continually presented to listeners in the media.

Creative thinking is also salient. Novel, unique ideas may be built upon factual information gained as well as ideas acquired from analysing. New ways then need to be found to use attained ideas. Sometimes, a brain storming approach may be very effective. Pupils with health teacher guidance might then indicate in how many ways a statement or paragraph might be interpreted. If a writer writes something like the following, but does not elaborate, then brainstorming may be very appropriate:

"Each person should do the best possible to protect the self from unwanted diseases. Healthful living is a key idea to avoid different illnesses. People of good health practice habits of healthful living. This is common knowledge which all know or should know".

In reading the above paragraph, the reader needs to determine what the writer has in mind when writing about healthful living. Pupils individually may present ideas in the class as a whole or within a committee as to some possible meanings. The more ideas generated the better and each needs to be recorded on the chalkboard as it is being presented. No idea should be rejected, but pupils need to stay on the topic of what the writer might have had in mind when writing about "healthful living". Duplication of ideas presented from pupils needs to be avoided. When the brain storming has been completed, pupils should be guided to summarise the statements into a few major conclusions (Ediger, 1996, Chapter Three).

Problem solving is an additional good way to reflect upon ideas gained from reading health information. Problem solving is useful in school and in society, and should be stressed frequently in health education lessons and units of study.

A first flexible step of problem solving is to identify a perplexing situation, or problem. The problem is one which has purpose for the class as a whole, a small group, a committee or an individual. The problem needs adequate delimitation so it possesses clarity and might be solvable. Research from a variety of reference sources needs to be done in order to secure information or a possible answer to the problem. The information obtained must relate directly to the identified problem. Selected problems may take a considerable amount of time to reach a solution whereas others can be solved rather readily. Most problems do take a considerable amount of time to solve and appropriate reference sources need to be available. Possible answers to the problems should be dealt with as hypotheses. Any hypothesis is tentative and subject to change. The hypotheses then needs to be assessed to see if they hold water and not leak. Additional study and reflective thinking helps in the assessment process of the hypothesis. This is necessary to arrive at a conclusion which is valid and reliable (Dewey).

Reflective thinking might be emphasised when pupils do journal writing. When ready, pupils may write in their journals major ideas gleaned from reading. Subordinate ideas to support the major ideas may also be put in writing. Writing journal entries assists pupils to recall what has been learned and could lean in the direction of identifying problems. Retention of what has been learned can be a major problem for pupils unless there are opportunities to review and rehearse information obtained. Journal writing offers these opportunities for reinforcing what has been learned. At the same time, ideas may be clarified when putting them into one's own words. Paraphrasing obtained subject matter requires thought and practice. These are useful skills presently for the learner as well as when he/she pursues higher education, following the public school years. Dialogue journal writing may be used as an alternative (see Education Week, Journey 11, 2001).

Additional ways of assisting pupils to understand subject matter include the following:

1. indepth discussion of content read. Here, questions come from pupils and clarification of ideas stressed in ongoing experiences and activities. The teacher needs to be a good asker of questions. Challenging experiences are then in the offing. Reading activities are selected based on what interests and engages pupils (See Adler).
2. seminar methods used in helping pupils comprehend content. Ideally, the questions for discussion should come from pupils, covering that which has been read. Identification of relevant questions and having related knowledge is vitally important in the seminar method. The health teacher is a guide and motivator of pupil progress. He/she is also a resource person to stimulate further pupil thinking. The late Carl Rogers (1902-1987) was a leading advocate of a pupil centred curriculum. A desire to learn comes from within the pupil who through curiosity has an intrinsic need to achieve. The teacher is one who is thoroughly interested in each pupil and helps learners to develop unique qualities. Ridicule and rudeness are definitely not a part of a learner centred teaching and learning strategy;
3. state mandated objectives and assessment, if in evidence within a state. The objectives, provided by the state, may be specific for teachers to use in teaching. The objectives are criterion referenced due to having the objectives available for teachers to use in teaching

pupils. The accompanying tests are criterion referenced tests (CRTs). These tests developed by each state within the nation attempt to measure what pupils have learned. They tend to be valid if they measure what has be taught and are clearly written, as stated in the objectives. The CRTs need to possess reliability in that they measure pupil achievement consistently, be it test/ retest, alternative forms, or split half reliability (See Slavin and Karweit).

Measurement and evaluation of pupil achievement needs to stress a variety of procedures. In addition to CRTs discussed above, the health teacher may write/use the following approaches:

1. discussions. Here, the health teacher may notice who participate and what each participant knows. This provides feedback to the teacher in terms of what needs to receive more emphasis in teaching be it knowledge, skills, and/or attitudes;
2. conferences. With individual or small group conferences, the teacher assists pupils to determine what has been learned and what is left to learn from ongoing lessons and units of study;
3. multiple choice tests, carefully written, may provide feed back to the teacher from pupil's results as to what learners have achieved. This provides the teacher with diagnostic and remediation information;
4. pupil's written products, with a variety of kinds of writing having stresses, including creative, narrative, and expository;
5. essay tests which assist in evaluating main ideas acquired, subordinate ideas to substantiate main ideas, major concepts, facts, as well as generalisations achieved. These achievements are harmonised to write sequential paragraphs when pupil readiness permits. The mechanics of writing are also assessed terms of pupil's present achievement and possible future optimal achievement;

6. continuous teacher observation of pupil progress needs monitoring. With the use of updated criteria, the teacher may observe how well each pupil is achieving relevant understandings, psychomotor development, and affective ends of instruction (Ediger, 2002, 7-10).

A quality health education programme is a necessity for optimal healthful living in school and in society.

REFERENCES

Adler, Mortimer J. 1981) *Six Great Ideas*. New York: Collier Books.

Brown, Kathleen J. (2003), *"What Do I Say When They Get Struck on a Word?* Aligning Teacher Prompts With Student Development", The Reading Teacher 56 (8), 720-733.

Cassel, Russell (2002), *"First Second, and Third Force Psychology Serve As The Only Means for Determining Pupil Readiness and Prison Reform"*, Journal of instructional Psychology 30 (2), 144-155.

Dewey, John (1916), *Democracy and Education*. New York: The Mac Millan Company.

Douillard, Kim (2002), "Going Past Doing: Taking Time for Reflection", The Language Arts 80 (2), 92-99.

Ediger, Marlow (1997), *Teaching Reading and the Language Arts in the Elementary School*. Kirksville, Missouri: Simpson Publishing Company, Chapter Two.

——(2000), *Teaching Science in the Elementary School*. Kirksville, Missouri: Simpson Publishing Company, Chapter Nine.

——(1998), *Teaching Reading Successfully in the Elementary School*, Kirksville, Missouri: Simpson Publishing Company, Chapter Three.

Ediger, Marlow (2002)—, *"Measurement Theory Versus Constructivism"*, Journal of Research in Education, 1 (1), 7-10.

Education Week (January 11, 2001, *"How High the Bar?"* pp. 53-56.

Slavin, R.E. and N.L. Karweit (1984), *"Mastery Learning and Student Teams: A Factorial Experiment in Urban General Mathematics Classes"*, American Educational Research, Journal, 21: 725-736.

19

Analysing the Goals of the National Reading Panel

The American National Reading Panel (NRP) stated five goals for teachers to use in teaching students. These goals are to assist young learners to become good readers. The panel was selected to study research results on what makes for good reading practices. The five elements which the NRP came up with are phonemics, phonics, vocabulary, fluency in reading, and comprehension. Each of these five elements are discussed separately here under.

Phonemics in Reading

The first element emphasised by the NRP was phonemics. Phonemics awareness stresses the importance of students hearing specific sounds in English. Words are made up of separate sounds. The word "had" has three separate sounds h/a/d. Each can be clearly enunciated. There are a plethora of words in which each letter in a word makes a consistent sound. The *man* family of words is an example in which several words pattern when changing the initial consonant. —ban, can, dan, fan, nan, pan, ran, tan, van. The word *hen* is spelled consistently between grapheme/phoneme, but few words pattern — den, men, pen. Then there are words spelled inconsistently such as cough, bough, dough, thought, through. Each of these words has an "ough" spelling, but the resulting sounds made are quite different. With the phonemic emphasis in beginning reading instruction, several issues arrive:

1. will students learn isolated sounds, unrelated to reading? Any word can be segmented into specific sounds — m/a/t/ch, th/ink, b/a/ll;
2. will each isolated sound to related to its corresponding grapheme?
3. will pictures be used in teaching phonemics? Thus, a picture of a bat, with its naming word, will be shown and students point to each letter as its corresponding sound is pronounced;
4. will chants with isolated phonemes be used to develop proficiency in reading readiness?
5. will students tend to separate sounds to the point that difficulty results in blending letters (sounds) to make words?

Phonics in Reading Instruction

Phonics has been taught over the centuries to help students in word recognition. Some teachers have used a systemic approach in teaching phonics. Here, there is a definite sequence in instruction with a basal phonics, text used in teaching students. The thinking has been that each student needs to be able to associate sound with symbol for independent reading to take place. Independence in word recognition, according to advocates, may then take place with heavy reliance upon phonics. Phonics instruction certainly has its strong points in having students learn to recognise words in reading which are spelled consistently between grapheme and phoneme. However, there are words which lack this consistency and might well need to be learned by sight. Questions which may be raised about phonics instruction in the reading curriculum are the following:

1. will students minimise comprehension by paying an excessive amount of time in sounding out words?
2. will reading emphasise sounding out words and thus minimise fluency of content read?
3. will phonics instruction crowd out reading for meaning?

4. will student interest in reading be minimised when heavy emphasis is placed upon phonics instruction?
5. will strong stress placed upon phonics truly make for better readers?

Fluency in Reading

As the third ingredient in a quality reading programme, students need to become fluent readers. Good teaching and much practice is involved when students become proficient readers. Reading experiences need to be challenging and satisfying. Interesting materials need to be in the offing for student reading. Growth and achievement in reading is ongoing and never reaches a terminal point. There is always room for a student to increase proficiency in reading. Thus, fluency in reading is an ever present objective of reading instruction.

Fluency in reading may be hindered when a student is unable identify words in context. Struggling to identify words hinders understanding of content. Failure to read in thought units also is a hindrance to attaching meaning to what is being read. Generally, a lack of fluent reading indicates the subject matter read is too complex for the involved student. Appropriate reading materials may be located for these students by using an informal reading inventory (IRI) in determining individual reading levels. Selected teachers may prefer, instead, to use a standardised oral reading test to ascertain a student's reading level. In general, a student, while reading, should be able to identify 95 per cent of the running words correctly and be able to answer 75 per cent of the questions covering subject matter read. A lack of fluency in reading is noticed when a student substitutes words, omits or adds words, disregards punctuation marks, and repeats, words read correctly. Teachers need to diagnose a student's reading to notice the kinds of errors made which hinder fluent reading. Teaching needed reading skills then becomes a necessity if fluency is to become a reality!

Vocabulary Development

A fourth, ingredient in a good reading programme, according to NRP, is student vocabulary development. This is essential. Many times, students have not done well in reading due to a limited vocabulary. Reading comprehension does emphasise having a vocabulary whereby meaning is attached to what has been read. A rich set of learning opportunities which permeate each school day are necessary to assist students to develop their listening, speaking, reading and writing vocabularies. When students do much reading to themselves with the use of library books, their vocabularies are being enriched and extended. The teacher needs to supplement these experiences by reading quality literature aloud to students. Special times may be set aside for Drop Everything and Read (DEAR) sessions whereby each student selects a library book to read to the self. As the student reads to the self, he/she increases strengths in vocabulary development. Each book read needs to be developmentally appropriate. The learner then understands content read. Meaning is being attached to acquired ideas.

When basal texts are being used in instruction, the teacher may introduce the daily, new vocabulary terms by printing each in neat manuscript letters on the chalkboard, students are then guided to identify each word correctly as well as go over the meaning of these words. It is best to go over the new vocabulary terms contextually within a sentence. Words are a part of a sentence, a paragraph and a sequence of paragraphs. The related illustrations in the basal, used by the teacher in teaching and the student in learning, might well provide a sense of meaning for each new vocabulary term. Students need to use the vocabulary terms in oral communication as well as in written work. Vocabulary terms acquired could also be recorded in a notebook for student review.

The Glossary in a basal as well as a grade level dictionary may provide necessary assistance to a learner in securing meaning of selected words in ongoing language arts areas. Vocabulary development must be emphasised in all academic areas as well as on all grade levels. When students attach meaning to the listening, speaking, reading, and writing vocabulary, they are well on their way to an enriched life style.

Comprehension in Reading

The ultimate goal in reading is comprehension. Individuals read to comprehend content. Comprehension may be on different levels of achievement. Thus, a student may comprehend on a literal level. He/she might then say in his/her own words that which has been read. If a student uses words directly from a textbook selection read, the learner may not understand what has been read. A higher level than literal comprehension is for the student to analyse what has been read. Here, facts are separated from opinions, accurate from inaccurate statements, as well as fantasy from reality. Creative reading is also important. Here, the student comes up with a unique interpretation of what has been read. He/she is able to develop unique and novel ideas pertaining to subject matter read. Originality of interpretation is salient. The student, too, needs to assess the worth of content read. This is the evaluation level of comprehension. Definite criteria may be developed to note the worth of content read.

When comprehending subject matter, it is noteworthy to be able to apply subject matter to new situations. Many uses can and must be made of acquired subject matter. With problem solving, the content may be used as a solution to an identified problem area. Thus within a unit of study, students with teacher guidance may identify a problem. The problem is a dilemma with multiple facets of possible solutions. A variety of data sources may be used to secure needed information. An hypothesis which is tentative results. The tentative hypothesis needs to be tested through additional study. The answer to the problem is then modified, accepted, or refuted. Problems chosen need to be on the developmental level of the learner. They should attract learner attention and provide motivation to preserve toward a solution.

Comprehension of content may also involve understanding printed directions, reading to secure a main idea as well as subordinate ideas and reading to obtain vital factual information. Comprehension is the ultimate goal of reading. Within the framework of comprehension are a plethora of skills, including using that which has been read. To use information obtained through reading, the content needs to be critically appraised.

Attitudes Toward Reading

To achieve well in reading, appropriate attitudes need to become a part of the self. They might well be the driving force in becoming a good reader. Attitudes result from ongoing reading and other experiences in the total environment of the learner. Success in reading is basic in becoming good reader. The reading teacher needs to start any student in reading where he/she is achieving. To go beyond this level may frustrate the learner and make for failure in reading. To limit the learner in reading challenging materials may well make for boredom and a lack of engagement in learning. From that baseline of where the student is presently achieving, the teacher needs to provide sequential learning opportunities which assist the learner to experience continuous optimal progress. The ideal of maximum achievement in reading cannot be overemphasised for each student.

REFERENCES

Astin, P. and C. Buxton (2000) *Science As Inquiry*, Boblinks, 10 (2), 10-15.

Blough, Glenn O., Julius Schwartz (1984), *Elementary School Science and How to Teach It*. New York: CBS College Publishing.

Condrey, Jean Friend (1996), "*Focus on Science Concepts*", The Science Teacher, 63 (4).

Dewey, John (1916), *Democracy and Education*. New York: The MacMillan Company.

Ediger, Marlow (1999), *Teaching Science in the Elementary School*. Kirksville, Missouri: Simpson Publishing Company, Chapter Seven.

——(1995), "*Designing Science Units of Study*", School Science, 33 (1), 14-15.

Melber, Leah M. (2003), "*True Tales of Science,*" Science and Children 41 (2), 24-32.

National Research Council (1996), *National Science Education Standards,* Washington, DC: National Academy Press.

Ward, Kathleen, et.al. (1996), "*Constructing Scientific Knowledge*", *The Science Teacher,* 63 (9).

Wolf, Kenneth (1996), "*Developing An Effective Teaching Portfolio,*" Educational Leadership, 53; 34.

20

Student Motivation in Reading

Motivation is a rather persistent problem in guiding students to read well. If a student lacks motivation, a low energy level will be available in learning to read. Through motivation, a learner is encouraged to achieve definite goals in reading. Persistence is there to aid students in goal attainment with adequately motivated behaviour.

Why Motivation is Important?

Students who lack motivation do not pay adequate attention to ongoing learning opportunities. Chances to learn then are minimised. Later on, these students need to make up deficiencies from the lost opportunities to learn. If a student does not concentrate and focus upon new words in reading on the chalkboard introduced by the teacher, the chances are these words will not be identified while reading the related content. The learner must put forth effort and energy to view each word carefully. Attempts need to be made by involved students to retain the correct identification of the new words. Otherwise, new learnings will be forgotten before their implementation in reading required subject matter. It is the student that must do the learning and, in this case, learn to identify words correctly, as they are being introduced by the teacher of reading. Adequate motivation on the part of the learner is necessary to attend to and retain identification of new words introduced by the teacher.

Attention and retention by the student is important in recognising new words whether the approach is through phonics instruction, syllabication, structural analysis, configuration clues, use of picture clues, or identification of words through contextual situations.

Why Motivation is Lacking?

Numerous reasons are given for students lacking motivation. Frequently, teachers are blamed for learners not being motivated due to poor teaching methods. This may be one reason. Teachers need to feel challenge covering the subject matter being taught. *Enthusiasm* of teachers might be reflected within learners. Thus, a teacher who enthusiastically tells learners what he/she has read demonstrates interest in reading content, as well as in teaching reading to each student, may well encourage the latter to read proficiently. Certainly, a motivated teacher teaching students to read creatively should have the enthusiasm reflected within learners.

There are numerous other reasons for students lacking motivation in reading. A variety of reading materials, including textbooks, library books, and other print materials must be available for learners to provide for *individual differences*. It certainly is not motivating for learners if the subject matter read is too complex or excessively easy. Each student needs to be ready for reading specific subject matter. Readiness factors to motivate students to read include having ample opportunities to see new words in print, attach meaning to each new word, have adequate background information, as well as have a purpose (reason) to read, prior to reading the involved subject matter. Motivation to read may be lacking due to students lacking readiness factors.

Subject matter to be read should be of *interest* to students. A lack of interesting reading materials can make for inappropriate motivation. With interest in subject matter being read, students possess a high energy level for reading. Motivation is inherent when each student is interested in reading the involved subject matter.

Reading teachers must use a *variety* of stimulating methods in teaching students. To learn inductively on the part of students, the teacher needs to ask challenging questions covering content read. Each question needs to be on the understanding level of students. Questions to motivate students need to lead to higher levels of thinking, such as the levels of analysis (separating facts from opinions, fantasy from reality, accurate from inaccurate content, as well as detecting bias, glittering generalities, and card stacking), synthesis (hypothesising), and evaluation (appraising subject matter read in terms of quality criteria).

Quality deductive methods to motivate student behaviour may emphasise a teacher modelling analysis, synthesis, and evaluation in reading. Motivated students apply what has been learned pertaining to higher levels of cognition.

Problem solving methods should also be utilised to stimulate student reading. Here, students with teacher guidance identify stimulating problems or broad questions. Information is gathered through reading and the use of audiovisual materials. A hypothesis is tested in action and revised if necessary. Problem solving methods are good to utilise when students select interesting problems pertaining to subject matter read. A variety of reading materials and non-reading activities assist in data gathering, as well as in checking hypotheses. Critical and creative thinking are emphasised in true problem solving experiences. Problems identified are new to involved students. Challenge is involved in choosing learning opportunities to solve the identified problems. If the same methods are utilised continuously, students will tend to dislike reading. Problems identified by students with teacher guidance integrated interest with effort. Interest provides for effort in learning. Motivation is then present.

Balance among cognitive, affective, and psychomotor objectives should be emphasised in teaching reading. A single domain of objectives, such as cognitive is not adequate. The development of the intellect (cognition) is significant in the teaching of reading. Students then need to learn to achieve skills in reading to follow directions, skim, or scan, develop sequence in ideas, as well as achieve main ideas and generalisation. Analysing what has been read and achieving unique ideas covering subject matter ideas and further relevant cognitive goals. Affective objectives, however, stimulate students to do well in the cognitive domain.

The affective dimension of objectives is equally important as compared to the cognitive domain. With desirable affective objectives, students learn to select and enjoy quality literature. When ready, a learner then enjoys characterisation, setting, plot, irony, and theme of literature read. An individualised reading programme needs to be in evidence in which the student feels motivated by selecting the little and achievement level of the library book. Hopefully, challenging library books will be selected by the learner. The teacher in a conference with the student needs to encourage, not force, increased interest in reading. Fascinating questions raised by the teacher and the student can be discussed within the conference setting. Evaluation of the success of each conference would emphasised students doing more reading and appreciating subject matter content.

The psychomotor level of objectives should receive adequate attention in the reading curriculum should receive adequate attention in the reading curriculum to motivate student learning. With psychomotor goals, students develop proficiency in using the gross and finer muscles, as well as skill in eye-hand coordination. Numerous fascinating learning opportunities can be stressed by the teacher in the psychomotor domain. Thus, after reading content from basal textbooks or through an individualised reading programme, learners may complete stimulating projects to reveal comprehension. These projects include:

1. developing a mural or pencil sketching;
2. making a diorama;
3. creating a pantomime or creative dramatics presentation;
4. completing a movie set, showing illustrated scenes of subject matter read;
5. writing a different beginning or ending for the study with accompanying illustrations;
6. constructing a model relating directly to ideas contained in a story or reading selection.

Teachers of reading then need to have students attain balance among cognitive, affective, and psychomotor objectives. Each objectives needs to stress, encouragement and motivation for learning.

Students may lack motivation in reading due to a lack of meaningful learning. The reader needs to relate the self to the selection being read. The reading teacher must make certain that students understand subject matter. Students who do not read well enough to benefit from the reading of the textbook need assistance. A good reader could orally read the contents to the disabled reader as the latter follows along in his/her book. If not overdone as a method, this can be challenging to both students. The disabled reader can then learn to identify words in the process as well as listen to the ideas read. Attaching meaning to the subject matter listened to is then possible. Motivation to read new materials may be a relevant end result. Gifted/talented readers need to read challenging materials; otherwise a lack of meaning is not possible when subject matter is boring and lacks maturity. These learners must be assisted to achieve optimally. This will be well above the grade level they are presently in. If a student with eighth or ninth grade reading abilities is asked to utilise textbooks written for fifth graders, it is no wonder that motivation to read is lacking. Or a fifth grader, reading on the second grade level, will lack motivation to read content written for average achievers in grade five.

The key to successful reading achievement of students is to match their present level of attainment with materials of instruction that are meaningful and possess challenge.

Recommendations to Improve the Reading Curriculum

Numerous recommendations have been made by experts to improve reading skills on the part of students. The writer would like to recommend definite quality criteria to assist students to achieve more optimally in reading.

First of all, with the accountability movement in vogue, basic essential skills for students have been identified on the state or local school level. These skills are generally listed as behaviourally stated objectives. The reading curriculum then becomes fragmented. Each student needs to attain then sequential precise ends. Too much time by the reading teacher needs to be spent on having learners achieve each behaviourally stated objective. Little time may be available to have students read subject matter in a holistic approach. Learning of isolated skills becomes relevant, rather than reading sequential ideas in order to learn. Certainly, comprehension of quality literature must be the end result, rather than acquiring isolated reading skills. Enjoying literature read should be a true motivator for students.

Secondly, the writer recommends that students have a greater voice in determining which sources to read from and which problem areas to solve, involving the processes of reading. Student-teacher planning of goals, experiences, and appraisal procedures emphasises a sound philosophy of education. Interest of student provides for effort in learning. Motivation is then present in the learning opportunities.

Thirdly, motivated, well educated and trained teachers should be able to make good decisions in terms of providing for individual differences in reading. With state mandated objectives or local district instructional management systems (IMS), decision making by the reading teacher is minimised Certainly, a quality motivated teacher should be able to determine scope and sequence better than can be done on the state or district wide level. Each teacher, regardless of age level of students taught or academic area taught, must be a teacher of reading. The making of decisions by the teacher may become a motivator in and of itself. This enthusiasm is reflected within learners.

Fourthly, state certification departments need to require in teacher preparation programmes that all prospective teachers have adequate course work in the teaching of reading. Schools of education preparing teachers need to be certain that all have demonstrated proficiency in the teaching of reading. Teachers need to possess adequate knowledge and skill in teaching word recognition techniques and diverse kinds of comprehension skills to develop within students. A love for the teaching of reading and an ability to motivate students is a must in teacher education programmes.

Fifthly, teachers need to stimulate students to enjoy and appreciate reading. It is a blessing to be a good reader. Nonreaders or those limited in the ability to read suffer grave consequences in society. The level of job attainment is lowered if an adult can not read at a required proficient level. Enjoyment of life is minimised due to not possessing needed skills in reading. Too frequently, the student and parents do not appreciate the opportunities to learn. Opportunities to learn involve the skill of reading.

Sixthly, teachers need to stimulate students to move to higher cognition levels, as compared to rote learning and drill experiences. Students should experience needed drill and practice in reading subject matter. However, life itself demands that learners be skillful in problem solving situations. Reading of content provides opportunities to students with teacher assistance to identify vital problems, gather related data and achieve answers to each problem. The ability to motivate students to higher levels of cognition is a must for the teacher.

Seventhly, students should experience life vicariously. It is impossible to experience, in many situations, desirable situations in life. Through reading or vicariously, learners may experience what is good, true, and beautiful. Undesirable situations in life are costly to experience directly. With vicarious experiences in reading, what is undesirable can be experienced in a relatively harmless manner. Learners need to be motivated to experience life vicariously.

Conclusion

A quality reading curriculum needs much planning. Careful attention to vital objectives, relevant learning opportunities to read, and important evaluation procedures can truly make for a quality reading curriculum. Hopefully, students will be motivated to read with quality planning in evidence from the teacher.

REFERENCES

Alexander, J. Estill (Editor), *Teaching Reading*. Second Edition. Boston: Little, Brown and Company, 1983.

Davis, Gary A. *Educational Psychology*. New York: Random House, 1983.

Harris, Albert, and Edward Sipay. *How to Increase Reading Ability*. Eighth Edition. New York: Longman, Inc., 1985.

Ringler, Lenore H., and Carol K. Weber. *A Language-Thinking Approach to Reading*. New York: Harcourt Brace Jovanovich, 1984.

Rubin, Dorothy *Diagnosis and Correlation in Reading Instruction*. New York: Holt, Rinehart and Winston, 1982.

21

Homogeneous and Heterogeneous Grouping in Reading Instruction

The reading teacher needs to use grouping procedures, which will assist each pupil to achieve, as well as possible. A single plan is not adequate. Dogmatically adhering to one approach may emphasise an agenda of the teacher, writer, or speaker, rather than guiding each pupil to do as well as possible in reading.

Flexible Plans of Grouping

There are plans of grouping in which it does not matter if homogeneous or heterogeneous grouping is involved. Individualised reading is an example. Here, a pupil chooses, from among alternatives, which books to read sequentially. A variety of topics need to be available as well as library books on different reading achievement levels. The learner may have a conference with the teacher after a library book has been completed.

With the use of experience charts, either heterogeneous or homogeneous grouping may also be used. Here pupils, based on an experience such as objects on a learning centre, provide ideas for the teacher to record on the chalkboard or with the use of computers. Ideas come from learners, not from the teacher. After the content has been recorded by the teacher, pupils orally read aloud the recorded ideas as the teacher points to each word. The experience chart may be reread orally as often as necessary. Here, pupils develop a basic sight vocabulary and enjoy actual reading activities.

Grouping of pupils with experience chart use may be either homogeneously or heterogeneously grouped. It may not matter, only slow learners may hold fast learners back from more optimal achievement.

Basal reader use in a heterogeneously grouped classroom may find learner on a variety of achievement levels read the same story with high achievement levels established. Peer grouping might be used to assist slower achievers "catch up" or attain the determined levels of reading achievement. In peer grouping, the fast reader might be held back while assisting the slower learner in reading.

Homogeneous grouping of pupils places the top achievers in one group, the middle achievers in a second group, as well as the slow readers in a third group. These three reading groups are formed within a heterogeneously grouped classroom. There are reasons for grouping homogeneously for reading instruction within a heterogeneously grouped classroom:

1. Each group, collectively, may achieve as optimally as possible;
2. No group is held back due to slower achievers with its group;
3. The fast achiever may motivate each other in the fastest group of the three.

A major reason given for heterogeneous grouping is that faster readers may assist the slower achiever in reading. However, the fast reader may be giving up time here in pursuing his/her own goals in reading. The gifted/talented also need a reading curriculum which was developed to assist optimal achievement.

Perhaps, a balance can be struck between the gifted/talented reader helping slower readers to achieve, as well as pursuing a purposeful, personal reading curriculum.

Grouping Homogeneously By Classrooms

Pupils may also be grouped homogeneously by classrooms with the top achievers being in one classroom, the average in the second, and the slowest in the third. The following are always salient when grouping learners for instruction:

1. Be respectful and accepting of all pupils as having extreme worth;
2. Show a feeling of "I care for you and want you to do well", for all pupils;
3. Avoid group names such as robins, bluejays, and starlings.

Flexibility needs to be a key concept in all plans of grouping. Thus, a pupil may be achieving more rapidly and needs to be placed in a higher achieving group.

Homogeneous grouped classrooms should not be frowned upon when they assist pupils to achieve as optimally as possible. Grouping should be used as a means of helping a pupil to learn to read as well as possible. The self-concept should be improved upon as a result of the group the child is in for reading instruction. No pupils should be held back from achieving optimally on an individual level. A major goal of teaching and learning is to guide individual, optimal achievement, not to follow an agenda in what an educator feels is democratic or equality. Individual, optimal achievement also needs to be emphasised in social or collaborative settings, challenging to each pupil regardless of ability levels. No pupil should be held from becoming the best reader possible with the intent being to provide for "equality". Equality has to do with providing quality in instruction so that each pupil is:

1. Prized highly
2. Recognised for contributions made, regardless of abilities possessed
3. Valued in any group setting
4. Praised and has esteem needs met
5. Achieving growing, and developing well

Regardless of the kind of grouping used, the negative can occur, such as:

1. Ridiculing and belittling pupils
2. Rudeness in working with others
3. Impatience in relating to pupils and teachers

4. Hostility and hatred in the social arena
5. Partiality to a selected group

Homogeneous versus heterogeneous grouping of pupils for reading instruction will not guarantee that the above five named negative behaviours will be minimised. A particular kind of grouping will not eliminate pupil behaviour, such as looking down upon others or being segregationist in thinking. Rather, attitudes and beliefs need to be changed so that all are highly important, teachers and pupils alike, in the social kingdom.

Criticisms of Homogeneous Grouping

There has been much unwarranted criticism of homogeneous grouping of pupils for instruction. The negative criticism has zeored in on the following:

1. Education becomes "elitist" if top achievers are grouped homogeneously. Why should it be "elitist" if the top achievers achieve as optimally as possible. It is undemocratic if these pupils are not given the best instruction possible, as should be done for all pupils;
2. Talented/gifted pupils should be in heterogeneous groups so that can help slower readers catch up;
3. Slow readers have no role models unless there are gifted/talented to set the pace for more optimal achievement;
4. Homogeneous grouping does not close the gap between fast and slow readers. Somehow, closing this gap is democratic. The reasoning here is fallacious. Should better readers then be held back to close the gap;
5. Research states that all pupils achieve better in collaborative endeavours with heterogeneous grouping. *Even if* a study indicates that pupils in heterogeneous/ collaborative groups do better than pupils in homogeneous groups, at the .05 level of significance, there are still 5 out of 100 that do not do better. Anyway, the quality of each research study needs to be evaluated. Most "research" studies have too many loopholes to be useful.

Conclusion

There are plans of reading instruction that can incorporate either heterogeneous or homogeneous grouping. With programmed reading, using textbooks or computers, each pupil achieves individually, ideally, as rapidly as possible. The pupil sets the pace for tutorial, diagnosis and remediation, gaming, and simulation programmes.

The Big Book approach may stress either plan of grouping. Of course, selected pupils will and do achieve more rapidly than do others.

The ideal in grouping pupils for instruction is optimal achievement for each.

22

The Middle School

The middle school, generally involving learners in grades six through eight, has gained some prominence in recent years. Reasons given for emphasising the middle school rather than the more traditional junior high school include the following:

Unquestionably, the middle school movement has been a force in education. It has focused national attention upon the long neglected early adolescent age group; forged a coalition of teachers, scholars, and researchers, concerned with the well-being of these students; and made proposals, and developed plans for improving their education.

Additional reasons include:

1. The middle school provide adequately for learners within a specific age group, learners in grades six through eight. The junior high school has become too much like the senior high school, with its emphasis upon the separate subjects curriculum and competitive athletics. This does not guide learners to develop well academically, socially, emotionally, and physically in terms of student growth and development characteristics;
2. Teachers and administrators need to specialise in teaching a given set of learners. Thus, educators, in their specialised undergraduate and graduate curriculum, may truly teach learners well in grades six through eight.

Issues in the Middle School

There are numerous issues which need resolving in grouping learners for instruction. The issues to be discussed involve the middle school-junior high school controversy.

First of all, the cost of constructing new school buildings may be high. Thus, it would appear that if a present junior high school building is in reasonable quality, or repair or modifications can effectively be made, that building should be utilised in teaching and learning. Perhaps, modifications in the curriculum can be made in which junior high school pupils may experience vital objectives, learning activities, and evaluation procedures. What is then emphasised in ongoing units of study might then harmonise with growth and development characteristics of junior high school students.

Secondly, should learners in grades six through eight be housed and taught in a separate school building (the middle school) as contrasted with those students in the present junior high school years (grades seven through nine)? In other words, is the age difference that much greater between the two plans of grouping learners for instruction to warrant making selected changes? It almost appears that regardless of the middle school or the junior high school plan of organisation, the teacher needs to provide for the interests, needs, and purposes of each learner. Each student needs to achieve optimally in every curriculum area.

Thirdly, if junior high school teachers are not able to provide adequately for each pupil, can middle school teachers do better? Regardless of the middle school or the junior high school plan of organisation, each teacher needs to guide optimal pupil achievement intellectually, physically, socially, and emotionally. Each teacher needs to develop and implement a philosophy of providing for individual differences.

Fourthly, a quality middle school needs to have effective supervisory leadership. The supervisor needs to stimulate teachers to develop relevant objectives, learning activities and evaluation procedures. Might an effective junior high school principal be able to provide equally proficient leadership? A plan for grouping learners may possess a name or title such as 'the middle school'. However, teaching-learning strategies may be no more or even less effective as compared to a comparable junior high school. Thus, a middle school might be justifiable if it can truly provide a learning environment guiding optimal learner progress for pre and early adolescents. William E. Klingele writes:

Modern middle school philosophy is based upon the needs of preadolescent and adolescent youths, often referred to as transcends. The middle school should be designed to separate these transcend-age youngsters from the younger elementary school children as well as the older high school adolescents. A main theme in the philosophy of the middle school is that it provides concern for a identity, self-concept, and personal security of the students it serves.

The middle school programme is highly child-centred with an emphasis on learning how to learn as opposed to rote learning. It is characterised by a great deal of student independence in which much of the responsibility for learning is placed upon the student. Much emphasis is placed on allowing students to explore and create on their own pace, thus allowing for individual differences. Students often have input into determining the schedule, which is characterised by a high degree of flexibility.

The middle school makes extensive use of multimaterial approaches, team teaching, and variable group size. The school is staffed with specially trained teachers, administrators, and auxiliary personnel who seek to provide a programme to assist transcends in making the transition from childhood dependence to adult independence, helping them bridge the gap between elementary school and high school.

Fifthly, ideals stated for middle school implementation may not be feasible under selected circumstances. Thus, class size as to numbers of learners in a set may well inhibit learners realising desired objectives. Or, selected students might continually disrupt a class and hinder other learners from achieving optimally A classroom may lack reading and non-reading materials to provide for individual differences among learners. Selected students may not be adequately mature to benefit from learning activities in which personal choices might be made, such as in the use of learning centres and open space education. Then too, teachers individually possess diverse philosophies of education. Philosophies, such as the following might be stressed by diverse teachers:

1. an activity centred curriculum. Pupils with teacher guidance may cooperatively plan, carry out, and evaluate purposeful projects in ongoing units of study. These activities may well include learners working on construction projects, art experiences, dramatic activities, and problem solving methods involving specific units of study;
2. an essentialist curriculum. Teachers and supervisors select, prior to instruction, vital objectives for pupil attainment. The objectives chosen generally reflect subject matter involving the three r's (reading, writing, and arithmetic). The teacher may choose learning activities for students to attain precise objectives. After which, the teacher might appraise if a learner has/has not achieved a specific objective. New teaching strategies need utilising for pupils who did not achieve a specific end;
3. a problem solving curriculum. Learners with teacher guidance identify relevant problems. Data is gathered from a variety of reference sources to answer the problem area. After which, a hypothesis is developed. The hypothesis is tested, and revised, if necessary;
4. a vocationally oriented curriculum. Relevant objectives are chosen pertaining to diverse significant careers in the world of work. Each student selects tasks relating to vital concerns in career education with instructor guidance. The learner, as well as the instructor, appraise the former's progress in attaining stated objectives. Practicality is a major concept to emphasis in career education. That which is functional and useful in society is then emphasised in units on career education.

The principal of the school must provide leadership in developing the curriculum so that each learner may achieve optimally. Roe and Drake write the following relevant duties of principles:

1. Stimulate and motivate staff to maximum performance;
2. Develop with the staff a realistic and objective system of accounting for learning (as contrasted to merely monitoring programmes and instructional processes in input terms as prescribed by the central office);
3 Develop cooperatively operable assessment procedures for ongoing programmes to identify and suggest alternatives for improving weak areas;
4. Work with staff in developing and implementing the evaluation of the staff;
5. Work with staff is formulating plans for evaluating and reporting student progress;
6. Provide channels for involvement of the community in the operation of the school;
7. Encourage continuous study of curricular and instructional innovations and provide help and resources for the establishment of those that are most promising;
8. Provide leadership to students in helping them to develop a meaningful but responsible student government;
9. Establish a professional learning resources centre and expedite its use;
10. Develop cooperatively with the staff a dynamic professional development and inservice education programme.

Conclusion

Numerous issues exist and need resolving in the middle school curriculum. The ultimate goal of instruction is to guide each learner to achieve optimally. Thus, pupils need to perceive interest, meaning, and purpose in ongoing units of study. Pupils in middle schools, as well as other means of grouping learners for instruction, need to achieve in an optimal manner vital understanding, skills, and attitudinal goals.

REFERENCES

Arnold, John, *"Rhetoric and Reform in Middle Schools"*, Phi Delta Kappan, March, 1982, pp. 453-456.

Klingele, William E., *Teaching in Middle Schools*, Boston: Allyn and Bacon, Inc., 1979. p. 3.

Roe, William H. and Darke, Thelbert L., *The Principalship*. New York: The Macmillian Company, 1980, p. 15.

23

Increasing Listening Comprehension

Students spend a considerable amount of time in listening to others in the classroom. It behooves the teacher to assist students to become good listeners and thus increase comprehension. With state mandated testing, there is a great need for optimal achievement. If a state mandated test is not passed, the student may not be promoted to the next higher grade level, nor receive a high school diploma. What might the teacher do to assist students to do better in course work, especially when listening is involved?

Improving Listening Behaviour

Definite objectives of instruction need to incorporate listening skills for students. One learns much through listening to ideas expressed. Then too, it reveals politeness to others when being a good listener. There are a plethora of additional reasons for being a good listener. These purposes are important to emphasise in teaching and learning situations.

When directions are asked for and necessary to get to a specific location, careful listening is needed. Generally, there are a sequence of steps to follow when securing these directions. Each step needs to be obtained through listening. Once the directions have been given, then the listener needs to follow them. These may be remembered incorrectly due to careless listening. At the time the directions are given, understanding needs to occur or clarification may be necessary. Otherwise, the listener needs to rely upon his/her memory. Good listening habits may be developed if one is determined to improve this skill.

In addition to learning to follow directions though listening, the teacher may assist students to become better listeners during a discussion. Ideas presented in a discussion must be understood if the student is to respond to what was said. It can be embarrassing if a student presents irrelevant ideas in a discussion due to faulty listening. It can also be embarrassing if the student is called upon in class to answer a questions and yet necessary listening skills were not used. During discussions, there is frequent time for students to develop listening skills. Diagnosis needs to be emphasised when attempting to understand why a student does not appear to listen in class:

- the student may be thinking of other things such as going fishing during the week end;
- the student's mind wanders for one thing to the next;
- the student lacks background information;
- the student cannot hear well;
- the noise level in the classroom is exceptionally high.

The teacher needs to diagnose reasons for poor listening and attempt to find out reasons for this happening. The student may need training and assistance to become a better listener. Or, the problem may be physical such as having problems with hearing. Remediation needs to be done whenever feasible. If a student appears to have no hearing problem, the learner needs to have definite objectives to work toward in becoming a better listener. Referrals need to be made for those who appear to have hearing problems (Ediger, 1999).

Third, games may be played to encourage careful listening. Thus, students may place their heads on the desktop without being able to see what is happening. The teacher may then do each of the following:

- pour water from a pitcher into a cup;
- crush a sheet of paper;
- tap a pencil point two times on a desk top;

- chew on a piece of bread;
- walk three steps, among other noises, to be made.

For each of the above, a student with his/her head down on the desktop may give the cause for a happening such as what is sounded like when water was poured into a cup. Hopefully, there will be a transfer of learning from the listening activity to a practical, setting such as listening to follow directions.

Fourth, purpose for an ongoing listening activity may be lacking. The student then feels there is no need to listen. If the teacher states a purpose or reason for listening, this may assist the student to feel a need to engage in better listening. The student may accept the teacher's stated purpose to listen. This is a deductive approach in stating a purpose for listening. Induction might also be used whereby the teacher asks the class why it is important, for example, to listen carefully as to why the Middle East conflict continues and is ongoing.

Fifth, interest is a powerful factor in learning. Learning activities for students should be chosen based on obtaining learner interests. Methods of teaching also need to encourage the interests of learners. Experiences for students need to be interesting regardless of what is taught. Even if students are studying the parts of speech in English, there is interesting methods to use in helping students learn these parts of speech.

Sixth, the teacher needs to provide for individual differences in listening abilities among students. There will be those who are good listeners presently. Maintaining these listening habits is important. Others need assistance in becoming better listeners. Listening to selected cassettes at a listening centre containing subject matter related to the unit being studied presently with relevant comprehension questions to answer may help many to become better listeners. Small group discussions with the use of self evaluation criteria for listening might well assist others to improved listening. Results of the evaluation should be studied and improvements made based on the self evaluation criteria. Poor listeners need to be seated near to where the teacher is located so that content may be clearly understood, especially in the case of learners with hearing problems. When teaching, the teacher needs to monitor, carefully, all students as continually as possible to notice if learners are attending and listening.

The teacher needs to take ample time to discuss with students reasons for good listening and what can be done to improve in this area Time taken to discuss good listening habits is time well spent.

Seventh, ample background information needs to be in the repertoire of all students when listening to a discussion. The background information is needed so that new subject matter discussed may be understood. The background information serves as an advance organiser. In this way, a student may organise subject matter better in relating the new ideas being discussed with what was learned previously. If ideas are presented chaotically, the student may have a very difficult time to listen as well as understand new content.

Eighth, questions raised of students during a discussion should be challenging and on their understanding level. The question raised should be asked first before calling on a student for an answer. In this way, the learner has a chance to reflect on the question and answer, before attempting a response. If a student does not know an answer, scaffolding may be used by breaking, the question down into easier component parts.

Ninth, meaning theory needs to be emphasised in listening situations. Thus, the content listened to must mean something to the listener. This might mean understanding the subject matter presented. It also may mean that the learner feels it is worthy of knowing. If the subject matter or skill to be taught lacks meaning, time needs to be taken by the teacher to develop necessary meanings. Nonsense learnings have little value to the student.

Tenth, learning styles theory needs to be emphasised. Students possess diverse styles of learning and teachers need to accommodate each, if possible. Thus some students prefer cooperative endeavours to work at. Listening habits may be a definite goal to emphasise in group work. Or when having a conference with the teacher after having completed reading a library book on an individual basis, student listening is very important and needs to be evaluated (Ediger, 1998).

Factors for Being a Good Listener

There are selected factors which research has shown to be important in good learning. Among others, these include the following:

- socio-economic status;
- a supportive family and school environment;
- learner attitudes;
- good study habits;
- locus of control;
- effective learning approaches used by the student;
- positive aspirations;
- effectiveness of student learning (Chandrakanthi, 2003).

By using research results, such as the above, the teacher can do much to assist students to become better listeners. Thus, the teacher may work with parents in helping the offspring to improve in listening skills. Suggestions might then be given on what to do to guide optimal student listening. In developing good attitudes within students, the teacher may provide learning opportunities whereby the student may develop feelings of success. Good study habits may well be encouraged in school with quality criteria for listening posted on a classroom bulletin board. These criteria need to be enforced in the classroom. The student, too, needs to evaluate the self in terms of improvement in listening habits. For locus of control students need to learn that becoming a good listener takes effort and is not due to chance factors. The locus of control then is within the student (putting forth effort), not due to external factors (luck). Learning approaches used by the student must stress getting to work on the task at hand immediately, not procrastinating. Being positive in life is always salient, even though things happen which might minimise aspirations adhered to. Effective learning requires the student to put forth effort and reach out to achieve.

As an additional factor, students need to learn to listen for a variety of specific purposes. One specific purpose is to listen for vital facts. To describe a character in literature, for example, there are a plethora of facts which are needed to describe the person. Or in a historical event, there are many specifics needed to tell about the Great Depression during the 1930s. Facts generally are considered to be building blocks for major understandings.

Second, students need to learn to listen for main ideas. Usually, there are too many precise items to acquire in listening. This makes it necessary to listen for a main idea. Facts usually can be put together to achieve a major idea. Main ideas are retained longer that are specific facts. Main ideas, too, are transferrable to other wholes in literature, history, among other academic areas.

Third, students need to learn to listen in order to achieve a sequence of ideas. Subject matter listened to may not make sense due to poor sequence or order of information remembered. Students may need considerable practice in listening for a sequence of ideas since it is a complex skill. The order of happenings in listening to literature and historical events may make for faulty or correct understandings.

Fourth, students need to listen to develop a concept. With concept development, the student organises information gleaned to a single word or phrase. For example, in developing the concept *medieval*, the student may incorporate the following:

- knights were warriors in their day;
- guild members produced needed goods to sell;
- manorial life was the system of farming stressed during medieval times;
- castles were at the heart of a manor and housed the nobleman and his family, plus weapons for warfare.

The above are a few ideas combined into a concept such as *medieval*.

Fifth, students should apply what has been listened to. The application may consist of answering test questions, making a model, doing a diorama, and/or writing a letter, among other experiences. If use is made of what was listened to, then forgetting of these learnings should be held to a minimum.

Sixth critical listening is important. When listening critically, the student is guided to separate ideas into component parts, such as in separating accurate from inaccurate ideas, the imaginary from the real, as well as the important versus ideas of lesser value, a student might then generalise on each separate set of ideas.

Seventh, students may engage in creative endeavours after listening to a cassette recording. A cassette has stressed, for example, the writing of a tall tale. Examples of tall tales were read are reasons were given for each being a tall tale. The student should then be ready to write a tall tale individually or within a committee.

From the discussion, there are a variety of specific purposes involved in listening. Students need to become conscientious listeners. With practice and encouragement, students may become excellent listeners. Continuous effort being put forth and a desire to become a good listener are musts!

The good listener:

- maintains an awareness of his own motives in listening. Develops own motives for effective listening. Analyses speech and adjusts to motives
- shares responsibility for communication. Considers the different techniques of the speaker. Assumes half the responsibility for communication
- arranges favourable conditions for listening. Adjusts for any personable hearing disability or poor room ventilation or temperature. Ignores outside or unnecessary distractions
- exercises emotional control during listening. Postpones personal worries. Does not permit an immediate dislike for a speech or speaker
- structuralises the presentation. Recognises conventional compositional techniques. Adjusts not taking to the organisational plan of the speech (Tiedt).

Students need to possess criteria for good listening in order to have a gauge to measure effectiveness of moving in the direction of achieving efficacy. A major way of learning is through listening. Listening skills need optimal development. Definite objectives need to be in the offing for teachers to use in guiding students to become quality listeners.

REFERENCES

Chandrakanthi, S. (2003), *Socio-Pedagogical Factors Affecting Language Skills Among Engineering College Students—A Study*. Coimbatore, India: Bharathiar University, Ph.D Thesis.

Ediger, Marlow (1998), *Teaching Reading and the Language Arts*. Kirksville, Missouri: Simpson Publishing Company, Chapter Seven.

Ediger, Marlow (1999), *Teaching the Language Arts in the Elementary School*. Kirksville, Missouri: Simpson Publishing Company, Chapter Ten.

Tiedt, Iris M. (1983), *The Language Arts Handbook*, Englewood Cliffs, New Jersey: Prentice Hall, Inc., 100.

24

Quality and Quantity in the Mathematics Curriculum

Mathematics, a basic in the curriculum, is heavily emphasised, along with reading, in state mandated testing. To have a good mathematics curriculum, carefully chosen objectives need to be in the offing and implemented in the instructional arena. These objectives need to stress a balance among cognitive, affective, and psychomotor ends. Teaching and learning contain a plethora of specifics which are necessary to adhere to. Thus to do the best possible, the pupil needs adequate nutrition. Sleep, and decent living facilities. Then too, the pupil must feel safe in school and in the home setting as well as experience en route safety between home and school. A school needs to be a place where pupils feel they belong and are accepted by others. Feelings of rejection are highly negative. The entire school system needs to work in the direction of pupils and school personnel being highly accepting of others in a multicultural environment. Also, a pupil desires to be known for something done well. The school and classroom setting need to provide opportunities for pupils individually to be successful learners and thus receive praise for achievement and progress. Self confidence in mathematics is a must in the curriculum (See Maslow, 1954).

Cognitive Objectives in Mathematics

Each cognitive objectives needs to be chosen carefully in mathematics. Quality sequence of objectives begins in the preschool years and goes throughout higher education. Thinking skills are vital in mathematics. Too many teachers stress rote learning and memorisation of mathematics content. This is not adequate. Pupils need to understand what is being learned. To understand means to attach meaning to ongoing lessons and units of study. Any number pair, for example, such as 8 + 7 may have a memorised answer but this is survey, not depth learning. Learners need to attach meaning to "8" representing a quality of objects which can be counted as a set. This is true no matter how large the addends are. The foundation for meaningful mathematics learnings must begin early in the child's life.

Logical thing needs adequate emphasis in mathematics. The communicative, associative, and distributive properties then should sequentially be stressed. A child may learn the logic in that 8 + 7 = 15, as well as 7 + 8 = 15. At any age level, this commutative property of addition saves much time in learning in that it cuts in half the number of addition facts to be learned. Logical thinking transfers in sequence to all branches of mathematics.

Critical thinking is salient in that pupils need to be able to analyse mathematical subject matter. For example, any value then such as 5123 might be analysed in terms of thousands, hundreds, tens and ones. Column addition stresses that the ones need to be added to ones, tens to tens, hundreds to hundreds, and thousands to thousands with the possibilities of regrouping and renaming. Later on, increasingly complex numerical values and reasoning will be involved.

Inherent in critical thinking is creative thought. Here, the pupil needs to be flexible in terms of using a variety of algorithms. There are diverse algorithms which might be used in coming up with answer in problem solving. Then too, problem solving requires identifying a problematic situation, gathering information, developing an hypothesis, and testing the hypothesis in a life like situation. Deliberations is involved. It takes time and effort to solve relevant problems. Within the framework of critical and creative thinking, problem solving is vital as well as useful. Subject matter is used creatively as needed to solve problems.

Being able to estimate well and check the estimation correctly is a vital skill. Estimating in mathematics is a highly useful and important skill in every day life. Mentally in being able to estimate well in specific situations is emphasised in terms of time, distance, volume, and area. A practical use of estimation must be stressed in the curriculum.

Being able to interpret graphic information correctly is necessary when gleaning information from the media. Thus, line, bar, picture, and circle graphs, need interpretation as to what is being conveyed. Knowledge of correct interval size and statistical procedures such as in using the mean, median, mode, quartile as well as standard deviation, among others, need to be taught developmentally. Meanings need to be attached to grouped and ungraded numerical data as well as descriptive and inferential statistics. Inferences need to be made of carefully collected and organised statistical data.

A rich mathematics vocabulary needs to be in the offing and integrated into each mathematical lesson and unit of study. Subject matter needs to be taught developmentally and sequentially in order provide learners with background information to master each new objective. No pupil should be left behind without a well defined scope and sequence programme of mathematics (Ediger and Rao, 2000, Chapter One).

Affective Objectives in Mathematics

Too frequently, affective objectives are minimised in teaching due to the inability to accurately measure if these kinds of objectives have been achieved by pupils. The teacher, through daily observation, may notice the quality of attitudes possessed by pupils. Growth in a desire to achieve more optimally in mathematics, as an attitude, provides opportunities for pupils to attain vital facts, concepts, and generalisations in mathematics. These learnings need to be reflected upon and communicated to others in an atmosphere of respect. Accepting others makes committee endeavours more enriching and pleasant. Rudeness and lack of tolerance toward others has no place in situations where pupils interact with each other.

Neat, legible, and accurate writing is necessary when communicating mathematical ideas in writing. Communication skills are important in mathematics, including the ability and desire to convey ideas orally. Processes and procedures in mathematics need to be conveyed which are meaningful to other pupils, the teacher, and parents in the home setting. Wanting to communicate clearly and accurately provides opportunities to develop thinking abilities. Each learning obtained provides a foundation for achieving increasingly more complex ideas. It takes understanding and quality attitudes to attach meaning to vital subject matter such as fundamental operations on number, linear measurement, area, volume, weight, ratio and proportion, among others salient learnings. The pupil needs to have an inward desire to learn and achieve. Quality attitudes then in the affective dimension aid pupils to achieve and accomplish. Having good attitudes go a long way in doing well in a developmental mathematics curriculum (See New, 2003).

Psychomotor Objectives in Mathematics

Ample and meticulous attention must be given to psychomotor objectives in the mathematics curriculum. These kinds of objectives emphasis pupils applying what has been learned. When application is made, pupils practice what has been learned previously. Retention of learnings is improved upon when facts, concepts, and generalisations are used by pupils. Using that which has been learned also makes it possible for review and practice to take place in a meaningfully way. However, in applying learnings, meaningless drills are minimised. Making application may mean using what has been learned in a new process, skill, or practical situation. There are a plethora of situations in which previously achieved ideas in mathematics may be used. The following are several suggested learning opportunities:

1. making mathematical models;
2. constructing items where mathematics is used in an ongoing unit of study;
3. dramatising a mathematical situation;
4. drawing diverse geometrical figures to show design and spatial relations;
5. modelling a process or procedure to share with others.

Then too in heavy day life, pupils need to use what has been learned in mathematics applied to practical situations. When items are purchased or sold, mathematics is needed in making these transactions (See National Council Teachers of Mathematics, 1989).

In all kinds of psychomotor, affective, and cognitive objectives being emphasised in teaching mathematics, the teacher needs to follow principles of learning from the psychology of education, including the following:

1. learning activities need to actively engage pupils. Pupils need to be wholeheartedly involved in ongoing lessons and units of study. The chances are a passive child will not learn much in mathematics;
2. pupils need to make sense of subject matter taught and learner. It wastes learner time if a lack of understanding results from the facts, concepts and generalisations being taught;
3. motivation is a powerful factor in learning. With quality learning opportunities, pupils should feel energised to learn, to do, and to accomplish. Adequate motivation provides an inward desire for pupils to acquire mathematical learnings;
4. learning styles need to be stressed in teaching pupils. Thus, selected pupils like to learn in collective situations whereas others prefer individual endeavours;
5. the teacher needs to select interesting activities to achieve objectives. This is important in order to secure pupil attention in the lesson presentation;
6. individual differences need adequate provision since pupils differ from each other in talents and abilities. Each pupil needs to achieve as optimally as possible in the curriculum;
7. a variety of appraisal procedures need to be used to ascertain pupil achievement. Achievement in cognitive, affective, and psychomotor objectives need to be evaluated in terms of quality criteria (See Peressini, 1997).

Appraisal Procedures in Mathematics

There are diverse evaluative procedures available to measure mathematical achievement. State mandated testing is one procedure to ascertain what pupils have learned. One kind is norm referenced whereby each pupil may be compared on a grade level with others in the nation. Thus, a local pupil's score may pertain to being on the 34th percentile, for example. This means that out of every 100 pupils having taken the test, 66 pupils are higher and 34 are lower in making the comparison. There are no accompanying objectives for the teacher to use in teaching when norm referenced tests are used. From pupil test results on the norm referenced test, there will be a spread of scores from the 99th down to the first percentile. Criterion referenced tests (CRTs), developed state wide, do have accompanying objectives for the teacher to use in teaching. The subject matter taught then is valid in terms of what will be covered, in general, on the test. The spread of scores from high to low will be much less from CRT results as compared to norm referenced testing. Norm referenced test writers plan for a spread of test results from the 99th to the first percentile whereas CRTs emphasise, if possible, that all pupils be successful in learning. The objectives furnished to the teacher harmonise with the CRT so that is a better chance for pupils to score higher on the CRT as compared to the norm referenced test (Ediger, 1995, 7-10).

Second, teacher observation may be used continuously. Here, the teacher may notice the kinds of efforts made by pupils and assist in remediation. The teacher may record the common kinds of errors made by pupils in class and then remedy these in small group or large group instruction. Errors made may be due to a lack of knowledge, carelessness, haste, incorrect copying of numerals to perform mathematical operations, a lack of legibility in writing numerals, and/or neatness, among others.

Third, teacher written tests may help ascertain what pupils have learned in mathematics. These might be multiple choice, true/false, matching, short answer, completion, and/or essay. Each kind of test has a different purpose for its use as compared to the others. For example, multiple choice test items may largely measure salient facts learned by children whereas essay tests may stress problem solving emphasising higher levels of cognition.

Fourth, a test may emphasise multiple languages to reveal information acquired in mathematics. Thus, a young child may show that 4 + 5 = 9 by using beads with a set of four yellow and five read beads, totalling nine beads whereas a different child may show the same addition fact with four white tally marks and five red tally marks on the chalkboard to indicate a sum of nine. The four basic operations on number may be shown in a plethora of ways including blocks, strips of paper, pencils, chalk, buttons, among others.

Fifth, daily discussions might well reveal what a pupil has learned in a lesson or unit of study. The pupil may indicate learnings acquired in a discussion by participating actively, showing a learning asked for with a drawing on paper or use of everybody show cards whereby a child may answer a question by holding up the correct card such as "five" in answer to an addition, subtraction, multiplication, or division number pair, i.e. 9 x 8 = , shown on a card.

Sixth, teacher made materials can be excellent to use in teaching. For example, two pupils may use flash cards in drill and practice. One person then shows a card and the other provides the answer. The flash cards are stacked face down on a pile. The roles of pupils may reversed after the first pupil is through responding to the face down pile of cards.

Selected teachers have also made excellent game boards with a pupil moving forward one space if he/she answers correctly to a number pair on a card, originally turned face down. The first child who comes to the end of the race track, by moving forward one space at a time for each item answered correctly wins the game.

Seventh, workbook exercises completed by pupils in meaningful activities may provide the teacher with much information about a pupil's achievement in mathematics. Working pages in a workbook for the sake of doing so has little value. Rather, there must be a clear pupil purpose for working an exercise.

Eighth, software programmes may well provide challenges to pupils in mathematics achievement. Tutorials provide new learnings to pupils. Each programme is sequenced by the programmer and each answer given provides immediate feedback to the learner. Continuous evaluation based on each response provided by a learner gives the teacher necessary information on a pupil's progress. Drill and practice programmes give the learner opportunities to practice skills in mathematics in which weaknesses have been exhibited previously. Pupils should experience drill and practice based on need and not for the sake of doing so. Simulation programmes emphasise life like situations in mathematics in which pupils solve realistic problems. Continuous feedback is provided pupils in problem solving. Gaming programmes provide the learner chances to use a game like approach in achieving new concepts and generalisations in mathematics. The game may be played individually or within a small group or committee. The computer monitor shows what the pupil has learned and which learnings are presenting difficulties (Ediger, 1989, 20-23).

Conclusion

Pupils need to have challenge, yet an achievable mathematics curriculum. Each pupil needs to learn as much mathematics as possible for use in school and in society. The objectives of instruction need to be chosen carefully by involved persons. The learning opportunities to achieve objectives need to assist in providing for individual differences among learners. Assessment must be ongoing and sequential to provide appropriate order of mathematical experiences for pupils.

REFERENCES

Ediger, Marlow, and D. Bhaskara Rao (2000), *Teaching Mathematics Successfully*. New Delhi, India: Discovery Publishing House, Chapter One.

Ediger, Marlow (1995), "*Current Concepts in Teaching Mathematics*", Philippine Education Quarterly, 7-10.

Ediger, Marlow (1989), "*Psychology in Teaching Mathematics*", Delta K, Vol. 27, No. 4, 20-23.

Maslow, Abraham (1954), *Motivation and Personality*. New York: Harper and Row.

National Council Teachers of Mathematics (1989), *Curriculum and Evaluation Standards for School Mathematics*. Reston, Virginia: NCTM.

New, Rebecca S. (2003), "*Reggio Emilia; New Ways to Think About Schooling*", Educational Leadership. 60 (7), 34-39.

Peressini, Dominic (1997), "*Parental Reform of Mathematics Education*", The Mathematics Teacher, 90 (6), 423-427.

Recent Trends in the Mathematics Curriculum

There are definite trends which need to be emphasised in the mathematics curriculum. These trends are relatively stable, but may be subject to modification in time. Trends do not stress what is here today but gone relatively quickly. Teachers and school administrators need to study, analyse, and think about which trends are salient to emphasise. By reading recent literature in educational journals and university level teacher education textbooks, observing quality instruction in the classroom, observing video tapes on teaching excellence, among others, the mathematics curriculum may be updated. Each trend needs to be studied indepth, and those deemed worthwhile when using recommended criteria might well be implemented in the classroom. Which trends might then be implemented in the school mathematics curriculum?

The Mathematics Curriculum

The mathematics teacher needs to follow important tenets from the psychology of education in teaching and learning situations. Thus, the teacher needs to:

- provide engaging activities for pupils so that an inward desire to learn is in evidence. Instead of passive learners, pupils need to be enthused and interested in ongoing experiences in mathematics. Intrinsic motivation to learn has long been an ideal in the curriculum.

Motivated pupils pursue and achieve in mathematics. They are able to attain challenging developmental objectives within the framework of appropriate learning opportunities;

- assist pupils to attach meaning to ongoing experiences in mathematics. Concrete and semiconcrete activities help pupils to attach meaning to vocabulary terms directly related to ongoing units of study. With meaning, pupils understand what is being taught. Vaugeness and guess work is eliminated from the curriculum. Then too, meaning attached to facts, concepts, and generalisations being emphasised in teaching and learning situations provides a foundation for achieving more complex learnings, which meaningless learnings do not provide;
- assist pupils to perceive purpose in learning. Unless the pupil sees reasons for achieving in mathematics lessons and units of study, the chances are he/she may not attain as much as would otherwise be the case. There are a plethora of purposes for achieving relevant ideas in mathematics. A few talented pupils may believe that it is valuable to learn mathematics for its very own sake. Others might be guided to learn for the sake of its use in daily life, and still others find it difficult to determine any purpose for its study. The mathematics teacher needs to assist pupils inductively or deductively to find values in accomplishing as optimally as possible. He/she may ask questions of pupils pertaining to the values of learning selected facts, concepts, and generalisations in an ongoing lesson. An inductive procedure of learning is then in evidence. Or, the teacher may state the reason(s) for pupils achieving the objectives of instruction. This is a deductive approach (Ediger, 1999, Chapter Ten);
- guide pupils to use their individual strengths in learning. Multiple intelligences theory lists eight different intelligences which individuals possess. Thus, the strongest intelligence needs to be used as possessed

by any individual student. *Verbal intelligence* may provide well for those who gain much from school mathematics through reading. A well chosen basal textbook might then provide learning opportunities which involve word problems, computation, and written work. A second intelligence, namely *logical thinking* or reasoning, may be used much in all facets of mathematics. Reasoning logically is used in obtaining structural ideas in mathematics. The commutative, associative, and distributive properties, as examples, stress much logic. Pertaining to the commutative property in addition and multiplication, a + b = b + a; a x b = b x a. *Interpersonal intelligence* may emphasise pupils working in committees for those possessing this intelligence. *Intrapersonal intelligence* involves working individually in ongoing mathematics lessons. Knowledge of multiple intelligences theory assists the mathematics teacher to study children carefully and use relevant theories to make decisions in the instructional arena. Using multiple intelligences theory helps children in using their own unique personal strengths to do mathematics (See, Gardner, 1993);

- use classroom management approaches which assist pupils to achieve more optimally. There are pupils who do better in a very quiet learning environment whereas others prefer a more busy like atmosphere in the classroom to achieve more optimally. Those who like a very quiet environment may be seated in divided study carrels whereas others who like a more business like humming noise may then work collaboratively in groups.

  Selected pupils like to have a more formal learning environment than others in the classroom. These pupils may like a structured teaching and learning situation such as direct explanations and directions pertaining to the new lesson in mathematics before proceeding with assigned work. Others may like a more open ended approach such as having a voice in decision making including teacher pupil planning of the curriculum.

There is also a dichotomy in selected pupils liking a step by step procedure of instruction to achieve a generalisation(s), as compared to those who prefer to begin with holism and then proceed to the parts in mathematics instruction. These factors in classroom management involve learning styles possessed by individual pupils (See, Searson and Dunn, 2001).

- integrate computers and technology into the mathematics curriculum. There are developmentally appropriate software packages which need to be brought into ongoing lessons and units of study in mathematics. These software programmes assist pupils to achieve vital objectives more effectively. The following kinds of computer programmes need to be used when it benefits pupils sequentially:

  1. tutorial whereby new learnings are developed by pupils to achieve objectives;
  2. simulation in which pupils respond to specific ordered items in order to solve a problem. Continuous feedback is provided each pupil in terms of being successful in problem solving;
  3. drill and practice whereby a pupil practices on certain basic number pairs. Where a pupil is weak, he/she receives additional practice in those specific areas of mathematics;
  4. games whereby pupils may learn mathematics knowledge and skills through a gaming situation. Two or more may be on each side. In providing the most correct answers each side attempts to win the game as maths items are answered correctly when presented on the monitor.

Multimedia approaches need to be used to provide for a variety of individual differences among pupils. Each material of instruction used should assist pupils to achieve as optimally as possible (See, Watts-Taffe, et. al., 2003).

Objectives of Instruction

Each objective needs to be determined carefully in mathematics lessons and units of study. The objectives should be challenging, but achievable. Knowledge objectives, as one of three categories, should consist of subject matter which is relevant for pupils to learn. Here, viable facts, concepts, and generalisations should be in the offing for learner attainment. Pupils need to comprehend what is taught so that application may be made of these learnings. What is of use in classrooms and in practical learnings must be analysed in order to separate that which is accurately done as contrasted with the inaccurate. Diagnostic procedures then must be used. After inaccuracies have been diagnosed, then a synthesis of knowledge needs to accrue. The synthesised ideas might then be applied in problem solving. Evaluation of the solutions to a problem needs to be assessed so that weaknesses in thinking and in solutions may be noticed.

A second category of maths objectives pertains to skills for pupils to attain. Skills emphasise a doing procedure by using the knowledge acquired. There are a plethora of valuable skills for pupil achievement. These include the following:

- reading maths content accurately in order to improve necessary skills. There are two dimensions here, the first is word recognition. Pupils may need assistance in word recognition. Assistance to be given here include:
    1. use of phonic clues. Where there is consistency between symbol (grapheme) and sound (phoneme) the pupil needs it learn to use a sounding out method of word recognition;
    2. use of context clues. The unrecognised word needs to be replaced with one which makes sense in relationship to the surrounding words in that sentence or paragraph. Meaning theory is in operation here in that the word used for the unknown one must make for meaningful subject matter;
    3. syllabication. A pupil may recognise a word by removing either a familiar prefix or suffix. After

the remaining word is recognised, then the prefix and/or suffix may be replaced so that pupils recognise what was initially an unknown word;

4. use of picture clues. For young children, especially, there may be selected illustrations on a page which may be referred to in identifying an unknown word.

To comprehend ideas effectively when reading, pupils need guidance and practice to:

1. reason and use logic in mathematical sentences and statements;
2. do analytic thinking in order to appraise what is salient from the non-salient in maths problem solving;
3. do creative thinking to come up with novel ideas in how to solve problems effectively;
4. apply learnings acquired in mathematics;
5. attach meaning to important vocabulary terms (Ediger, 1998, Chapter Fourteen).

A third category of maths objectives for pupils to achieve are attitudes. Thus, to achieve optimally, the pupil needs to:

1. develop a positive attitude toward mathematics in school and in society;
2. have a desire to increase knowledge and skills in mathematics;
3. achieve a positive attitude toward problem solving;
4. assist others to attain as optimally as possible with equity being a key concern;
5. be able to stay on task in ongoing maths lessons and units of study (See Kennedy and Tripp, 1991).

State mandated objectives in mathematics exist in all fifty states in the union. There is much pressure placed upon pupils to achieve satisfactorily on these tests. Equally much pressure is being placed upon mathematics teachers to secure adequate, annual yearly progress (AYP), achievement results from pupils. Pupils are tested annually in grades three through eight in mathematics and reading. A pupil may be held back in promotion if he/she fails the state mandated test in any of these grade levels, three through eight. Also, a pupil does not receive a high school diploma in many states unless the mandated mathematics and reading tests have been passed. A failure to comply with the criteria may well make it that a state does not receive federal monkeys from the No Child Left Behind (NCLB) Act. Cavanagh (2003) wrote the following:

"Three rural Vermont school systems are making an unusual attempt to avoid the penalties their schools face under the No Child Left Behind Act, through a deft shifting of the federal funding they receive under the Title One Programme.

Officials of the three districts believe the move will allow them to put off, at least temporarily the consequences provided under the federal law for schools that fail to make 'adequate yearly progress' on student test scores.

District administrators say they are not trying to shirk the federal mandate to improve their schools, nor are they rejecting the Title One money outright. They say they want to surely avoid what they view as overly harsh federal penalties that would prevent them from making academic strides on their own.

By shifting federal Title One money, the school system hopes to fall under the potentially less serious consequences specified under Vermont's accountability programme for non-Title One schools. Vermont, along with every other state, submitted such a plan to the U.S. Department of Education earlier this year to demonstrate how it would comply with the testing and accountability requirements of the No Child Left Behind law."

In addition to required state mandated testing, voluntarily the teacher needs to assist each pupil in developing a portfolio showing daily work performed by pupils in the classroom. A random sampling of representative pupil work should be included in the portfolio. Thus, the following may become a part of a pupil's products in a portfolio:

1. evaluated daily pupil written work in mathematics;
2. diagrams, charts, graphs, and listed formulas for finding area and volume, completed by the pupil;

3. teaching and learning aids made by the pupil including a place value chart, a fraction and a decimal chart, and a mathematics vocabulary chart, among others;
4. snapshots of teaching aids made which otherwise would be too large to place inside a portfolio;
5. a video tape showing the quality of the pupil's interaction in cooperative learning experiences;
6. cassette recordings of oral book reports given in class. These should be library books written on mathematical content;
7. self evaluation device used to assess the learner's perception of his/her own achievement;
8. teacher written test results (Ediger, 2002, 7-10).

The teacher may write quality tests to ascertain pupil achievement in mathematics. Proper standards need to be used with clarity in writing test items to use in determining what pupils have learned. Written by teachers, multiple choice tests are generally used to measure progress of learners. With four distractors, it is more difficult for pupils to guess the correct answer when responding to multiple choice items as compared to true/false tests. True/false can minimise the guessing facet by having pupils write the correction within a 'false' test item. Matching, completion, and short answer tests may also be written to determine if pupils have acquired salient facts.

Essay tests provide opportunities for pupils to use writing skills as well as higher levels of cognitive knowledge acquired. These tests need to have each test item adequately delimited so that only the important ideas are incorporated. Otherwise, the content written to answer an essay test question may become voluminous. However, enough needs to be written for each essay question so that it truly is a response which indicates a pupil's knowledge and writing skills. There is this problem whereby an essay test question may become too broad in scope as compared to being too narrow. When an essay question becomes too narrow, it may be better to write it in short answer or completion test item form.

All teacher written tests should be aligned with the objectives of the unit title or course being taught. There is qualify help available for teachers in selecting relevant objectives in the mathematics curriculum. The National Council Teachers of Mathematics (NCTM, 1989) gave much attention in choosing vital objectives for pupils to achieve. They presented NCTM standards for elementary education with the following topic, as an example:

K–4

— Estimation

— Number sense and numeration

— Concepts of whole number operations

— Whole number computation

— Geometry and spatial sense

— Measurement

— Statistics and probability

— Fractions and decimals

— Patterns and relationships

Grades 5–8

— Number and number relationships

— Number systems and number theory

— Computerisation and estimation

— Patterns and functions

— Algebra

— Statistics

— Probability

— Geometry measurement

Pupils should have ample opportunities to experience a high quality mathematics curriculum. The chosen objectives, learning opportunities, and assessment procedures need careful selection and be aligned with each other.

REFERENCES

Cavanagh, Sean (2003), *"Vermont District Seek to Avoid Federal Consequences,"* Education Week, 23 (5), 1, 15.

Ediger, Marlow (1999), *Improving the Teaching of Elementary School Mathematics*. Kirksville, Missouri: Simpson Publishing Company, Chapter Ten.

——(1998), *Teaching Reading Successfully in the Elementary School*. Kirksville, Missouri: Simpson Publishing Company, Chapter Fourteen.

——(2002), *Measurement Theory Versus Constructivism"*, Journal of Research in Education, 1 (1), 7-10.

Gardner, Howard (1993), *Multiple Intelligence: Theory into Practice*, New York: Basic Books.

Kennedy, Leonard M., and Stave Tipps (1991), *Guiding Children's Learning of Mathematics*. Belmont, California: Wadsworth Publishing Company.

National Council Teachers of Mathematics (1989), *Curriculum and Evaluation Standards for School Mathematics*. Reston, Reston, Virginia: NCTM.

Searson, Robert and Rita Dunn (2001), *"The Learning Style Teaching Model"*, Science and Children, 38 (5), 33-36.

Watts-Taffe, et. al. (2003), *"Preparing Inservice Teachers to Integrate Technology with the Elementary Literacy Programme,"* The Reading Teacher, 57 (2), 130-138.

26

Psychology in Teaching Mathematics

Numerous reputable psychologies are provided to assist mathematics teachers to guide each student to achieve optimally. The teacher of mathematics should study the diverse psychologies of education to implement the best teaching strategy possible. The lay public focuses on student achievement in the 3 r's or basics. Mathematics represents a highly salient basic. Students need to achieve well in mathematics to do well in school and in society. The societal arena demands mathematics proficiency within students. Learners in school need guidance to fulfill those responsibilities. Teachers need to select objectives; learning opportunities and appraisal procedures which assist each learner to achieve as well as is possible.

The balance of this chapter will emphasise specific psychologies of education, applicable to teaching-learning situations in the classroom.

Behaviourism in the Mathematics Curriculum

Precise, measurably stated objectives and their use is the heart of behaviourism. These objectives are selected prior to their being implemented in the classroom. Generally, no student participation has been emphasised in selecting these goals. Behaviourism can be emphasised with state mandated objectives in terms of core competencies and key skills. On the state level, precise measurably stated objectives have been chosen. The department of education of each state selects a cross section of educators within their borders to agree upon the stated ends. The mathematics teacher then plans learning opportunities to have students attain each objective.

A second example of behaviourism emphasises instructional management systems (IMS) on the district level. The central office then selects a cross section of teachers within the district to select salient objectives in mathematics. Again, the classroom teacher must emphasise each objective in teaching-learning situations.

The mathematics teacher, without stated mandated objectives or IMS, may write and implement specific ends for student attainment. Teaching strategies need selecting which insures that students attain desired ends.

An early pioneer in measurably stated objectives and their use was B.F. Skinner (1904-). Dr. Skinner emphasised programmed learning in either textbook or software form. The ingredients of programmed learning include:

1. sequential items of small amounts of information acquired by students in each step of learning;
2. students responding to a test item, such as a multiple choice item, based on information presented in book or software form;
3. learners receiving feedback based on the response made;
4. reinforcement being rather common with high frequency of correct responses made.

Behaviourism, in its diverse manifestations, emphasises that a student either does or does not achieve an objective as a result of instruction. If an end is not attained, the mathematics teacher needs to try a different teaching strategy.

Behaviourism appears to be a dominant psychology of education emphasised in the teaching of mathematics. With the popularity of behaviourism, the writer recommends:

1. each objective in mathematics be carefully selected in terms of being useful in school, as well as in society;

2. students achieving success in attaining sequential objectives;
3. a variety of challenging learning opportunities being provided for learners to attain each end;
4. students experiencing meaning, interest, and purpose in achieving desired ends;
5. critical and creative thinking, as well as problem solving, receiving ample attention in the mathematics curriculum;
6. appraisal procedures being varied, valid, and reliable to evaluate learner progress.

Humanism in the Mathematics Curriculum

Humanism, as a psychology of learning, emphasises students being heavily involved in determining objectives, learning opportunities and evaluation procedures. Each student is guided to attain self realisation. The late A.H. Maslow, humanist psychologist, listed five sequential levels for individuals to move through to achieve realisation of the self. These include:

(a) assisting students to meet physiological needs, such as adequate food, clothing and proper shelter;

(b) helping learners to feel safe and secure in their environment;

(c) guiding students in meeting love and belonging needs;

(d) developing situations in which esteem needs of students are being met;

(e) assisting learners to achieve self actualisation.

Only after the above sequential needs of students have been met can students achieve optimally, according to humanism, as a psychology of learning. It certainly behooves any school system to meet needs of students in order that increased achievement can be in the offing.

To pinpoint the mathematics curriculum more thoroughly, input from learners in selecting objectives, learning opportunities, and appraisal procedures is highly important. There are several excellent ways of emphasising humanism in the mathematics curriculum. One plan is to utilise learning centers. More tasks than any one student can complete would be at the diverse centres. Students individually learn to make decisions. They choose which tasks sequentially to complete and which to omit. Each learner then selects what is perceived to be of interest, meaning, and purpose. Students do not need to work on tasks perceived to be of little or no value. Sequence, in selecting ordered tasks, resides within the student. A psychological curriculum is then in evidence. Internally, the student makes choices in terms of tasks in mathematics to pursue.

A second plan of humanism, as a psychology of education, is to use a contract system. In a contract, the student and his/her teacher plan cooperatively specific learning opportunities for the former to complete. There must be considerable input from the student on the contract for humanistic psychology to be in evidence. The date the contract is due must be indicated together with the student and the teacher's signature.

A third plan of humanism is in the offing when the teacher lists, for example, ten activities for students to consider to complete in mathematics. Each student may choose five or more to complete. The student here has input as to what to pursue and what to omit.

Humanism emphasises a humane mathematics curriculum. Humanness is defined as students being able to decide from among alternatives which learning activities possess value and need to be completed satisfactorily.

The writer, in evaluating humanism, in teaching mathematics recommends that:

1. worthwhile tasks be developed for students to pursue sequentially. Trivia is to be omitted for learners to pursue;
2. students be guided to stay on task and not digress from achieving relevant objectives;
3. tasks be written on diverse levels of achievement to challenge each student to achieve as much as possible.

The Structure of Knowledge

During the 1960's and early 1970's much emphasis was placed upon mathematicians on the higher education level identifying structural ideas for public school students to attain. The structure of knowledge emphasised underlying principles that provided a framework for an academic discipline. Thus, in the academic discipline of mathematics, selected broad generalisations provided a structure for students in ongoing lessons and units. The key ideas then, among others, included the communicative property of addition and multiplication, the distributive property of multiplication over addition, the property of closure, and the identity elements.

The structure of knowledge approach, as identified by Jerome Bruner of Harvard University and his associates emphasised that public school students utilise methods of learning utilised by mathematicians on the higher education level. An inductive procedure is then in evidence. Students are guided by the teacher to learn by discovery in moving from the specific to the general to achieve structural ideas. Materials to use in teaching students to acquire content inductively include inactive (manipulative items), iconic (pictures, drawings, slides and filmstrips emphasising main ideas), and symbolic (abstract content such as printed words and numerals).

The structure of knowledge approach has much to recommend itself. The writer recommends that:

1. teachers emphasise structural ideas in a spiral curriculum. However, the spiral curriculum should not be excessively repetitious. There is built in review in the structure when these key generalisations receive attention at more complex levels in the mathematics curriculum;
2. induction receive adequate attention in teaching-learning situations. However, continued use of inductive methods are time consuming to use. The mathematics teacher needs to inject meaningful explanations also at definite points in ongoing lessons and units;

3. creative teaching in using diverse methodologies be emphasised thoroughly. Methods and subject matter have to be adjusted to the present achievement level of each student. Students differ from each other in many ways, such as interests, purposes, and present levels of achievement.

Diagnosis in Mathematics

The mathematics teacher must utilise the concept of diagnosis in teaching-learning situations. To diagnose means to pinpoint specific difficulties students experience in computation, concept development, and problem solving. Students need assistance to overcome errors made.

Robert Gagne in his book *The Conditions of Learning* (New York: Holt Rinehart and Winston publishers, 1985) advocates a hierarchy of objectives be stated in measurable terms for student attainment. If a learner cannot achieve a specific end, the teacher needs to move to a sequential easier objective. Reversing to easier ends is necessary until the present attainment level of the involved student is found. The last three levels of Gagne's hierarchy are especially important to know when teachers diagnose difficulties students experience in mathematics. The three in sequence are concept learning, rule learning, and problem solving. Thus, if a student cannot solve a problem in mathematics, the teacher needs to assist the former to determine if he/she understands involved rules. For example, if the problem to be solved involves finding the volume of a cylinder, the student must understand the involved formula — $r^2\pi h$. If the learner does not understand the rule to determine the volume of a cylinder, he/she needs assistance in attaching meaning the concepts. The separate concepts are radius, radius times radius, pi, and height. After the concepts have been learned, followed by the student acquiring the rule, the chances are that the problem can be solved in finding the volume of a cylinder.

Diagnosis is involved when the mathematics teacher assist the student to pinpoint specific weaknesses in a lesson or unit. Assistance and guidance needs to be provided to the learner to overcome identified deficiencies. Robert Gagne provides a quality model for mathematics teachers to follow in helping learners to progress sequentially. The diagnosis and remediation concepts in Gagne's hierarchy of objectives can give much help to teachers in guiding each student to attain as much as possible in mathematics.

In using diagnostic-remediation procedures in the teaching of mathematics, the writer recommends that:

1. students attach meaning to each sequential step of learning;
2. learners be assisted to perceive holism and sequence in subject matter learned. Diagnosis is available if a student fails to attach meaning to ongoing rules (generalisations) and concepts in order to solve problems in mathematics.

Conclusion

Relevant principles of learning from the psychology of education need to be implemented in teaching-learning situations. The teacher of mathematics must assist each student to attain in an optimal manner.

Four schools of thoughts were discussed in the psychology of education. These were behaviourism, humanism, the structure of knowledge and diagnosis based on a hierarchy of objectives.

The writer recommends that mathematics teachers:

1. implement tenets of behaviourism with its measurably stated objectives. Higher levels of cognition must not be hindered with the use of behaviourism in teaching-learning situations;
2. provide ample opportunities for students to engage in decision making. Learners need to have chances to select sequential learning opportunities, as advocated by humanism;
3. stress the structures of knowledge so that students may perceive that subject matter is related;
4. adequately diagnose and remediate student problems in lessons and units. Students need to perceive mathematics as being holistic and not isolated specifics in diagnostic/remediation situations.

27

Science Learning and the Student

Each student need to achieve optimally in science. Each part of the science curriculum needs careful planning. The objectives section is of utmost importance. The objectives determine what students are to achieve. All states in the union need to test students in science during the 2008-2009 school year, in addition to reading and mathematics which is presently being emphasised in testing student achievement. Thus, students in grades three through eight must be tested annually and each must pass, before being promoted to the next grade level. This means that students must study hard and achieve optimally. No longer is social promotion adequate. Furthermore, each student must pass the exit test before being granted a high school diploma. State mandated tests are a part of the No Child Left Behind law of 2002 and there are penalties if a school has too many failing students. Thus, if a school does not meet the Adequate Yearly Progress (AYP) standards two years in a row, that individual school is listed as failing and students may then enroll in a school which shows passing results.

It behooves the teacher to choose carefully which objectives students are to achieve. The objectives to be selected need to emphasise knowledge and skills ends which are useful to the student presently as well as in the future.

Science Objectives and the Learner

Which objectives, then, should students achieve in any science unit of study? Vital science facts, concepts, and generalisations need identification and implementation in the classroom. The subject matter identified may then be used in problem solving situations. Thus, within a science unit of study, the students need to choose a problem area which has significance and is relevant. Students may work individually or in a committee for possible solutions to the problem. Multi-media must be available to use in gathering information directly related to the identified problem. Media to be used should include the internet, videotapes, science equipment for experiments and demonstrations, library books, demonstration teaching, films, filmstrips, illustrations, among other necessary materials. After searching for viable information, an hypothesis is developed which is directly related the problem. The hypothesis is tentative and is to be tested with additional learning opportunities. Adequate verification is needed to truly come up with scientific information. Scientific experiments and demonstrations are the heart of science in a hands on approach to learning.

Within the framework of problem solving, students need to develop needed skills in thinking critically. To think critically the student needs to be able to analyse subject matter in terms of being factual versus opinion, accurate versus inaccurate and relevant versus irrelevant.

In addition to critical thought, the student also needs to think creatively. Unique ideas are necessary, in many cases, to solve problems. The "tried and true" might not work as solutions. Thus, novelty and originality of decisions must be made. Flexibility of ideas is then needed in the decision making arena.

Quality attitudes should be an end result of all learning opportunities in ongoing science units of study. These attitudes should include the following:

1. wanting to learn more about the world of science;
2. wanting to get along well with others;
3. wanting to be actively involved in doing science experiments and demonstrations;
4. wanting to become proficient in problem solving;
5. wanting to use flexibility in thinking skills;

6. wanting to increase proficiency in using science equipment;
7. wanting to develop adequate skill in reading, writing, and mathematics, especially as these basics relate to the science curriculum;
8. wanting to integrate all academic disciplines, as needed, into the science curriculum;
9. wanting to work cooperatively with the science teacher as well as peers in the classroom;
10. wanting to do enrichment work in science lessons and units of study.

Role of the Science Teacher

In addition to choosing objectives and aligned learning opportunities, the science teacher needs to use appropriate methodology in the instructional arena. A very important factor in teaching science is to obtain the interests of students. A high quality experiment or demonstration, an illustration, and/or concrete objects, related to the unit title, generally will do much to encourage learner attention in the ongoing lesson. Arousal of interests indicates that students are eager to learn and achieve.

Second, students need to have adequate background information to achieve the new objective(s). With important possessed background information, the student is in a better position to perceive sequence in learning. Relating the old with the new subject matter assists the learner to assimilate ongoing learnings.

Third, students need to attach meaning to new learnings encountered. Understanding of new subject matter is a must! It will become increasingly difficult to understand important facts, concepts, and generalisations if meaningful learning is not in evidence. To attach meaning means for the learner to make complete sense of what is being studied.

Fourth, student motivation is salient. With good motivation, the student may reach out and accomplish. The sky is the limit for the student if he/she is motivated to learn more in science. An enrichment centre might then provides choices for the student to acquire vital learnings *High expectations and challenge* are key ideas to emphasise in the instructional arena. Objectives, however, should be attainable.

Fifth, purpose is an important factor in learning. Thus, if students perceive reasons for learning, they should achieve at a higher level. The teacher may state the purpose at the beginning of a learning opportunity or inductively assist students to ascertain reasons for achieving a given objective.

Sixth, learning by discovery as well as teacher directed learning should be emphasised. Ample time needs to be given to productive learning by discovery or inductive learning. With inductive learning, students present hypotheses, for example, in answer to a problem in a science experiment. Brain storming is another approach to inductive learning, if quality criteria are followed, such as:

1. all participate and no one dominate in providing possible answers to a question or problem area;
2. respect for the thinking of others is necessary;
3. no one should dominate the brain storming experience;
4. each answer/hypothesis should be recorded on the chalkboard so that duplication of statements is not in evidence;
5. responses given by students need to be clear and concise;
6. no value statements are made pertaining to each answer/hypothesis given;
7. responses given may be regrouped following the brain storming session in terms of being related answers/ hypotheses.

Seventh, a variety of evaluation devices need to be used to assess student achievement. State mandated tests may be one way. This test should provide feedback on what students have missed so that remedial measures may be taken. Since state mandated tests are given once a year, the science teacher must be a good evaluator along the way and assess continuously. Thus, teacher written tests with high validity and reliability should be used. Essay tests, multiple choice test items, true/false, completion, short answer, and matching tests may be used to assess student achievement. Results from the test need to be used to ascertain where, specifically, students exhibit strengths and where assistance in teaching and learning must be emphasised.

Conclusion

Student achievement in science is an important area of personal development. The world of science surrounds the individual with technological improvements, innovations in ideas, and the natural environment. Thus, in medical practices and human health, in agriculture, in transportation, in structural buildings, in communication, the individual perceives what science has accomplished for the individual. The natural environment can be very favourable for human progress with adequate food and fiber production, as well as detrimental with its natural disasters.

REFERENCES

Astin, P, and C. Buxton (2000) *Science as Inquiry, Boblinks*, 10 (2), 10-15.

Blough, Glenn O., and Julius Schwartz (1984), *Elementary School Science and How to Teach it*. New York: CBS College Publishing.

Condrey, Jean Friend (1996), "*Focus on Science Concepts*", The Science Teacher, 63 (4).

Dewey, John (1916), *Democracy and Education*, New York: The MacMillan Company.

Ediger, Marlow (1999), *Teaching Science in the Elementary School*. Kirksville, Missouri: Simpson Publishing Company, Chapter Seven.

——(1995), "*Designing Science Units of Study*" School Science, 33 (1), 14-15.

Melber, Leah M. (2003), "*True Tales of Science*", Science and Children 41 (2), 24-32.

National Research Council (1996), *National Science Education Standards*, Washington, DC: National Academy Press.

Ward Kathleen, et. al. (1996), "*Constructing Scientific Knowledge*", The Science Teacher, 63 (9).

Wolf, Kenneth (1996), "*Developing an Effective Teaching Portfolio*", Educational Leadership, 53; 34.

28

Guidelines for Teaching Science

There are selected guidelines which need to be used as major criteria for science instruction. They serve as standards for teacher use in the instructional arena. In a world of science, the student needs to become increasingly proficient in knowledge, skills, and attitudes, involving subject matter in different branches of the sciences. Thus, the earth, biological, and physical sciences, as well as their related branches, must become relevant in the lives of students. A kindergarten through grade twelve sequence needs to be planned and implemented in the school curriculum. Which guidelines then need careful attention when planning a quality science curriculum?

Making Connections in the Science Curriculum

A quality science programme emphasises that subject matter be related so that students might benefit from an integrated curriculum. Thus, biology, chemistry, and physics possess facts, concepts, and generalisations which cut across each academic discipline. It becomes easier for students to engage in problem solving, a major objective in teaching, with an integrated curriculum. To solve any problem in science requires knowledge and skills from different subject matter areas. Needed knowledge may also come from the social sciences. There are times when a teacher may wish to focus on one academic discipline, alone, such as biology. The latter may be stressed so that indepth learning is necessary.

Objectives need to be selected carefully so that relevancy is in evidence. Then too, there needs to be a balance among the different branches of science. Each is important. In state mandated tests, one branch of science may not be tested upon. Others may have many test items such as geology, for example. Test writers need to be certain that validity is stressed when items are written so that what is tested upon has chances of being taught in the classroom setting. Thus, connections between what is tested upon and what is taught needs adequate emphasis.

Democracy in the Classroom

Each science unit must stress democratic living whereby respect for others is in evidence. If rudeness, put downs, and crude behaviour are practised, then academic achievement goes downhill. The student who was minimised by others might not learn to like science. Democratic rules of conduct need to be developed and enforced with the following rules:

1. caring for others;
2. assisting others when needed;
3. helping to keep the classroom neat and tidy;
4. maintaining a quality working environment;
5. working harmoniously.

Democratic living is important in science so that learners become involved in civility and good citizenship. To become a participating member in society, the students needs to begin these behaviours early and sequentially. Definite objectives need to be implemented which encourage tenets of excellence in human behaviour. Learning activities to achieve these objectives may be emphasised in large and small group experiences. Assessment in terms of the stated objectives needs to be emphasised continuously and be ongoing. The concept of "respecting others", alone should assist students to do better in science. If students are respected, they will feel more at ease in asking relevant questions as well as request help as needed to continue in ongoing lesson.

Encourages Curiosity in Learning

Students need opportunities to bring to the class something which deals with their unique interests. Items of interest might include an insect, a beautiful rock, a small jar of pond water containing a few tadpoles, a picture of a scene on or near the planet Mars, and floodwaters rampant in a given region. The items(s) of curiosity may spur on a discussion or individual research. What interests the student has tends to propel further learning. New interests may also be developed. In fact when teachers teach, one purpose is to instill within the learner a desire to learn the new. In introducing a new science unit, the teacher needs to use initiating activities which encourage learning. Which selected initiating activities might stimulate curiosity and interest in learning about animals, for example?

1. have an attractive bulletin board with a caption on farm animals, circus animals. Zoo animals, and pets;
2. use the classroom aquarium with small goldfish, develop an interest centre with tadpoles (frogs) in a small jar, a turtle in a terrarium to represent a reptile, and a canary in a cage to represent a bird. A pet cat (mammal) may be brought to the classroom by the parent of a student for a short periods of time. Students might then observe and discuss five categories of animals with backbones such as fish, amphibians, reptiles, birds, and mammals;
3. display library books available for reading on animal life and how animals with backbones are classified. These books should be briefly introduced to students to motivate reading of contents;
4. have an enrichment centre from which students may choose initiating science activities. An activity may be chosen as a part of other initiating activities;
5. show and discuss an AV presentation which relates directly to the ensuing unit in science.

Hands on Approaches in Science Teaching

Hands on procedures of teaching and learning need to be experienced by students. Here, the student is actively engaged in achieving and not a passive recipient of science learnings. Experimentation should be the heart of science learnings. Students with teacher guidance should do many of the experiments. Where possible hazards may exist, the teacher should assume responsibilities for performing the experiments. Safety goggles should be worn by students to make for safety.

There are numerous experiments for students of all ages to perform within related units of study.

1. In a unit on Magnetism and Electricity, two small boxes of items may be prepared by the teacher. In one box, there are items which are attracted by magnets such as metal nails, paper clips, coins of different sizes, a piece of copper, as well as other metals versus pieces of paper, small pieces of woods, a small piece of plastic, and cloth in the second box. Students may hypothesize which objects will/will not be attracted by a magnet. With a bar and a horse shoe magnet, the student may experiment to find out which materials are and are not attracted by the magnets. Each hypothesis needs to be analysed and explained to find out which materials are and are not attracted by the magnets. Each hypothesis needs to be analysed and explained.
2. In a science unit on Plants in our community, two plants may be taken which are of similar stock and quality. Each is placed in a pot with soil of similar quality. The point is to keep all variables the same, except for one which will be tested. The first variable to be tested might be the amount of sunlight plants need to order to grow. Otherwise, the amount of moisture, fertiliser, among other items, is kept constant. Thus, one plant is placed in sunlight while the other has a paper bag placed over it. After three days approximately, the paper bag may be removed to notice comparisons with the other in sunlight. Results for the happenings should be discussed in depth and recorded.
3. In a science unit on insects and animals life, students may observe different insects in a cage feeding on

diverse forms of plant life. The insects in one cage may consist of grasshoppers. Leaves from different trees, grass, and flowers may be available for feeding purposes. Recordings should be made of what transpires over several days of time.

4. Students may raise questions of observations made including:
   - How are rocks formed?
   - How do tadpoles change into frogs?
   - Why do some animals have backbones whereas others do not?

Students need to use reference sources to locate vital information. Hypotheses are then developed and evaluated.

Inservice Education for Science Teachers

Teachers together with principals and supervisors may discuss what needs to be done to upgrade the science curriculum. Through reading and research, teachers may realise that there are definite needs which may be identified and closure attempted in the teaching of science. Problems may be identified such as the following:

1. Which objectives should students achieve?
2. Which unit titles are relevant for students in science?
3. Which sequence is best to follow in teaching science?
4. Which experiments and demonstrations are appropriate for students in a given grade level?
5. Which standards should students follow to use science equipment safely and effectively?
6. Which criteria should teachers use to appraise learner achievement?
7. Which learning opportunities should be used to align with the stated objectives?
8. Which procedures should be used to assist students to reading science materials more effectively?

9. Which standards might be used to ascertain the scope of each science unit of study?
10. Which methods may be used to guide inductive learning for students?

A general session involving all science teachers in a school or several schools might be conducted to identify major problems in science instruction. Committee endeavours may be used to help teachers work on problem area of their very own choosing. Individual work may help a science teacher to focus on a specific problem area faced in the instructional arena. Consultant assistance needs to be available as well as a professional library of science materials to guide teacher achievement.

Current Events in Science

A good current events curriculum can do much to assist students in science learning. A daily, student centred newspaper available for learner use, is a necessity in the classroom. Internet use has made great inroads into the school curriculum, the current events included. Here, students may read about updated scientific phenomenon such as the following:

1. exploration of the planet Mars;
2. knowledge of asteroids located between the planets Jupiter and Mars;
3. weather phenomenon and forecasts;
4. reports of hail, earthquakes, folding and faulting, volcanic eruptions, mudslides, avalanches, floods and soil erosion, tornados, and hurricanes;
5. history of ancient plants and animals from diverse geological periods of time.

Each of the above examples of current events items might well provide time for indepth discussions and additional research on scientific phenomenon.

Reading in Science

Students need to become proficient readers in order to gather relevant information in science. The science teacher needs to be a teacher of reading as well as of science. Students who have difficulties in word recognition need assistance so that increased fluency in reading is an end result. Word recognition techniques may well need to be taught. These might well include the following:

1. use of phonics so that a student may associate sounds (phonemes) with letters (graphemes);
2. use of syllabication to identify the unknown word;
3. use of known parts within a word to help in its identification. These known parts are known as phonograms;
4. context clues. If an unknown word is met in print, then the reader must substitute a meaningful word. If this is not satisfactory, then the initial consonant maybe used to ascertain the correct word. Context clues plus the initial consonant of the unknown word should make for correct word recognition.

Word recognition techniques are tools to use to read for meaning and understanding. Understanding comes in a plethora of forms. Thus, students do need to read for salient facts in science. These facts should not be trivial but major in nature to assist students to understand the world of science. Facts are to be used by the student to develop a foundation for more complex levels of thinking such as in conceptual thinking. A concept consists of may facts. A concept such as *sedimentary rock* consists of limestone, shale, and conglomerate, among other kinds of rocks. Reading, to form generalisations requires a more complex level of reading. Generalisations join concepts into a meaningful sentence such as, "Three major classification of rocks are sedimentary, igneous, and metamorphic". Each of these may provide additional generalisations when describing how they are formed.

In addition to reading for facts, concepts, and generalisations, students also need to read analytically. Here, the learner separates such items as facts from opinions, major from minor ideas, as well as accurate from inaccurate ideas. Another higher level cognitive objective is to have students read creatively. The student then needs to read content to develop unique ideas and originality of thought.

Qualify, novel hypotheses in problem solving are always invited. Flexibility and fluency in thought are landmarks of creative thinking.

Students in the Science Curriculum

Teachers need to know much about and understand students being taught in the classroom. The abilities, interests, and needs of each student must be studied and accepted by the science teacher. Multiple intelligences theory (Gardner, 1993) has much to offer when student behaviour is being studied. There are then selected intelligences possessed by students which need consideration for implementation:

- verbal intelligences consisting of reading and writing;
- logical intelligence which uses reasoning abilities;
- musical/rhythmical as in writing lyrics and setting them to music;
- intrapersonal intelligence whereby these students achieve at a very high level individually in working by the self;
- interpersonal intelligence in which students achieve at a very high rate by working within a committee or group;
- bodily/kinesthetic which stresses skill in muscular dexterity;
- scientific intelligence emphasising objective thought such as in the scientific curriculum;
- artistic intelligence stressing creative and uniqueness in expression as in the art curriculum.

The teacher needs to be well versed in different intelligences possessed by students and how these may be used to assist each student to optimise instruction in many fields of knowledge and skills. Hopefully, attitudes will improve to move in the direction of further achievement and progress.

REFERENCES

Blough, Glenn O., and Julius Schwartz (1995), *Elementary School Science and How to Teach it*. New York: Holt, Rinehart and Winston.

Ediger, Marlow and D. Bhaskara Rao (2001), *Teaching Science Successfully*. New Delhi, India: Discovery Publishing House, Chapter Two.

Ediger, Marlow (1996), *"Evaluation of Pupil Achievement"*, Education Magazine, 45-53.

Gardner, Howard (1993), *Multiple Intelligences: Theory into Practice*. New York: Basic Books.

Holt Science and Technology (2002), *Earth Science*. New York: Holt, Rinehart and Winston.

Mehlinger, Howard D., (1996), *"School Reform in the Information Age"*, Phi Delta Kappan, 77 (6), 405-406.

Morrow, Lesley Mandel (2003), *"President's Message"*, Reading Today, 20 (6), 6.

National Research Council (1996), *National Science Education Standards*, Washington, DC: National Academy Press.

29

Sequence of Learning in the Science Curriculum

How should learnings be sequenced for learner attainment? Two recommended approaches will be discussed.

Measurable Objectives

The science teacher determines the order of ends for learner achievement when precise objectives are utilised in teaching situations. State mandated objectives are also predetermined for students to attain. The ends need to be written in ascending order of complexity. Thus, a learner must attain the first objective before working toward achieving the next sequential goal. Success in learning is optimalised if the teacher truly has written properly sequenced ends.

If an objective is not related to a previously stated end, the involved student may experience difficulty in goal attainment. This is true if the new goal to be achieved is exceedingly complex. It is difficult to order measurable ends to optimise learner achievement.

Reason given for emphasising specific objectives in teaching students are the following:

1. It is possible to measure if a learner has/has not attained a precise goal. If the student is successful in achieving the desired outcome, he/she may then progress to the next ordered end. Thus, the teacher is certain that the involved learner is ready for the next sequential goal.

2. The teacher is in the best position to order objectives for students. With an appropriate educational background, the teacher should understand the present achievement level of each learner. Only then might a teacher sequence learnings appropriately for each student.
3. The teacher should pretest each student prior to implementing a new science unit. With the concept of diagnosis being emphasised in the pretest, the teacher may determine learnings each student is ready for, in terms of sequence.
4. Sequential goals, as originally established, may be changed, if evidence warrants, to stress a rearrangement of objectives. Improved sequence in learning should be a relevant end result.
5. Students may achieve at a higher rate if teachers decide upon sequential ends for each student to attain. A structured curriculum is then in evidence.

Behaviourists advocate the utilisation of precise objectives, sequentially ordered by the teacher, for students to achieve. Achievement by learners must be observable by the teacher. What resides within the learner is not important. Only that which is measurable as to learner achievement is deemed worthwhile, since the teacher has no other avenue to gauge student progress.

General Objectives

A less structured science lesson or unit is in evidence if open-ended goals are stressed compared to the use of precise objectives. Any learning situation will possess structure, in degrees. General objectives allow interpretations as to what learners are to attain within the diverse understandings, skills, and attitudinal ends learners are to attain. Anarchy, however, is not emphasised in learning. Rather, flexibility is a key concept. Direction and guidance is provided as to what students are to learn within the framework of general objectives. Achieving precision in learnings acquired is not emphasised. Rather, students may achieve on a continuum is subject matter, abilities and the attitudinal dimension.

Utilising learning centres is a means of stressing general objectives in the science curriculum. There needs to be an adequate number of centres and tasks so that students individually may truly choose which activities to pursue and which to omit. Thus, learners in a class achieve, not the same, but diverse goals. Learning to make choices and pursue chosen tasks is highly relevant. Selections are made on the basis of personal learner interests. Style of learning is also unique in that preferred routes of learning vary from student to student. Self-actualisation is vital for students in that optimal progress is possible if sequential tasks are meaningful to students. Quality of decisions made, interests developed, style of learning possessed, as well as achieving self-actualisation cannot be measured precisely. However, in general, with teacher observation, progress of students can be evaluated in an open-ended, flexible way.

Why should students be involved in sequencing their own learnings?

1. sequence resides within the learner only, and not within teachers, textbooks, or other activities predetermined for students;
2. student interest is higher in learning when being personally involved in selecting experiences, compared to teachers selecting sequential experiences;
3. purpose in learning comes from learners. If students select their own activities, generally purposeful experience are an end result. Thus, reasons for learning are inherent in ongoing lessons and units;
4. meaningful activities are chosen if students select sequential experiences, contrasted with the teacher ordering activities for students;
5. selected students have styles of learning which emphasise selecting and chosing sequential tasks.

Conclusion

One of the authors has compared two recommended schools of thought involving sequencing activities for students.

Behaviourism emphasises the teacher predetermining what students are to learn, whereas humanism emphasises rather heavy student involvement in ordering personal experiences in the science curriculum. Whichever means are utilised to order student experiences, the science teacher needs to guide learners to achieve optimally.

30

Organising the Social Studies Curriculum

Teachers, principals, and supervisors need to analyse, synthesise, and ultimately implement a desired plan for organising the social studies curriculum. A major question then arises pertaining to who should sequence learnings for pupils. Should the teacher or should the learner basically sequence experiences in the social studies curriculum?

The Logical Social Studies Curriculum

There are selected educators who feel that teachers are in the best position to order learnings for pupils. Thus, the teacher through education and experiences, generally, can determine which activities should provide sequential learnings for each pupil. Logical thinking must then be utilised in selecting objectives, learning activities, and evaluation techniques to provide continuity in achievement in the social studies for learners on an individual basis.

To develop a logical social studies curriculum, the teacher may:

1. Select and arrange measurably stated objectives for learners to attain sequentially;
2. Choose programmed materials in which programmers have sequenced learnings for pupils;

3. Utilise management systems of instruction for pupils. Thus, for example, pupils may achieve continuity in learning through the use of the SRA Map and Globe Skills Laboratory, published by a commercial company—Science Research Associates. The teacher manages the purposes and experiences for learners as contained in the SRA kit/box of materials for pupil learning;
4. Utilise reputable single/multiple series social studies textbooks. The teacher following sequential units and content contained in these basal texts assists pupils to order their experiences in a logical curriculum. Workbooks related to the accepted textbooks may also be utilised in teaching situations to provide continuity in learning for pupils. The utilisation of audio-visual materials along with the textbooks and/or workbooks guides the teacher in further providing for individual differences among learners;
5. Develop and use subject matter units. The teacher might pretest, assign, and then test pupils in specific sequential subject matter learnings acquired.

There are selected assumptions underlying rationale in achieving a logical curriculum for learners. These assumptions include the following:

1. Professionally trained adults can do a better job of choosing sequential learnings for pupils, as compared to involving learners themselves in attaining continuity in experiences;
2. Vital concepts, generalisations, and facts can be ordered by adults for pupils to achieve effectively in a sequential manner;
3. Relevant subject matter learnings can be predetermined by teachers for pupil attainment. If pupils are involved in selecting content for mastery learning, the irrelevant and insignificant may become an end result;

4. Content achieved logically by pupils basically will be applied/transferred personally by the latter in new situations or in problematic encounters;
5. Pupil achievement can be determined rather precisely when measuring gains against precise behaviourally stated objectives. These objectives/ends have been written sequentially by the classroom teacher/teachers;
6. Teachers can develop/maintain pupil interest and meaning in learning with carefully ordered experiences and activities.

The Psychological Social Studies Curriculum

In developing a psychological curriculum, sequence in learning must be perceived for the learner's own unique perception. In contrast, a logically developed curriculum in social studies emphasises the teacher/team of teachers determining continuity in learning for involved pupils. Thus, considerable input from pupils must be in evidence from pupils in terms of choosing objectives, learning activities, and appraisal techniques in a psychologically oriented curriculum. The learner then may achieve/perceive sequence in ongoing units of study. To develop a psychological curriculum, the following approaches may be utilised:

1. Pupils with teacher guidance identifying and solving problems in the social studies;
2. Learners individually choosing the learning centre, as well as the task to pursue, within the framework of unit teaching in the social studies;
3. The pupil and the teacher cooperatively developing an agreed upon contract for the involved learner to complete. The date for completion of the experiences may also be a part of the contract.
4. Pupils with teacher guidance selecting ends, experiences, and evaluation techniques in ongoing social studies units.

5. Pupils choosing the order of learnings within a flexible framework in ongoing units of study in the school/class setting.

There are numerous assumptions directly related to a psychologically developed social studies curriculum. These assumptions include the following:

1. Sequence in learning can only be perceived by the individual involved in learning. The teacher does not do the actual learning, and in all reality cannot determine sequence for others;
2. The interests of pupils can be actuated through their active involvement in planning objectives, experiences, and methods of evaluation;
3. Meaningful learning accrues if the involved learner perceives continuity in learning;
4. Individual differences may best be provided for when the learner personally achieves continuity in experiences;
5. Pupils perceive purpose in learning when they experience order in ongoing learning activities.

Summary

Teachers, principals, and supervisors need to resolve the logical-psychological curriculum controversy in terms of which approach assists each learner to achieve optimally. Pupils individually possess diverse styles of learning in the social studies, as well as in all other curriculum areas in the school/class setting.

31

Challenging All Students in the Social Studies

Social studies as a curriculum area lacks challenge for selected students. Boredom or a lack of meaning in the social studies seems to be in the offing for these students. The social studies teacher, in many cases, appears to lack a repertoire of learning opportunities to challenge all students in class. These teachers need to experience motivation and renewal through inservice education.

Social studies is a major curriculum area and necessary to stress quality citizenship. Students need to have opportunities to learn, achieve and grow in the social studies curriculum as a separate subject as well as in an integrated curriculum area. These learnings across the curriculum will assist students to realise the relationship of content rather than each having a divided component part.

Challenge in the Social Studies

To feel challenge, each student needs to have learning opportunities which harmonise with his/her present level of achievement. If learnings are too difficult, students may not feel it is worth it to pursue and achieve. If the activities are too easy, then students may feel bored and lack interest. The teacher truly has a difficult task to determine present achievement levels of each student as well as ascertain possible of optimal achievement. The student too must accept responsibility for putting forth as much effort as possible. Together, the student and the teacher with parental support may experience quality in the social studies. There needs to be encouragement for individuals to strive do, engage in, and grow in understandings, wisdom, moral devilment, and ethical behaviour. Also, the social studies may have not only general education purposes but also vocational and vocational interests. What are selected procedures which may be used to develop a challenging social studies programme for all students?

First, the teacher needs to know the approximate reading level of each student. When a student reads aloud a significant paragraph to classmates at the beginning of a new school year, the teacher may obtain a working knowledge of reading achievement of that pupil. This procedure may be carried over for the first two weeks of school. The teacher may notice if the learner can read approximately 95 per cent of the running words correctly without previous practice. The book is generally considered to be on his/her reading level if this is done. A second component for a book to be on the reading level of a student is when three out of four questions may be answered correctly covering subject matter read. The teacher may obtain a gauge by raising a few questions covering what has been read. The teacher may determine reading levels by having a student or two each day read aloud a paragraph to classmates and then answer questions covering the content. Classmates hear the subject matter read aloud pertaining to the unit taught. Never should students feel embarrassment when reading aloud or when answering questions orally in the classroom. Respect for others is a key concept when teaching citizenship and democratic living. The results from the assessment of reading achievement are to be used in making adjustments in the social studies curriculum. A variety of learning opportunities may challenge and yet be used to provide for diverse achievement levels (Ediger and Rao, 2003, Chapter Seven).

Second, students need to experiences a variety of library books which supplement the social studies curriculum. These library books need to be about diverse general and reading levels to provide for individual differences. Students need encouragement to read a plethora of library books which assist in clarifying meanings in the social studies. These books may also be read, during sustained silent reading (SSR) and in the individualised reading programme (See Dahl, et. al. 2003).

Third, students need develop breadth, and indepth study by making graphs (picture, line, bar, and circle), tables, and charts (vocabulary, narrative, organisational, time lines) in ongoing units of study. These devices assist students to understand and attach meaning to what is being studied. Students may work in committees and collaboratively develop graphs, tables, and charts. There needs to be a reason for their development and not merely for the sake of doing so. For example by developing and viewing a picture graph, students may see at a glance how corn, wheat, and oats production differ among the leading agricultural states in the nation. The picture graph needs to be made neatly, have a title, show effort in its making and be accurate.

Fourth, adequate, emphasis needs to be given to multicultural units of study. Students need to have opportunities to learn about diverse cultures in society. A major goal here is to respect and accept diverse cultures being studied. An appreciation of diverse cultures needs to be stressed. Each culture has contributions to make in the areas of music, dance, foods, games and recreational activities, architecture, work and jobs, transportation, level of technology, and communication means. Learning activities need to be varied in order to provide for students of different abilities (See Parker, 2001, Chapter Five).

Fifth, students do possess different intelligences. Students do show more strengths in one intelligence as compared to another. They might also show abilities in several or even in all intelligences such as in verbal/linguistic, scientific, logical/mathematical, visual/spatial, musical, bodily/kinesthetic, interpersonal, intrapersonal, and existential. Social studies teachers need to be aware of these different intelligences and integrate them into each unit of study. Strengths and interests of students must be considered when developing the curriculum (see Gardner, 1993).

Sixth, good human relations and classroom climate need adequate emphasis. A classroom needs to posses characteristics which assist students to achieve as optimally as possible. A tense, highly competitive, rigid, formal environment will not assist students to learn optimally. Nor does a disruptive school climate help students to achieve. Rather, a learning environment must be conducive to help students achieve. Standards need to be developed and enforced pertaining to a wholesome learning environment.

Seventh, a variety of learning opportunities need to be in the offing to help students use their individual learning style to achieve, grow, and develop. Thus concrete materials (objects, items, excursions, realia, and models), semi-concrete materials (films, filmstrips, slides, illustrations, CDs, DVDs, use of transparencies and the overhead, internet, software and the computer, and video tapes) as well as abstract materials (textbooks, library books, encyclopaedias, pamphlets, and scripted materials) should be used in teaching and learning situations. With the use of a variety of activities, the social studies teacher needs to involve learners in becoming motivated students, not passive recipients of knowledge and skills (Ediger, 1995, Chapters Six and Seven).

Eighth, a quality evaluation programme needs to be in the offing. Teacher written tests, student self evaluation, objective and subjective assessment must be in the offing. Objective evaluations provide numerical results pertaining to student work whereas subjective evaluation involves judgements made to assess the following student made products: dioramas, murals, models, puppets, and bulletin board displays.

Portfolios developed by each student, with teacher guidance, make it possible for observers to see the actual work of students. The following are possibilities for a student portfolio:

- written summaries, conclusions, outlines, essays and reports;
- cassette recordings of oral book reports and read aloud give in class and within committees;
- art work including pencil sketches, murals, water colour work, and picture photos as they relate to ongoing units of study;
- construction work including the making of games played in other regions; model urban, village, and rural scenes; as they help to clarify that which was studied;
- paper/pencil test taken and the results discussed in class;

- assessment of the self in terms of criteria developed by students with teacher assistance (Ediger and Rao, 2003, Chapter Eight).

Ninth, there needs to be proper balance among social science disciplines for unit teaching in the social studies. Thus, the following need to be in emphasis:

- history with its relevant stress upon events of the past as they illuminate what is being studied in ongoing units. Primary and secondary sources need to be used in data gathering by students;
- geography with its salient regions and geographical phenomena directly related to relevant subject matter in the curriculum;
- economics with its goods and services needed by people in society;
- anthropology and sociology with emphasis placed upon culture in the social studies;
- political science and its stress placed upon rules, regulations, as well as laws (local, state, federal, and international) as they affect human behaviour (National Council for the Social Studies, 1994).

Tenth, appropriate methods of teaching must be used. Inservice and continuous education of the teacher is necessary. The teacher needs to select the objectives, learning opportunities to achieve the chosen objectives, and evaluation procedures to assess student achievement.

Methods of teaching to be used in implementing the social studies curriculum need to follow relevant principles of learning from educational psychology:

- learning activities for students should be interesting and engaging;
- learning activities for students should be sequential so that students experience proper order of facts, concepts, and generalisations;

- learning activities should be purposeful in that students need to perceive reasons and justification for learning what is relevant in social studies;
- learning activities should provide for different ability levels of students in the classroom;
- learning activities should be meaningful so that knowledge and skills are understood by learners;
- learning activities should motivate students to learn;
- learning activities should challenge students to achieve higher, but reasonable expectations;
- learning activities should emphasise life long student learning.

The above principles of learning should assist students to achieve optimally. Each student needs to learn as much as possible to be successful, presently as well as future.

Philosophy of Instruction

There are vital philosophers of instruction which the teacher needs to have adequate knowledge of the most important philosophy to emphasise in teaching social studies is experimentalism. Experimentalists believe in the use of problem solving strategies. Why? They believe that change is a key factor in life. Society is constantly changing. With change, new problems arise which need to be solved. One cannot know the real world as it truly exists; only approximations of the real world may be known. The person in wishing to solve problems desires to know reality as it truly is and move closer to this reality with problem solving.

The student then identifies a problem. The problem needs to be clarified so it may be tentatively resolved. Information needs to be obtained so that an hypothesis may be developed. The hypothesis is tentative and subject to change with its assessment. These are not rigid steps, but rather they are flexible and open ended. Problem solving is practical for use in school and in society (See Dewey, 1916).

There is also room for idealism as a philosophy in teaching social studies. Idealism is an idea centered school of thought.

Idealists believe that one cannot know the real world as it truly exists, but a person may receive ideas of it only. Subjects matter, being idea centered, then becomes salient for students to learn. Carefully selected knowledge ends must be chosen. There is much content for students to learn and each generalisation and its supporting facts must be relevant. Student motivation for subject matter attainment is vital. Subject matter may be chosen for the solving of problems, but not necessarily so. It has its values for students to use in school and in society. Abstract learnings are then salient for student achievement. A good background of subject matter will be useful for students as they become adults in the societal arena.

Behaviourism as a third philosophy has its origin in believing that everything which exists can be measured. Thus, what students are to learn must be stated with the use of measurable objectives. These objectives are precise and students may reveal through testing if an objective has/has not been achieved. Only that which can be measured as an outcome is stated as an objective. The objective to be achieved by students is stated prior to experiencing leaning activities. Test items are aligned with the measurably stated objectives. Much emphasis is then place upon testing to notice if the objectives have been achieved by students. State mandated objectives are based upon the philosophy of behaviourism.

A fourth philosophy and somewhat opposite of behaviourism is Constructivism. Constructivism is based upon the student developing his/her own truths. With constructivism, students do more of selecting of what to learn as compared to behaviourism. Then too, the objectives of instruction are generally not stated prior to learning but rather emerge as the learning activity for students progresses. Students sequence their very own learning with teacher guidance. The teacher motivates, encourages, and helps students in learning. Competition among and between students is not stressed, nor emphasised. Portfolio development harmonises well with constructivism. This is an opportune way to reveal student achievement and not by state mandated test scores. There certainly is room for constructivism in the social studies in which students may volunteer to do art and construction experiences. Written work of different kinds such as prose, poetry, and subject matter may be written as they relate to ongoing units of study in the social studies. Student input into the curriculum is very important with teacher/ pupil planning of the curriculum (See Stumpf, 1971).

The social studies curriculum must be built upon using vital strands of unit teaching. Students should develop high qualities in citizenship development. This must be done through teaching and learning situations in a carefully developed social studies curriculum and implementing relevant philosophies of education.

REFERENCES

Dahl, Karen, et. al. (2003), *The Reading Teacher*, 57 (4), 310-319.

Dewey, John (1916), *Democracy and Education*. New York: The Macmillan Company.

Ediger, Marlow and D. Bhaskara Rao (2003), *Psychology and the Curriculum*. New Delhi, India: Discovery Publishing House, Chapter Seven.

——(2003), *Teaching Social Studies Successfully*. New Delhi, India: Discovery Publishing House, Chapter Fourteen.

Ediger, Marlow (1995), *Philosophy in Curriculum Development*. Kirksville, Missouri: Simpson Publishing Company, Chapter Nine.

Gardner, Howard (1993), *Multiple Intelligences: Theory into Practice*. New York: Basic Books.

National Council for the Social Studies (1994), *Curriculum Standards for the Social Studies*. Washington, DC: NCSS.

Parkar, Walter, Walter C. (2001), *Social Studies in Elementary Education*. Upper Saddle River, New Jersey: Prentice-Hall, Inc., Chapter Five.

Stumpf, Samuel Enoch (1971), *Philosophy, History and Problems*. New York: McGraw—Hill Book Company.

32

Teaching History in the Classroom

Considerable attention is being given to the importance of teaching history. History and its study is vital for students in order to become good citizens in society. Students need to understand the events in time which made for their native land as well as for the world. They may then analyse strengths and weaknesses of their nation in its dealings from the beginning until the present. This is a difficult task for any student on any level of instruction. However, now is a good time to begin, whatever the developmental level of the learner. Indepth study is recommended since this makes for better understanding as compared to survey learnings.

What Makes for a Good History Curriculum?

There are a plethora of dimensions which make for quality lessons and units of study in history. The objectives need to be clearly stated with relevant knowledge, skills, and attitudinal ends of instruction being in the offing. Knowledge objectives will be plenteous in number to achieve and need careful screening to implement what is truly worthy. Facts, concepts, and generalisations which are enduring need to be separated from trivia. Vital facts are the building blocks for students in achieving concepts. In return, relating significant concepts make for important generalisations.

History emphasises a study of the past. It assists in understanding sequence of events which have in its totality made for the present. To realise the present, however, students need to realise the struggles, the successes, and the attempt to develop meaning therein. Change then is a key concept for students to understand in ongoing units of study in history. One can trace the history of transportation, for example, from the beginning of time such as walking; using horses, mules, and donkeys; early ships and water canals; trains, cars, trucks, buses, and modern rail transportation. Refinements are always in the offing of transportation methods such as power steering, air bags, automatic drive, on star, and computerised parts, among others in vehicles. Life does not stand still but is changing, modifying and developing.

It is good to assist students to develop time lines pertaining to changes in history. A drawn illustration together with its accompanying printed event may be neatly placed on a line with sequential dates to show the succeeding event such as:

1. Jamestown colony was founded in 1607;
2. Plymouth Rock colony in 1620;
3. Massachusetts Bay Colony in 1630.

Addition colonies and their beginning in time may be added on the time line when they are being studied sequentially.

In addition to change being a key idea for students to understand in history, learners also need to understand interactions among people and how a society adapts to new situations. The United States has indeed become nation of many nationalities and cultures since its beginning. After World War Two ended, many immigrants arrived from war torn areas of Western Europe. People, too, looked for a better life when leaving their native land and coming the United States after:

1. the Korean War which ended in 1953;
2. the Vietnamese War which was brought to a halt in 1973.

Many immigrants have come from Mexico when seeking jobs and a better future. Those who speak another language than English do provide challenges to teachers when providing for individual differences among students. Immigrants do need to communicate in the major language of a nation in order to benefit more fully from its many institutions in society. A multi-cultural curriculum then needs to be in the offing. Contributions from other nations must be recognised and diversity stressed when choosing objectives and learning opportunities to achieve these ends.

Technology and inventions play an important role in history. There are a few survivors living today who remember when the automobile was just arriving on the American scene. These people remember when there were paths for automobile transportation instead of roads! This was as late as the early 1920s. Trucks, also, came into being at that time to haul farm crops and a few manufactured items. Sixty per cent of the population were involved in farming. Much heavy *manual* work went into producing grain, meat and fiber. The pull type combine, pulled by a tractor, to cut wheat came into being in the early 1930s.

With technology, modern ways of living have produced refrigerators, ranges, dishwashers, computers, television, CD and DVD players, among other items of convenience and utility. Modern farms have self propelled combines, hay balers, tractors with hydraulic lifts, implements such as plows, disks, and grain drills which readily attached to the tractor. Less than two per cent of the population is presently engaged in farming. Technology has certainly made its inroads in a study of history.

The average life span of the individual has increased much from fifty years to seventy five years, since the beginning of the twentieth century in American society. Progress in medical science has done much to curb heart disease, diabetes, cancer, lung disease, and pain, among others. Polio, a deadly, crippling disease as late as the 1950s has been eliminated. Much money goes into educating the lay public to encourage more healthful living practices.

Philosophical beliefs have been identified within specific periods of time in history. The early Massachusetts Bay Colony, begun in 1630, tended to stress Puritanism in religious beliefs to govern and rule its colony. The Puritans had left England for the New World to seek religious freedom and economic benefits. They wished to continue to separate themselves from the Church of England. Puritan rules were strict pertaining to punishing those who did not believe and act "correctly". They believed strongly in absolutes in religious beliefs. God determined human history and was angry at those who failed to follow Puritan beliefs. Toward the lates Colonial years, religious beliefs had changed much with deism being in strong evidence, especially by framers of the United States constitution. Deism emphasised the importance of science, human progress, perfectibility, and freedom of expression. They believed in a God who had set the world in motion and then left it up to human beings to progress and move forward. Today, much stress is placed upon experimentalism, as a philosophy of life, with its problem solving approach. Problems need to be identified and solved in the societal arena.

Presently in American society, there is a divided camp between conservatives who favour a very strong form of capitalism, freedom from any form of abortion, complete opposition to same sex marriages, and strong military intervention in foreign affairs. To the somewhat opposite end of the continuum, liberals represent those who are more inclined to emphasise national health care, more money spent on education, taking care of the needy, and more money spent domestically, in general. A strong military is stressed by both sides, conservatives and liberals, of the spectrum.

From the above names trends, among others, objectives need to be selected which harmonise with democracy as a form of government and as a way of life.

Selecting Objectives in Historical Units of Study

Knowledge objectives must be weighed and carefully considered since there is much subject matter which may be taught. History objectives then need to be chosen carefully from among the following periods of time:

1. Colonial America, beginning with the first permanent colony in 1607;
2. Growth and settlements in the colonies up to the American Revolution in 1776;
3. The American Revolution, and a new nation, 1776-1815;
4. Expansion, the Westward Movement, and Issues pertaining to slavery;
5. The Civil War (1861-1865) and Reconstruction (1865-1877);

6. Development of the United States in terms of railroads, manufacturing, and industry;
7. Involvement in World War One (1917-1918) and World War Two (1941-1945) involving sacrifices of life on the battle fields, as well as cost of military equipment used in war;
8. Contemporary America with its many inventions, techniques, and beliefs to make for a better society. However, intermittent involvement in wars included the Korean War (1950-1953), and the Vietnamese War (1962-1973).

From the above named periods of time and unit titles, the history teacher may choose relevant objectives. These knowledge objectives should incorporate vital facts, concepts, and generalisations. The following knowledge objectives might be worthwhile for students to achieve pertaining to colonial America:

1. The student will give three reasons why many colonies grew rapidly in the new world;
2. The student will give four reasons which hindered some colonies from growing even more rapidly than they did.

Each objective needs to be clearly stated. The teacher, also, needs to choose learning activities which assist students to achieve the stated objectives of instruction. Periodically, the teacher needs to evaluate with students the correctness and appropriateness of each response.

A few states have state mandated objectives and their accompanying tests which measure if students have achieved criteria in social studies for their grade levels in grades three through eight, and also in grade ten as an exit test. Most states, at the present time do not test for student achievement in history and the social studies, but do test in reading and mathematics, as mandated by law. Many educators believe strongly that history and the social studies should also be mandated by each state for testing purposes. The thinking is that the academic areas being tested receive more attention than those not being tested in state mandated testing.

Knowledge or subject matter objectives should emphasise different levels of cognition and skills involved. Certainly, students should not stay merely with the learning of facts, but also achieve more complex ends such as:

1. understanding what has been taught so that meaning is involved in learning;
2. using that which has been learned;
3. thinking critically as in separating facts from opinions, fantasy from reality, and accurate from inaccurate statements;
4. thinking creatively by coming up with unique ways of solving problems;
5. assessing the values or worth of information being considered.

Quality attitudes also need to be developed within students. These attitudes need to include that students:

1. develop a love for learning;
2. respect and accept each other as human beings having much worth;
3. assist each other, as needed, to achieve objectives;
4. identify problem areas in history and the social studies;
5. analyse subject matter;
6. use subject matter in novel and unique ways to meet specific purposes;
7. apply what has been learned to new situations in the social studies curriculum and in life;
8. want to be a good citizens;
9. place good human relations high on the list of objectives to achieve;
10. participate eagerly and fully in ongoing lessons and units of study.

Learning Opportunities to Achieve Objectives

Learning opportunities to achieve objectives should be engaging, interesting, and purposeful. They should assist students to become motivated individuals. Multi-media approaches should be used to provide for the needs of individual students. Multi-media stresses the concrete whereby students learn from realia and real objects and items. Semi-concrete materials stress the use of CDs, DVDs, illustrations, study, prints, transparencies and the overhead projector, video tapes, films, and filmstrips. Pictorial forms and inherent in the semiconcrete. Abstract materials are the most complex for many learners since letters and numerals in symbolic form are used in reading and learning. Thus, textbooks, library books, encyclopaedia entries, work books, written work, and primary sources consisting of letters, diary entries, artifacts, biographies, autobiographies, among others, may be classified as abstract materials of instruction.

To use each of the above concrete, semiconcrete, and abstract materials, diversity of methods may be used to provide for individual differences in the classroom. The following methods of instruction might then be used:

1. learning by discovery or induction;
2. deduction whereby ideas move from a speaker to the classroom audience;
3. problem solving procedures;
4. committees at work, dyads, as well as individual endeavours;
5. peer mediated instruction and teaching;
6. heterogeneous and homogeneous grouping;
7. large group, small group, and individual projects;
8. cross grade grouping;
9. use of learning centres and self selected tasks;
10. enrichment learning which goes beyond assigned lessons.

The teacher of history needs to study students and ascertain under which conditions each learner may achieve most optimally. It is good if a teacher has quality aid service available. Retired teachers may make for a good source of teacher aid service. Properly trained aids may assist the regular teacher by reading historical content aloud to students having problems in reading. They may also listen to students read aloud certain portions of difficult as well as important textbook content. Other tasks for the aid might well involve the following:

1. evaluation of student written work;
2. listen to and assess oral student book reports;
3. make materials for teaching history;
4. assist students with dramatizations involving incidences in history;
5. work on one with very low achieving students.

Assessment of Student Achievement in History

There are a plethora of quality ways to assess learner achievement. If a state mandates testing in history, hopefully there will be feed back to the teacher on what can be done to assist student achievement. All test items should be valid. Thus with state mandated objectives as a guide, the teacher may use these guidelines in teaching. If the test is aligned with the objectives, the history teacher should have considerable assurance that what is taught will relate directly to items on the lest. This is especially true if the state mandated test has also be pilot tested for reliability either through test/retest, split half, and/or alternate forms of reliability.

Systematic testing, using teacher written tests, may assist the history teacher to ascertain which facts, concepts, and generalisations students have left to achieve. Learning activities might then be provided to minimise students errors made on the test. Testing, according to the writer, should be done to determine how successful the instructional process has been. Testing, to compare students in achievement has very few, if any, benefits. Rather, testing and test results may be helpful as teaching tools and that tool being to find out if additional learning activities need to be provided due to students having missed out on responding correctly to any item. Test items should be varied, in kind, to provide for diverse learning styles of students. Thus the following kinds of test items may be administered to students:

1. true/false, with corrections made by the learner to change a "false" test item to that of being "true";
2. multiple choice, with each distractor being plausible;
3. completion, with adequate information given so that a student may respond to a meaningful test item. —, —, and — are in —, is not meaningful to the student in making responses;
4. matching, whereby a student matches column A with column B. There needs to be more items in one column as compared to the other so that the process of elimination may be minimised when students respond to a matching test;
5. essay, in which students may engage in problem solving. These kinds of test items may be quite open ended which truly might encourage problem solving. To make for more objective scoring, a rubric should be carefully designed and used;
6. short answer, in which students respond to a question but the required answer may consist of a phrase or sentence.

Teacher observation may be an excellent way to ascertain student achievement. Quality standards need to be used here. Teacher observation may well be continuous and ongoing.

33

The Psychology of Learning and Adult Education

Educational psychologists have definite recommendations to make in guiding optimal adult achievement. Continuous education is important for all individuals. Society emphasises a changing environment. Inventions, technology, and values seemingly change much in time and space. Thus, each person must modify, reconstruct, and evaluate the self to determine which goals need attainment in order grow, develop, and achieve. Changeless situations do not exist. Rather individuals must adjust to changes in society. Also, it is good to forecast changes so that one can be a leader in bringing new concepts and generalisations to fruition Leadership is needed much in society to solve local, regional, state, national, and international problems. One should, of course, develop extreme proficiency in solving personal problematic situations.

The Psychology of Instruction

Instructors of adult education should follow tenets of the psychology of learning to assist students to attain as optimally as possible. In a changing world which requires abilities to be developed as much as possible, learners in adult education must attain optimally. Quality attitudes assist in achieving as much as individual abilities permit. The instructor needs to guide students to develop attitudes which assist optimal attainment.

Thus the instructor guides learners to be successful in coursework taken. Sequence in learning is based upon what learners have achieved previously. New facts, concepts, and generalisations obtained are related directly to what was achieved previously. With quality sequence are order in learning, the adult learner may attain feelings of success and develop a positive self concept. A good self concept guides students to achieve higher goals in life. Low self concepts greatly hinder students from attaining that which is possible. Objectives for student attainment not be so high that failure to achieve is an end result. Nor should be objectives be stated at such a low level of complexity that a lack of challenge is in evidence. Challenge for learners is salient if they can be successful students in adult education.

Purpose for learning is important. Thus adult learners need to accept reasons for goal attainment. To guide students to perceive purpose, the instructor of adult education must explain why it is important for learners to achieve each salient objective before it is being stressed in an ongoing lesson. A deductive procedure may be used in that the instructor explains to students why it is salient to achieve an objective. The explanation is provided by the instructor and exists for student use in developing purpose for learning. The use a different approach, the instructor may use an inductive method. With induction, the instructor asks adult learners why it is important to learn specific content and skills as stated in the objective being stressed for student attainment. Responses must come from students when providing reasons for learning. Questions raised by the instructor must relate directly to establishing reasons for adult learners to perceive purpose for participating in an ongoing activity. The activity to participate in and the goal to be attained become one and not separate entities. Active participation by learners to the questions raised by the instructor is needed. Inductive teaching stresses that students themselves are guided by the instructor to establish reasons for learning. Purpose for learning may also be emphasised through the use of extrinsic rewards. Thus the instructor must praise learners for quality individual or group participation in ongiong activities and experiences. Praise received stresses feedback to learners that goal attainment by students is in evidence which should be purposeful to students. Instructors must not hesitate to praise students for achieving well within in a class or course.

Interest in learning is a powerful factor in guiding students to achieve. With interest, the student attends to ongoing presentations. Attention is then focused on content presented by the instructor and from answers to questions raised by students. Active involvement by students in definitely preferable to a learner being a passive recipient of ideas and skills.

Specific Psychologies of Learning

The instructor of adult education classes needs to study and implement selected tenets from diverse schools of thought in the theory of learning developed by educational psychologists. Behaviourism as one theory of learning emphasises establishing precise objectives prior to instruction for learner attainment. Each course then in adult education must have specific objectives which leave no leeway in interpretation. After instruction, the student has or has not attained a specific objective. With precise measurably stated objectives, the instructor must choose learning opportunities that relate directly to the objective being emphasised in teaching-learning situations. Activities chosen assist adult learners to attain that which is stated in the objective, no more nor less. After instruction, the instructor measures which students have or have not been successful in goal attainment. Those learners who have been unsuccessful in achieving the desired goal need a different teaching strategy so they too can be successful in achieving stated ends.

Precise objectives (using behaviourism as a psychology of learning) need to be arranged in sequence so that adult students may attain as much as possible. The instructor arranges the objectives sequentially to secure optimal learner progress. A logical sequence is then in evidence when the instructor orders the objectives in ascending levels of difficulty.

When teaching toward objectives or ends, the instructor is stressing an outcomes based approach in adult education. Since measurement is frequent to determine if learners have attained each precise objective, measurement driven instruction is being stressed. Testing is a major means of ascertaining the amount of achievement each adult student is making. Results in testing from each student may be given as per cent of responses correct, percentile rank, quartile deviation, and/or standard deviation. Numerical results are then in evidence.

Reinforcement theory within the framework of behaviourism states that the instructor rewards students frequently. Praise for work well done by students can be an excellent way of reinforcing learning.

Toward the other end of the continuum, the instructor may use humanism as a psychology of learning to provide for individual differences. Humanism advocates heavy input from students in developing the adult education curriculum. Thus the instructor invites questions from students in ongoing lessons and units of study. These questions may well stress problem solving and emphasise student concerned in adult education. Projects to be completed for the course should be determined by the learner with instructor guidance. Term papers and other written requirements need to involve the student when selecting topics to write about. The instructor decides upon the written work as a requirement, but the learner decides upon the topic and title to pursue within the framework of the course. At frequent intervals during the duration of the course, students within committees may decide content to be discussed. The content assists in clarifying course objectives, or it might guide learners to engage in-depth thinking pertaining to vital facts, concepts, generalisations, and skills inherent in the adult education course. Critical and creative thinking should then be in evidence.

A contract system might also be stressed to emphasise humanism as a psychology of learning. The contract may be developed with each student somewhat toward the beginning of the semester or duration of the course. With background information, the student with instructor guidance plans what should go into the contract for the former to complete. Included in the contract could be the following:

1. reading activities and their summaries;
2. constructing projects related to the objectives of the course;
3. drawings made of procedure or plan of operation;
4. developing a term paper on a self chosen topic stressing content relevant to the class being taken;
5. tape recording a talk on a vital area of concern within the framework of content relating directly to course content.

Humanism as a psychology of instruction stresses learners being actively involved in choosing objectives, learning opportunities, and evaluation procedures in the ongoing course. Learning is its very own reward. Intrinsic motivation is then in evidence.

Summary

Using tenets of the psychology of learning when teaching students guides adult students to attain more optimally in the curriculum. Students individually need to achieve as much as possible. Thus the instructor needs to determine when behaviourism or humanism should be stressed in ongoing activities. Both psychologies are highly reputable and should be used to guide optimal learner achievement. Instructors need to evaluate the self in terms of how well students achieve in the adult education curriculum.

34

Evaluation and the Psychology of Learning

A study of diverse schools of thought in the psychology of learning may provide useful guidelines in evaluating the school curriculum.

Advocates of programmed learning for example, believe that programmers are in a significant position to determine what pupils are to learn. Thus, in a programmed textbook, the pupil may read a sentence, several sentences or a short paragraph, respond to a completion item, and then check his/her response with the correct answer given by the writer of the programmed materials. The learner is then ready to respond to the next sequential items using the same or similar approach in learning. The sequential steps of each item to be learned by pupils are small indeed. Thus, learners make few errors generally when working on programmed materials. These materials must be on their present achievement level.

Teachers, principals, and supervisors may then appraise the school curriculum in terms of tenets of the psychology of learning in the civilization of programmed materials. Stimulus-Responses (S → R) school of thought is then involved in learning. The sentence, sentences, or a short paragraph read by the pupil is the stimulus; the answer written by the learner is the response. Reinforcement in learning is involved when the pupil is correct in responding to any item in programmed learning. Success in learning is important!

Teachers, principals, and supervisors may also evaluate the curriculum in terms of using specific, measurable objectives in teaching-learning situations. The following criteria are generally important to follow when writing specific, behaviourally stated objectives:

1. pupil achievement may definitely be determined if a learner has or has not achieved a stated objectives;
2. observable evidence is available to teachers, parents, administrators, and other interested individuals if a pupil has or has not achieved a specific objective.

The behaviourally stated objectives are written by the teacher prior to teaching a given set of learners. These ends may be written sequentially for learners to achieve.

Teachers, principals, supervisors, and interested lay people may wish to appraise the school curriculum in terms of using precise objectives whereby observable evidence is possible as to pupils having or not having achieved desired ends. Specific objectives also emphasise the utilisation of the Stimulus → Response school of thought in terms of how pupils learn. The learning activity to achieve an objective is the stimulus, whereas the reactions made by learners to these tasks are the response or responses to achieve behaviourally stated objectives.

A rather different school of thought in the psychology of learning is humanism. Humanists stress the following criteria in the psychology of learning:

1. pupils need to select, from among alternatives, what to learn (ends or objectives) as well as the means of learning (tasks or learning activities);
2. creative endeavours are important for learners;
3. self-actualisation or the realisation of the optimal self is a very important concept for emphasis in teaching-learning situations;
4. relevant needs of learners must be met for optimal learner achievement to take place;

5. perception of learners is an important consideration when choosing goals, learning activities, and appraisal techniques.

Humanists definitely do not stress the following, generally, in teaching-learning situations:

1. the teacher choosing objectives, learning experiences, and appraisal procedures for pupils;
2. the use of measurable, specific goals in the school-class setting;
3 accountability movements which emphasise precise ends being utilised in the school curriculum;
4. large group instruction in the classroom;
5. the use of lectures and strong emphasis placed upon explanations in teaching-learning situations;
6. a formal classroom environment stressing the importance of pupils being quiet and sitting still;
7. much significance placed upon subject matter learning to the exclusion of learning more about oneself and about other human beings. Humanists generally would advocate adequate use of values clarification content in the curriculum.

Diverse schools of thought in the psychology of learning provide content for educators and lay citizens in evaluating the curriculum. Questions, such as the following, arise in utilising the psychology of learning in appraising teaching-learning situations:

1. Who should choose objectives for learner achievement? The programmer? The teacher? Pupils with teacher guidance? How much involvement should there be by interested lay people in selection desirable ends?
2. Who is in the best position to select and sequence or order learning experiences? Behaviouristic approaches? Humanistic emphasis?
3. Who should be involved in assessing progress of pupils?

REFERENCES

Ediger, Marlow, *The Elementary Curriculum, A Handbook*, Kirksville, Missouri: Simpson Publishing Company, 1977.

Goodwin, William L., and Herbert J. Klausmeier, *Facilitating Student Learning*, New York: Harper & Row, Publishers, 1975.

Morris, Van Cleve & Young Pai. *Philosophy and the American School*, Second Edition, Boston: Houghton Mifflin Company, 1976.

Mouly, George J., (Ed.), *Readings in Educational Psychology*, New York: Holt, Rinehart & Winston, Inc., 1971.

35

Promoting Oral Communication Experiences

Speaking with others is a very common occurrence. Here, the speaker sends messages to a listener. He/she has certain obligations to the listener such as speaking clearly at an appropriate pace, and making certain that clarity of ideas are being communicated. Messages need to be understood so that the listener may respond. Speakers, whether in conversation or in presenting a talk in an auditorium, have a plethora of responsibilities to provide for meaningful communication.

A variety of oral communication activities need to be in evidence in the classroom setting so that practice is given in effective use of the spoken language.

Discussions in the Classroom Setting

Ample time needs to be given in using discussions to ascertain learner achievement in oral language use. There are definite standards to follow when students are involved in a discussion. Each student should participate actively, but no one dominate the discussion. Interaction should occur among students, not between the student and teacher only. Indepth discussion of ideas presented need to be encouraged. Students must present ideas which make for meaningful oral communication. If a student does not understand a comment, he/she should be encouraged to ask for clarification.

From the total classroom discussion, students may work within committees to further intensify discussions. Here, problems may be identifies and a variety of reference sources used to secure necessary answers. The content gathered needs discussion in order to develop an hypothesis. The hypothesis is tentative and may be revised as evidence warrants. Problem solving involves perseverance until the activity has been completed. Ideas presented need to be analysed, synthesised, and appraised.

Project Methods of Instruction

Many students like to do projects in science such as making scientific equipment useful in unit teaching. Social studies units also provide opportunities to project methods of instruction. Making a model farm scene emphasises cooperation and the use of oral communication. The author when supervising student teachers in the public schools, observed the enthusiasm which many students revealed when working harmoniously on a science or social studies project. He was especially amazed at learners working on projects for the annual science fair. A committees of students was developing a solar collector. A second committees was working on a model scene in which erosion of soil was being controlled, while a third committee, made model forms of prehistoric life using paper mache'. Enthusiasm and interest ran high in the classroom!

Interaction among students in oral language use is salient in project methods of learning. There is much cooperative planning to be done in doing a project. Thus, there needs to be an agreed upon committee purpose, planning to carry out the purpose, the actual doing of the project to its completion, and then the assessment phase to notice the quality and worth of the project.

Oral Book Reports

There should be time in the curriculum for oral book reports. The oral part needs to stress quality enunciation, intonation, and pitch. Also included should be appropriate pauses where need be to indicate punctuation marks. The subject matter contained in the oral report should be accurate, reflect completeness, and indicate good sequence. The presenter should use an online to facilitate ease of communication. A good self concept should be developed when reporting ideas. With practice and a supporting environment, students may develop confidence in the self and improve the quality of book reports given in the classroom.

Related to oral book reports is for the student to present a report on a specific topic. Here, the student needs to use a variety of reference sources to secure needed data. Reference sources might well include encyclopaedias, internet, CD, ROMs. CDs, video tapes, textbooks, trade books, among others. The scope of the topic should be specified, followed by quality order in presenting the ideas to the class. The report must be presented at a rate of speed in which students can comprehend content presented. Eye contact is important to consider for the reporter. The posture and mannerisms of the reporter should be one which facilitates in securing the attention of listeners.

Impromptu Speaking

Impromptu speaking is fascinating to many learners. Here the student is presented with a topic relating to the unit being taught in class. The student is given five minutes, for example, in getting the speech organised. He/she then presents the talk to classmates and the teacher. Quick thinking is necessary in preparing for and giving an impromptu speech. Readiness needs to be in evidence on the part of learners when considering impromptu speaking.

Why might impromptu speaking be considered important? Individuals need to be able to "think on their feet." Being able to recall ideas quickly can be highly valuable in society. The recalled ideas may be quite random unless the speaker is able to develop some kind of order pertaining to what is said.

Reading Poetry Aloud

Poetry may be taught as an entire unit of study or it may be integrated with each academic area of study. It is good to obtain a meaningful overview of a poem so that its contents are understood. The selected poem may be read orally together as a class or within a committee. This assists all students to identify the inherent words correctly. They can see the words as they are being pronounced in unison, thus providing not being able to identify a word. Students individually might then practice reading the poem. Poetry should be shared and enjoyed. Parts may be discussed if there are difficulties in interpretation.

As time goes on, each student may wish to make a collection of desired poems. Students also will wish to write diverse forms of verse, such as in the following:

1. couplets which contain two somewhat equivalent lines with ending words rhyming;
2. triplets with three lines and ending words rhyming;
3. quatrains with four lines and ending words rhyming;
4. limericks with lines one, two, and five rhyming as well as lines three and four rhyming;
5. haiku verse with three lines containing five, seven, five syllables for each of three lines of verse respectively;
6. tanka verse with five lines containing five, seven, five, seven, seven syllables respectively per line;
7. free verse contains no planned rhyme and the length is open ended.

The teacher should frequently read different kinds of poetry aloud to students. Interesting poetry which capture student attention should be chosen. There also should be chances for each student to select and read poetry aloud to others. Small groups make it possible for students to have opportunities to read poetry aloud more frequently to others. If there are multiple meanings being attached to a line or two, brain, storming may be used to suggest interpretations.

Choric Reading

Choric reading emphasises that students join in together for the refrain of a given selection which is read aloud. The teacher reads a short selection, followed by students collectively following in with the refrain. Wanda Gag's *Millions of Cats* is an excellent trade book for use in choric reading. The teacher or student has an introductory selection to read followed by the refrain. The refrain represents repetition and is of high interest to students. The author when supervising university student teachers in the public schools observed students reciting the following familiar tongue twister in choric reading:

I saw Esau sawing wood
And Esau saw I saw him
Though Esau saw I saw him saw
Still Esau went on sawing

With choric reading, students need to blend their voices. Clarity of voice is important with proper pitch, stress, and intonation. Careful attention also needs to be given to pauses (punctuation).

The writer has also noticed primary grade pupils, when jumping rope, do creative chants. Collectively, the involved pupils move ahead on their own in developing and saying the chants together. Choric reading is indeed an enjoyable experience for pupils!

Readers' Theater

When readiness is in evidence, reader's theater is a challenging experience for students. Here, students may take an appropriate literary selection and arrange it into selective parts, according to the characters doing the actual speaking. Many literary selections have numerous speaking parts in direct quotation. Other literary selections may need to be arranged into direct quotations, involving separate speakers. There are, of course, commercial companies who list reader's theater selections. These need to be on the developmental level of students. Each student may volunteer for an oral reading role. Parts might also be assigned according to the teacher's judgement. The author would suggest students volunteering for a reader's position. The presentation should have educational values and not be a highly polished performance, unless students do exceedingly well on motivated efforts with teacher guidance. There are no props or background scenery. Each reader must do well in oral reading. Practice is important. In addition to oral reading of a character's part, there also need to be one or more readers to read the background information on the setting of the literary selection as well as facets of characterisation and other none characterisation parts, necessary for a meaningful presentation. Readers need to stay strictly on task in oral reading of sequential parts. Gestures, facial expressions, and voice inflection are important. Participants are generally seated in a semi-circle, facing an audience. Classmates might well be an audience. The final presentation may also be presented to visitors from other classrooms and, possibly, at a school assembly.

The Reader's Theater presentation may be assessed in rubric form based on the following criteria:

1. effort put forth by each reader;
2. cooperation on the part of participants;
3. clarity of ideas presented with proper enunciation;
4. good attitudes revealed toward reader's theater;
5. words pronounced and identified correctly.

Each member needs to practice reading his/her part until optimal achievement is indicated. Everyone should have opportunities to enjoy reader's theater participation.

A Story Telling Club

Story telling has become quite popular in society. A well remembered story was told a few years ago while the author was attending an evening session at the Grand Canyon. The speaker played the role of John Wesley Webb in the latter 1860s and early 1870s. Webb had lost an arm during the Civil War and presented his experiences as a pioneer rafting on the unexplored Colorado River. The presenter told first person experiences rafting on the dangerous Colorado river. It truly felt as if the speaker had gone through those tense times. The audience of 62 sat silently in suspense until the forty minute talk was completed. The presenter was indeed an outstanding story teller.

Story telling involves person who can communicate clearly and in an interesting manner. The content needs to develop and maintain listener interest in stories presented. It takes practice to be a good story teller. Many times in ordinary conversation, a conversant tells a brief story in context. It is a talent to be able to hold the attention of listeners throughout a told story. Pitch needs to be varied and voice inflection used. A story teller needs to be a keen observer of everyday life's situations. The everyday happenings provide interesting ideas for a story. Sometimes, state, national, and international happenings provide content for stories.

There are schools which have story telling clubs. Students need to avail themselves of the opportunities to join a club of personal interest, such as a story telling club. A teacher sponsors the club and organisers it to become functional as soon as possible so that students may learn about and practice the art of story telling. How much structure the story telling club should have depends upon local needs. Officers can be elected with students serving a very active role in the doings of the story telling club.

Sharing of Library Books

Students have a need many times to share library book content. The could be narrative, expository, and creative content such as poetry. One method of sharing information from library books is to have multiple copies of a paperback read by four participants, approximately. After the completion of having read the paperback, students may arrange in a circle so that face to face communication is possible. Involved students have the responsibility to:

1. keep the discussion moving satisfactorily;
2. have everyone participate and on one dominate;
3. present meaningful ideas;
4. listen carefully to others;
5. ask for clarification of ideas if necessary.

Informal Debates

Debates are excellent ways of viewing issues. Thus, one person or group may take the position of one side of the issue while another person or committee takes the opposite side in the debate. It takes knowledgeable individuals of an issue to be able to debate well. Much study, thought, and subject matter, as well as skill in debating, need to be in the offing. A highly competitive debate is not advocated here, but rather a debate which stresses considerable knowledge of an issue as well as positive attitudes considerable knowledge of an issue as well as positive attitudes toward others. The informal debate may be a precursor for formal debates in competitive situations such as on the distract and state levels. Topics for debates may come from social studies unit being emphasised. The teacher may choose the topic or teacher/student planning may be used. The pros and cons of each position need to be clarified. Practising debate skills is necessary in order to do well.

There are a plethora of topics for debate purposes, such as in the following:

1. when intervention by a nation, if at all, is necessary in a war;
2. prevention of poverty in a nation, is it possible?
3. is national health insurance a dream only, within a nation?
4. guaranteeing a job for all in a nation, possibility or myth?
5. how should old age benefits be implemented and financed?

The topics chosen for debate need to be developmentally appropriate. Adequate resources need to be available to secure information. A variety of reference sources need to be in the offing. Teachers need to introduce diverse kinds of materials used to find information such as those of a concrete nature, semi-concrete, an abstract. Individual difference need to be met.

In closing, teachers need to be aware of the many opportunities available for students to participate in oral communication experiences.

REFERENCES

Ediger, Marlow (1978), "Write On," *School and Community*, 65 (2), 12.

Ediger, Marlow, and D. Bhaskara Rao (2000), *Teaching Reading Successfully*. New Delhi, India: Discovery Publishing House, Chapter One.

Ediger, Marlow (1986-1987), "Reading Readiness and the Learner", *Minnesota English Journal*, 27 (2), 43-49.

Ediger, Marlow (1976), "Objectives and Oral Communication", *California English*, 12 (4), 7.

Ediger, Marlow (2001), "The School Principal: State Standards Versus Creativity", *The Journal of Instructional Psychology*, 28 (2), 79-83.

Ediger, Marlow (1999), "Teaching Reading in the Social Studies", *Arizona Reading Journal*, 26 (1), 15-18.

Ediger, Marlow (2000), "Speaking Activities and Reading", *Reading Improvement*, 37 (3), 136-144.

Ediger, Marlow (2000), "Writing, The Pupil, and the Social Studies", *College Student Journal*, 34 (1), 59-68.

Gardner, Howard (1993), *Multiple Intelligences: Theory into Practice*, New York: Basic Books.

Searson, Robert, and Rita Dunn (2001), "The Learning Style Teaching Model", *Science and Children*, 38 (5), 22-36.

36

Cooperative Learning Versus Competition Which is Better?

Most educators appear to advocate cooperative learning in the curriculum. Pupils then are to work together harmoniously to achieve objectives in the curriculum. Heterogeneous grouping is also recommended so that mixed achievement levels of pupil work in a committee setting. These educators emphasise democratic living in the classroom when pupils are grouped heterogeneously as compared to homogeneously. Cooperative endeavours stressed democracy as a way of life, according to may educators, as compared to competition among pupils in the classroom. If full inclusion is emphasised, then a committee in cooperative learning may truly be heterogeneously with increased diversity in terms of pupil abilities. Let us examine the philosophy of cooperative learning and heterogeneously grouping more fully.

Cooperative Learning

As we read journal articles and other teacher education materials we feel that most educators advocate cooperative learning throughout much of the school day. There is a distinctive kind of reasoning emphasised by advocates. Pupils may then learn from each other. Perhaps, more can be learned from peers as compared to the teacher. Learners are cooperative beings and like to work together with other pupils. Cooperative learning can be emphasised in all curriculum areas and throughout most or all of the school day. Pupils are serious achievers when working together with peers. Each one desires to do his/her fair share of work within a committee. Fast learners can assist the slower pupils to achieve well. They can learn from the slow learners in return. Pupils need to learn to get along with each other and to respect the abilities of others. Diversity in the curriculum is to be stressed.

We believe there are numerous loopholes in the reasoning of cooperative learning advocates. We emphasise that not all pupils by any means are cooperative. There is rivalry, hostility, and aggression among pupils. To be sure, there are many pupils who are cooperative beings in wishing to work well together with others in an harmonious manner. One has only to observe pupil behaviour to notice that pupils are both cooperative and non-cooperative beings. We thoroughly agree that pupils should learn to work well with others in school and later in the work place. But to what degree in terms of the total length of the school day should pupils work on cooperative endeavours? My thinking is that pupils should work in committees effectively since life itself consists of working well with others. However, there are many times when individuals need to work by the self. All of us find ourselves working on tasks and responsibilities by the oneself, without involvement of others. Thus there needs to be rational balance in the school curriculum between working with others as well as working individually on tasks and activities.

There is seemingly a learning style which pupils possess that prefers working with others on lessons, projects, and activities. These pupils, no doubt, might well prefer a committee or cooperative learning experience. Together, the pupil may achieve more than working individually. These pupils might be motivated more so with other learners than working by the self. Learners may motivate and challenge each other in a committee setting and yet efforts are harmonised to attain a togetherness in an educational endeavour. Pupils need to be highly accepting of each other in cooperative learning. They must respect diversity among pupils and ideas. The use of ridicule and sarcasm is to be frowned upon. Rather, the pupil needs to encourage broad participation by members of the team. Group cohesion is necessary so that the goals of cooperative learning are being attained. The committee may be evaluated together as well as individually in their team contributions. All need to participate actively and achieve maximally. Failure for one or two to achieve in cooperative learning hinders optimal attainment for these pupils. Each must be serious in preserving and working toward objectives. The individual needs to blend his/her efforts with those of others on the team. All on the team must participate optimally, no one dominate the committee endeavours. Learners should stay on the task at hand, not digress from agreed upon goals. Tasks need to become clear through interacting with each other. Achievement toward goals must be reviewed periodically in order to notice how much progress has been made and how much further the committee needs to go in order to achieve agreed upon goals.

The teacher in cooperative learning becomes a guide, a stimulator, and one who encourages, but not one who lectures nor dispenses information. He/she is a resource person who has much knowledge of keeping pupils on task. The teacher as resource person has numerous materials and necessary information from which pupils in cooperative learning may gather what is needed to achieve objectives. As a helper and facilitator, the teacher is motivated to assist pupils to be creative, to engage in critical thought, and to identify and solve problems. Higher levels of cognition are necessary here. The teacher knows how to relate to learners in order that higher levels of cognition on the pupil's part in teaching and learning is in evidence.

There are selected questions that need to be raised pertaining to cooperative learning. These are the following:

1. how much time in the school day should be given to cooperative learning?
2. how should committees be formed for cooperative learning?
3. who selects members of a committee?
4. how permanent should committee membership be?
5. how flexible should committee membership be if a pupil wishes to change to a different committee?

Frequently, we have received the impression that writers/speakers in education recommended continuous cooperative endeavours in a classroom. Certainly, learning opportunities need to be varied. Little is mentioned as to who should choose committee members. The teacher may make the choices. Pupils could also volunteer to serve on a committee. Random selection could be used to determine committee membership. Committee membership could be very short indeed for a particular group, perhaps a day or several days. Membership could be rather enduring also, such as planned tasks that last six weeks or so. There are different types of tasks such as those that are short in duration, such as planning refreshments for an end of the school year party. Cooperative learning members could also be together for an entire thematic unit of six weeks such as planning and making a model bedouin village in a unit on the Middle East. There will be pupils who do not like the project or a selected pupil on the committee. What is the answer here? This happens even if members have been chosen carefully using desired criteria.

Competition in the School Curriculum

There are a few educators, not many, who advocate a competitive curriculum. Many reasons are given for the competitive philosophy. Generally, it is based upon the free enterprise system. The US is not keeping up with Japan and Germany in world trade. US pupils need to be more competitive and be first in the nation in mathematics and science as advocated by the National Governors Conference in 1989 with Education 2000. Warnings are given by newsreporters as to low achievement in mathematics and science of US pupils as compared to those of other industrialised nations. Goals have been established on the state and local levels in order that learners may measure up to these levels in terms of what is deemed necessary to be first in the world in mathematics and science. Competition here rather than cooperation is emphasised.

The voucher system has many supporters in the US. Parents receiving the voucher money may redeem it at an other school which they deem to be better than the local school. The voucher money, if it becomes law, stresses that per pupil costs of education for a school year at the local school would equal the voucher that may then be used at the receiving school There are advocates of parents being able to use the voucher money in either public or parochial schools. Advocates believe with competition, bad schools and teachers will have no clients and therefore not be in existence. The better schools with more clients than ever will serve as models for other teachers to emulate. Competition for numbers of pupils in a school under the voucher system in strictly competitive. Poor schools will go out of business.

Merit pay has numerous advocates in the US. With merit pay teachers rated as being superior or excellent receive additional pay for their quality services. Those supporting merit pay believe that teachers individually will work harder and do a better job of teaching once they are rewarded for doing outstanding work. Differentiated pay is then desired among teachers. No longer would the single salary schedule then be in operation. The latter is based on the number of years of teaching experience and the level of attained education at colleges/universities as being sole determines of salary to be obtained by a teacher. Critics state that mediocrity is rewarded in teaching with the single salary schedule. If merit pay is implemented, competition for the higher salaries would then definitely be in evidence.

Open enrollment also emphasises the free enterprise system. Here, parents choose for their sons and daughters which kind of a school the latter are to attend. The chosen school may bypass many local schools and school systems. Parents and the child do the choosing not the local school or the locally assigned teacher. The purpose is competition in parents choosing which school and teacher is best for their offspring. Teachers and schools not selected may need statewide superintendents and newly retrained and reeducated teachers.

In a few states, e.g. Kentucky and New Jersey, schools must measure up to a definite standard in terms of standardised test results, or the state will take over deficient schools. There is competition here in a school not being delinquent as to pupil achievement revealed by test results.

The US Secretary of Education may list state by state how well pupils are achieving in different curriculum areas. This is called that wall chart. States are compared against each other in terms of pupil achievement, money spent on education per pupil, and average daily attendance of pupils. With competition among the different states in terms of wall chart figures, personal pride of each state to improve in education might be an end result when making these comparisons, according to selected educators and many lay people.

There are schools that have arranged contracts with commercial companies to teach their children. Educational Alternatives Incorporated (EAI) from Minneapolis, Minnesota is an example. EAI agrees with the school district how much achievement and the cost of services will be involved in a given school year. EAI then assumes responsibility for administration and instruction of the involved schools. There is competition here between the public schools and commercial companies in terms of who can provide the best education for pupils. It might well be true that school administrators and teachers remain the same with EAI as compared to earlier arrangements. EAI still does the training of teachers to use methodology as they deem to be good and profitable.

Additional means of competing with the public schools in terms of teaching pupils is to have charter schools and magnet schools.

When supervising student and cooperating teachers in the public schools, we have observed the following to encourage competition among pupils in the classroom setting:

1. a chart on the wall showing the names of each pupil in class indicating how many words were spelled correctly for each week using the basal spelling text. Gold stars were received by the top spellers, followed by silver stars for the next best set of spellers. Other colours of stars were situated next to the name of the pupil indicating his/her spelling achievement;
2. the teacher announcing to the entire class now many problems each pupil solved correctly from one lesson from the basal text in mathematics. The announcements were made for each day of pupil practice in mathematics using the basal textbook;

3. pupil test results in social studies were posted on the bulletin board ranking learners from high and low in achievement. The teacher commented on how well or how poorly individual pupils here had achieved;
4. prizes announced prior to beginning a new unit in science. These prizes were to be awarded to pupils depending upon how many total points each received a result of participating in different projects and tasks;
5. the pupil of the day selected by the teacher being presented with and wearing "the king's or queen's hat. There was much competition among pupils in class in being able to wear this hat for a day.

There are many additional examples which can be given whereby competition can and is being emphasised in the classroom setting. Pupils are compared with each other as to term projects, daily assignments, oral reports, oral reading, and test results, among other items. A major purpose of standardised tests is to compare on pupil against another. A parent, after receiving information of test results from his/her offspring, may, during informal conversation, compare test results with parents of other children. We have heard parents reprimand their children for not doing better on a standardised test. Generally, the reprimand emphasises why the child did not do better than so and so. Many parents are highly competitive in wanting their offspring to be a cheer leader, member of the first team in football or basketball, have a leading role in the school play, and/or being a class officer.

Competition can be healthy; it can also be destructive. Cooperative learning can be positive as well as negative. It all depends upon what transpires in either competitive or cooperative situations.

We will first discuss healthy competition. Here, pupils respect each other even though one or more persons in a given situation do not experience victory. Healthy, competition can bring out the best within the person. Efforts and perseverance is involved! There can be much interest on the part of all in competition be it between individual or within a committee competing against another committee. I recommend the following guidelines for stressing competitive events:

1. those competing should be somewhat equivalent in talents, skills, and abilities;
2. those competing should have positive attitudes toward each other;
3. those competing should have a desire to participate and learn;
4. those competing should have definite goals to achieve in the competitive event;
5. those competing should realise that not all individuals can be winners. Best it is if all pupils be winners! This is definitely possible.

Questions that might be raised about competitive behaviour in the classroom setting include the following:

1. does competition increase hostility among pupils toward each other?
2. does competition hinder pupils in achieving affective objectives?
3. does competition work against the learning style of selected pupils?
4. does competition compare involved pupils unfavourable due to differences in abilities, interests, and capabilities?
5. does competition increase achievement of pupils?

Teachers might wish to encourage positive competition among individuals in the classroom setting. Competition is neither good nor bad, but it depends upon how it affects individuals.

We all need to realise that as adults, we compete in numerous ways such as of jobs and occupations, promotions, marriage partners, good grades in classes taken, and for leadership responsibilities in society, among others.

Cooperative learning has its advantages and disadvantages. The advantages are the following:

1. pupils do have opportunities here in learning to work together with others;

2. selected pupils have as tneir fovourite learning style the working together with peers, rather than working individually;
3. goals in life can be achieved in cooperating with each other, rather than through dog eat dog approaches;
4. learners can realise that school and learning may be enjoyable through cooperative learning;
5. pupils need to learn to assist each other in the school and classroom setting. We human beings are dependent upon each other for survival.

Questions which need to be raised about cooperative learning include the following:

1. might pupils become highly competitive in a negative way within a committee setting?
2. might personality clashes hinder pupil achievement in committee settings?
3. might there be learning styles whereby selected pupils do not do well in group work, but would achieve better in more competitive settings? We would like to emphasise here the pupils individually may compete against their past performance with intent of making continuous progress;
4. might there be a rational balance between individual and committee endeavours in the curriculum which could benefit most pupils?
5. might there be leaders who do their best in cooperative learning?

There are no clear cut answers to these questions. Even well designed research studies have their many weakness. Human beings write test items for the measurement device, ensuring much subjectivity in a research study. Objectivity occurs when all conditions are kept similar in giving the tests to the experimental and the control groups. Or can they be similar/same? No, they are not. Pupils feel differently from one time to the next. Not all pupils find that revealing what has been learned occurs best through testing. There are pupils who like authentic means of revealing what has been learned better as compared to being tested.

Conclusion

Educators need to reexamine the cooperation versus competition philosophies in teaching pupils. Which approach is better of the two? It is hard to say. Neither approach is in and of itself is good. There can be negative teaching in either approach. We have seen bad teaching as well as good teaching in either case. Merely having cooperative learning or saying that one has cooperative learning does not make for goodness or badness. What truly matters is how each approach affects learners in the school and classroom setting. We would recommend having rational balance among the two approaches. Pupils need to learn to work harmoniously with others as well as work well on an individual basis. Each pupil should strive to achieve optimally when working individually. After all, life in school and in society consists of both!

37

Decision-making on Which Level?

There are many choices to be made in terms of selecting objectives, learning activities, and appraisal procedures. Decision made affect the welfare of students. Quality choices may well guide students to achieve optimally, whereas negative or mediocre decisions hinder learner progress.

Major debates are in evidence pertaining to who should make decisions in the curriculum. The level of decisions made can be the prerogative of the federal, state, system level, building level, or in the classroom setting. Which level or levels should decisions be made pertaining to developing the curriculum? The writer will discuss decision-making on each of the above named levels.

The Federal Level

Numerous laws have been made on the national level to improve the curriculum. PL94-142 Education for all Handicapped Pupils emphasises decisions made on the national level. PL94-142 was passed by Congress and signed into law by the President. A key feature of PL94-142 is the concept of mainstreaming. The least restricted environment is a second key concept in PL94-142. Thus, a handicapped student is to be placed, as much as is feasible and good, into a regular classroom. Each student that is mainstreamed needs to have an approved IEP (Individual Education Plan). The IEP spells out in measurable terms what a mainstreamed pupil is to learn in a given school year. Mainstreamed pupils then are to achieve that which is stated in the IEP.

Decision-making on Which Level?

There are many choices to be made in terms of selecting objectives, learning activities, and appraisal procedures. Decisions made affects the welfare of students. Quality choices may well guide students to achieve optimally, where negative or mediocre decisions hinder learner progress.

Major debates are in evidence pertaining to who should make decisions in the curriculum. The level of decisions made can be the prerogative of the federal, state, system level, building level, or in the classroom setting. Which level or levels should decisions be made pertaining to developing the curriculum? The writer will discuss decision-making on each of the above named levels.

The Federal Level

Numerous laws have been made on the national level to improve the curriculum. PL94-142 Education for all Handicapped Pupils emphasises decisions made on the national level. PL94-142 was passed by Congress and signed into law by the President. A key feature of PL94-142 is the concept of mainstreaming. The least restricted environment is a second key concept in PL94-142. Thus, a handicapped student is to be placed, as much as feasible and good, into a regular classroom. Each student that is mainstreamed needs to have an approved IEP (Individual Education Plan). The IEP spells out in measurable terms what a mainstreamed pupil is to learn in a given school year. Mainstreamed pupils then are to achieve that which is stated in the IEP.

There are numerous problems involved in implementing PL94-142. There are selected classrooms in which many pupils are mainstreamed to the point that a regular classroom consists mainly of handicapped pupils. When special education classes were first implemented and specially trained teachers taught handicapped students, the pupil-teacher ratio was low. Thus, for example, the teacher of a set of mentally retarded pupils could provide appropriate help for the latter. In a regular classroom with many handicapped students, the teacher has a difficult time to provide for the diverse levels of achievement. With a pupil-teacher ratio of 25 to 1 including mainstreamed students, it is indeed difficult to assist each student to achieve much.

The writer is not opposed to mainstreaming but believes that too frequently the regular classroom contains an excessive number of handicapped students. Many of these handicapped pupils could be given better instruction in a special education classroom.

Special education classroom need to follow and implement recommended criteria. These standards include:

1. each pupil needs to be respected;
2. a low student-teacher ratio needs to be in evidence;
3. specially educated teachers need to feel that a mission is involved in teaching the handicapped;
4. adequate teaching materials need to be in the offspring to teach each handicapped pupil;
5. effective criteria need to be utilised to place handicapped students in classes whereby optimal achievement may accrue. Standards based on race, creed, or religion should not be utilised to place pupils into a regular or special education classroom. Pupils individually should be placed into a classroom where he/she has opportunities to achieve optimally.

Wrong standards in placing into regular or special education classroom are utilised when:

1. schools fear lawsuits and shirk responsibilities in securing the best education for each pupil. Thus, a handicapped student may do very poorly in a regular classroom due to a high student-teacher ratio, as well as the involved teacher not having been educated to deal with handicapped pupils. Even if parents desire their handicapped student be placed in a regular classroom, the needs of the learner comes first. Selected needs can be met in a special education classroom, continuously;
2. beliefs exist that democracy is in evidence if all or most learners exhibiting handicaps are educated in the regular classroom. Democracy is in evidence only, if each pupil experience a curriculum which encourages, not hinders, optimal achievement.

Pupils who are disrupters in a regular classroom reveal considerable ability (average or higher capabilities) need to have a curriculum designed to meet their needs to attain as much as possible.

A low student-teacher ratio needs to be in evidence here so that each pupil experiences quality supervision and assistance.

The least restricted environment facet of PL94-142 has meant too frequently that the majority of students with single or multiple handicaps are mainstreamed into the regular classroom. The teacher then in hindered in providing for individual differences in the classroom.

The State Level

Many changes are occurring on the state level which are labelled as reforms. The changes amount to opinion, rather than reform. Numerous states in the union have Instructional Management Systems (IMS) or similar procedures mandated. IMS emphasises the utilisation of precise, measurably stated. The basic philosophy of IMS pertains to what is salient to learn can be measured. What students have learned in measurable terms needs to be recorded by the classroom teacher. Generally, the data is listed as to when a pupil attained each objective.

There are numerous problems inherent in IMS and similar philosophies of education:

1. There is more to learn in life as compared to that which is measurable. Critical thinking, creative thinking, problem solving and quality attitudes in the real world defy measurement. And yet these traits and concepts emphasise life in its fullest dimension.
2. An excess amount of teacher and pupil time is taken in testing and measuring student achievement. Life in the real world does not consist of teasing and passing tests.
3. The classroom teacher should have adequate time available to do a quality job of preparation for each day of teaching rather than recording tests results. Recording test results involves secretarial work rather than professional teaching.

Numerous states have laws pertaining to state mandated career ladder plans. Career ladder plans are to reward good teaching by having teachers judged worthy to move up to different levels in a hierarchy, such as level one, level two, three, and higher if the state emphasises an increased number of levels. To spriral upward on each of the sequential levels, the teacher needs to do quality classroom teaching, as well as meet other criteria. With the highest level in a career ladder plan, the teacher may have released time from teaching to serve as a mentor. The mentor assists in staff development for a school, as well as helps individual teachers to improve the quality of teaching. The mentor may also be heavily involved in developing curriculum materials. Moving upward on each level in the career ladder plan increases the salary or pay of the classroom teacher.

Many questions need clarifying pertaining to career ladder and mentor teacher plans.

1. Will evaluations be fairly done so that quality teacher can move up to higher levels on career ladder plans?
2. Will adequate funding be available to reward *all* teachers who deserve upward movement on the career ladder?
3. How will non-rewarded teachers accept those who have moved up on the career ladder?
4. Do teachers accept peer leadership when mentors are utilised to improve the curriculum?
5. Will teachers feel that the concept of fairness was involved in releasing selected individuals from teaching duties to become mentors?

System-wide Level

Within a school system, many changes have been made in education. A school system could require numerous staff development programmes for teachers. Generally, staff development is carried on after the school day has ended. An ambitious administration may desire to change from what is to what should be in the eyes of the educational leaders within the school system. Perhaps, most teachers do not perceive the changes as being worthwhile. It could well be that the advocated changes would not harmonise with desired tenets of educational philosophy. Change is made for the sake of change which is something that educators have previously warned against.

Changes made system-wide can be dictated and dogmatic. A prestigious administrator may be able to command key people for a school system to move in the direction he/she wishes. Before teacher develop awareness, workshops and faculty meeting are already in existence to emphasise staff development. Perhaps, staff development programmes emphasise research results which state that the principal needs to be a strong leader, teachers need to have high expectations from pupils, objectives need to be clearly stated, and time on task is important. Staff development programmes are then developed to implement these research tenets.

There certainly are weaknesses in the above named research results. The writer is an existentialists as a philosophy of life. He believes strongly in making choices and decisions individually and accepting sole responsibilities for decisions made. Existentialists believe that one exists first and then finds essences or goals in life. These goals must be developed by the individual. They cannot come from others unless authentically one truly accepts one or more goals from others. To be human, however, means to choose and to make decisions. If others make decisions for the self, the person no longer is human. Yes, some choices to be made will be awesome.

Existentialist educators would then question as to what is meant by strong administrative leadership to improve the curriculum. Selected educators in articles published in professional educational journals state research that emphasises strong administrative leadership as a key to reform in education. If the administration of a school system believes in directorial powers as representing strong leadership in curriculum development, the writer would be very much opposed to research results that indicate "good schools have strong administrative leadership". An existentialists, however, advocates strong administrative leadership which *releases* creative abilities within others in the school system.

38

An Analysis of Teacher Education Online

Teacher education online is receiving considerable attention in the educational media. When there are new opportunities and technologies in education, the business world enters the market place competition. There are universities that offer an entire baccalaureate degree (Bachelor of Science in Education...BSE) in teacher education. Others offer a few courses online which apply to the BSE degree. Little research has been done to make comparisons between the online versus the traditional BSE. A few universities have expanded their offerings to include an entire online Master of Arts degree in teaching. Bold, new approaches are then being pursued in offering innovative procedures in preservice and service teacher education.

Advantages and Disadvantages of Online Programmes

There are a plethora of reasons given for offering teacher education programmes online.

First, there is the convenience factor. Thus, the consumer may choose the time which is most convenient to work in his/her teacher education degree. Working at home online saves the hustle and bustle of driving to a campus. Students who drive several hundred miles to take a graduate course, for example, may now spend that same time online.

Second, a self motivated student may pursue online work more rapidly as compared to those who are prone to put off in their pursuits. Effort and energy must go into doing one's very best in meeting demanding online teacher education requirements. Perseverance is a key concept to follow when working individually toward completing online requirements.

Self motivation, too, is important in traditional teacher education programmes. There also are others to help set the pace for hither energy levels to pursue a teaching degree. Vygotsky's research (1978) indicates that learning occurs best within a group where ideas are shared and analysed through critical and creative thinking. The significant other may then be a motivator for the individual learner as a perspective teacher. Highly knowledgeable, motivated teachers are a necessity to serve as models in teaching and learning situations. Vygotzky (1978) indicates that thought occurs, not in a vacuum, but in a social situation where others are involved and actively participating. Then too, motivation for learning is a part of being with the significant other when sharing ideas.

Third, a preferred style of learning is involved when pursuing online course work with individual endeavours, an intrapersonal learning style. An intrapersonal learning style is then involved as compared to a student preferring collaborative endeavours such as in interpersonal model (See Dunn and Dunn, 1979). Under which conditions does a student achieve more optimally, intrapersonally or interpersonally? This is a question which needs careful considerations. Online teacher education involves intrapersonal approaches whereas student teaching in a public school classroom certainly does stress interpersonal dimensions of learning.

Fourth, teacher education online emphasises a virtual reality. A variety of audio-visual materials in virtual reality are used in teaching students. However, the concrete and actual reality are not there. Virtual reality is one step removed from actually observing and participating in a classroom pertaining to preservice or in service education. Ausubel (1978), a leading educational psychologist, stressed the importance of the semi-concrete, such as in audio-visual aids use, to be less complex and more effective in teaching and learning situations as compared to the concrete.

Thus, for example, the instructor may point to a specific facet of an illustration to show *active engagement* by students in learning. In an actual classroom then, there are too many variables when noticing this same concept. Ausubel believed that delimiting a concept to pictorial form, initially, to what is to be taught or emphasised makes for more clarity as compared to the many variables observed first hand in any classroom. Hands on experiences as well as abstract methods of instruction may then follow semi-concrete activities in teacher education.

Fourth, the student can pace his/her own progress in online teacher education programmes. Thus, the student may move forward at a slower rate or more rapidly, depending upon optimal individual approaches in learning. Perhaps, it is vacation time to take the family on a three day outing, this can be done and postpones working online during those days.

In traditional teacher education programmes, the university, student needs to follow the designated educational courses as offered. Thus, there are semesters devoted to class work in each of the following: educational psychology, foundations of education, curriculum development, testing and evaluation, field experiences, and student teaching. A student may miss a day or more due to illness, but each absence places the student at a disadvantage due to subject matter missed in a course or sequential experiences omitted in student teaching. In student teaching, the days missed will need to be made up at a suitable time (See Ediger, 2000, 244-249).

Fifth, teacher education may lack appeal for many due to online experiences alone or solely. The contents stress a virtual reality, not concrete in nature. Thus the student does not have opportunities to interact with others in an interesting manner. The author in thinking back of his own undergraduate teacher education programme reflects frequently about what was and what was not liked. This deals with the affective dimension. Certainly, working together with others in committees or studying together with others for an upcoming final examination made for enjoyment and appeal! Usually, some humour was involved in being together with and working harmoniously with others. Maslow (1954), in his theory of human motivation, emphasises the following sequential, hierarchical needs which all desire to have fulfilled: psychological such as adequate nutrition, shelter, and clothing; safety including security from all dangers; belonging such as wanting to be accepted in a group, esteem needs including a desire to be recognised for accomplishments and achievements; and self actualisation in becoming the kind and type of person desired. Thus belonging needs and esteem needs, in particular, emphasise a desire to be with and work with others.

Sixth, online teacher education may well have an advantage of a learner not comparing himself/herself with others in the immediate environment when using computer technology. Less tension and anxiety may then be experienced. How the student will be graded from online testing covering the course taken will make for comparing one student with another. These comparisons will be made by those involved in grading and recording test results at the sponsoring university (See Ediger, 2000, Chapter Six).

And yet, a certain amount of healthy tension and anxiety may be a true motivator for individuals. One, perhaps, cannot avoid being compared with others in society. Assessment of each individual goes on continually in the societal arena be it in jobs/ professions involved or possible marriage partners. However, the intensity of preferences should stress the Golden Mean of Aristotle (Ediger, 1995, Chapter Three). Thus, a person should not go overboard with involved anxiety nor be too relaxed in life's endeavours.

Eighth, there are selected kinds of communication with others which are possible in online teacher preparation. These include chat rooms and threaded discussions. In most cases, online teacher education will stress an internship or student teaching in a public school (Education Week, February 14, 2001).

However, these kinds of human interactions are quite limited as compared to traditional university campus based collaboration in teacher preparation. The latter is very much based on the possibilities of prospective teachers becoming caring, perserving, person centred and humane professionals in teaching. Working with and learning in a socio-centred environment is important in teacher education.

Ninth, appropriate standards for quality assurance are lacking in online teacher education programmes. Perhaps, much of this is due to the newness of these courses. Certainly, university students taking course work on the internet will want assurance that the course offerings are approved by a major organisation in the preparation of teachers, such as the National Council for the Accreditation of Teacher Education (NCATE).

Tenth, logging on problems are in evidence when working in online teacher education. There may be problems such as 20 per cent of the time being spent in attempting to being connected online. "Freezing" may be quite common as a further problem in getting online.

Commuting to the university campus and being there on time for classes in traditional teacher education programmes also has its problems. Costs for dormitory rooms, tuition fees for course work on campus, and driving experiences, among others, also takes its toll in financial obligations of the university student. Modern society has its many conveniences as well as its many frustrations.

What is the Answer?

There are no easy answers. Solutions to problems are ongoing and continuous. High quality, fully licensed and certified teachers are needed in each classroom. Teachers need to have adequate subject matter knowledge in their area of speciality as well as be able to implement recommended pedagogy in teaching and learning situations.

The recent advertising blitz by the US Department of Education stems from the recognition that teacher-training programmes are under-enrolled to meet the future demand for classroom teachers. The advertisements feature testimonials of adults remembering with fondness past teachers and appreciating their positive influence. The ads end with the solgan "Be a hero...be a teacher..." (Davenport 2000-2001).

This is quite different from the usual public school bashing that has occurred in the news media. The lay public and the media need to be careful on what is being bashed. The author believes strongly that positive information from society is important on how to modify and improve the public schools. Thus, diagnosis and remediation are musts in any work endeavour. From what is to what should be must be continuous and ongoing. Problems need to be identified and solutions offered. Bashing actually has no role to play in making needed improvements. Too frequently, there are agendas which bashers have and these agendas may not be in the interests of public school/private school education. Negative criticisms offer no solutions for improvement (See Ediger, 2000, 173-178).

Harmonising university campus based teacher education programmes with those of being online has many advantages. The following may then be emphasised:

1. selected courses may be taken online such as those where lecture predominates due to large course enrollment on a campus. Thus, a history class, as an example, may be taken in the home setting. There are others which are in the same category including educational psychology. Large lecture classes on campus may be no more personal than working online;
2. a major problem quality assurance in that any class taken online has met standards of excellence and is approved by an appropriate reputable, accrediting agency;
3. students should choose those courses to complete online which make for a quality degree programme in teacher certification. Thus, a student may prefer to work intrapersonally in online course work;
4. cost and covenience are two important factors in taking online courses. A mother, for example, with small children may be able to complete online courses at home when convenient, but could not spare the time nor the money for baby sitting to drive to a campus setting;
5. ample time must be spent in actual field work in a public school prior to student teaching. There would be no reason that on online teacher education course could not be correlated with public school field experiences.

The field experiences would then involve working with children in multiple tasks faced by fully licenced teachers in the classroom. Ample time must be given to practising what has been learned in methods of teaching classes online to their implementation in the regular classroom.

Searson and Dunn (2001) present the following learning style model for teachers to follow:

1. Most individuals can learn;
2. Students with diverse learning style strengths respond differently to instructional environments, resources, and approaches;
3. Everyone has different strengths;
4. Individual instructional preferences exist and can be measured reliably;
5. Given responsive environments, resources, and approaches, students attain statistically higher achievement and attitude test scores in congruent treatments. They also behave better in style-responsive environments;
6. Most teachers can use learning styles as a cornerstone of their instruction;
7. Most students capitalise on their learning style strengths when concentrating on new and difficult information.

The above learning styles model of teaching pays much attention to individual differences among students. Thus, "one size does not fit all", but each person is unique and learns in different ways. The teacher needs to assist students to capitalise on personal appropriate strengths to achieve as optimally as possible.

Ediger (2000, Chapter Seven) emphasises the importance of teacher following tenets of educational psychology to guide more optimal student achievement in the classroom, including the following:

1. obtaining student interest in teaching and learning situations;

2. assisting students to attach meaning and understanding pertaining to concepts and generalisations stressed in ongoing lessons and units of study;
3. attending to diverse levels of achievement, skills, and attitudes in the classroom so that individual differences among learners receive adequate attention;
4. providing background information so that learners may benefit from the related new knowledge and abilities being presented;
5. establishing student purpose for ongoing objectives to be achieved.

Thus, there are criteria for learning styles approaches and what is advocated by educational psychologists to emphasise in teacher training courses/classes. It might be easier to stress certain of these standards in online course work more so than traditional procedures in teacher education. This would be true of *intrapersonal* methods of instruction with its one on one relationships. Others, such as establishing purpose or reasons for learning, might be better implemented in course work on the university campus by a capable instructor.

Thus, teacher education changes. Technology has brought on a plethora of changes including online programmes. On university campuses, teacher education changes rather continuously with its implementation of numerous technologies including video-taping of student teacher performance and providing almost instant feedback to those involved in the supervisory process. John Dewey (1916) was a leading advocate of change being gradual and sometimes coming on rather quickly in the educational process.

Multiple Intelligence Theory (Gardner, 1993) has much to contribute in terms of how students reveal what has been learned. These intelligences possessed by individuals are the following: verbal/linguistic, visual/spatial, logical/mathematical, musical/rhythmic, intrapersonal, interpersonal, bodily/kinesthetic, and scientific. Those who excel in verbal/linguistic intelligence, no doubt, tend to do well in reading, writing, and test taking as compared to the person possessing scientific intelligence who may indicate what has been learned through science experiments/ demonstration as well as objective thinking.

Teacher educators and classroom teachers/school administrators in the public schools need to continually study, analyse, synthesise, and assess present progammes to teacher education with the intent of moving from *what* is to *what should be*.

REFERENCES

Ausubel, David (1978), *Educational Psychology: A Cognitive View*, New York: Holt Rinehart and Winston.

Davenport, Will (2000-2001), "Kristal Kleer American Association Technical Education Association (2 and 3), 32, 34.

Dunn, Rita, and Kenneth Dunn (1979), "Teaching Styles/Learning Styles", *Educational Leadership*, 36 (4), 238-244.

Dewey, John (1916), *Democracy and Education*, New York: The Mac Millan Company.

Ediger, Marlow (1985), *Philosophy in Curriculum Development*, Kirskville, Missouri: Simpson Publishing Company, Chapter Three.

Ediger, Marow, (2000), *Teaching Mathematics Successfully*. New Delhi, India: Discovery Publishing House, Chapter Seven.

Ediger, Marlow (2000), "Purposes in Learning Assessment", *Journal of Instructional Psychology*, 27 (4), 244-249.

Ediger, Marlow (2000), *Teaching Reading Successfully*, New Delhi, India: Discovery Publishing House, Chapter Six.

Ediger, Marlow (2000), "A Teaching of Reading Book Club," *Reading Improvement*, 37 (4), 173-178.

Education Week, February 14, 2001, 20 (22), 1 and 4.

Gardner, Howard (1993), *Multiple Intelligences: Theory into Practice*. New York: Basic Books.

Maslow, Abraham (1954), *Motivation and Personality*. New York: Harper and Row.

Searson, Robert and Rita Dunn (2001), "The Learning Style Teaching Model," *Science and Children*, 38 (5), 22-26.

Vygotsky, Lev (1978), *Mind and Society*, Cambridge, Massachusetts: Havard University Press.

39

Philosophy of Kindergarten Education

Kindergarten is a very valuable part of a student's education. Here, the student has left the home setting for a definite period of the day to be with other learners of a similar chronological age. The young child also interacts with a qualified teacher, certified to teach on the kindergarten level. An aid may assist the kindergarten teacher in teaching pupils. Diverse philosophies of kindergarten education are in evidence in present day schools.

History of Kindergarten

Friedrich Wilhelm Froebel (1782-1852) has been called the originator of kindergarten education. Froebel emphasised a definite philosophy of instruction. He believed that young learners should be active participants in learning. Too frequently in Froebel's day, students were passive in listening to teachers lecture. Physical punishment was utilised to discipline students. Students suffered from blows received from teachers. Rote learning and momorisation were methods used to teach students.

Friedrich Wilhelm Froebel emphasised respecting and liking children. Children should enjoy learning. Games needed to be utilised to assist pupils to like school. Rather than pupils being evil beings. Froebel advocated that children were born as good individuals. Freedom was very important for pupils in the kindergarten. Froebel was fond of nature. At one time, he was apprenticed as a forester. Kindergarten, meaning a garden for children, is very close to the idea and concept of nature.

Froebel had definite materials made for use in teaching. These materials assisted pupils to achieve the major goal of becoming creative individuals. The first kind of materials were called *gifts*. The items here pertained to the world of mathematics. One kind of gift was six spheres. To Froebel, the sphere represented perfection. There are no edges on a sphere. A point in the centre is equadistant to all points on the surface of the sphere. Pupils were to be creative in using the spheres. A second kind of material called gifts was a set of cylinders. Each cylinder had smaller cylinders inside. The smaller cylinders could be pulled out and put back together again to make the large cylinder. A third kind of material called gifts emphasised the use of cubes by pupils. Each cube could be separated into smaller cubes and put back together again to form the large cube. Additional gifts were physical representations of lines, points and planes.

The teacher, according to Froebel, was not to dictate to pupils uses for the gifts. Rather, pupils were busy utilising these materials based on their own creative needs and purposes. However, pupils were required to place the small cylinders inside the large one, or the small cubes were to be put back together to make a large cube, after each separate learning activity. The form or shape of gifts could not be changed.

A second kind of item emphasised in Froebel's kindergarten was called *occupations*. Several occupations were engaged in by pupils. Materials, comprising occupations changed in form or shape when utilised by kindergarten pupils. One kind of occupation emphasised pupils different colours of dots to make a pattern on paper. Or, pupils would string beads of different colours and shapes. Paper could be folded and different designs cut with the use of scissors. As an occupation, Froebel was very strong in recommending clay modelling by pupils. All of these activities stressed the use of materials in which the form or shape changed physically.

As a third kind of activity for kindergarten pupils, Froebel advocated the use of mother play songs. When pupils sang a song, such as content on gardening, there would creatively dramatise the tilling of the soil, planting of seeds, watering the plants, and hoeing the weeds. Sometimes, pupils would hold hands and form a circle when singing songs. Froebel was struck by the idea of having pupils in a circle. The circle, like the sphere, represented perfection in geometrical figures.

Friedrich Wilhelm Froebel believed that schooling should represent joyous occasions for learners. Play and learning needed to be integrated. Kindergartens should be spontaneous, creative, and free.

Opposite of Froebel's thinking would be:

1. physical punishment of pupils;
2. rote learning of subject matter;
3. a teacher determined curriculum;
4. a formal school environment.

The kindergarten was to be a place where pupils enjoyed ongoing learning opportunities. From within, pupils had much say so in how the gifts and occupations were to be utilised. Pupils were to feel safe, secure, and loved. On Froebel's tombstone are the words, "Come, let us live for our children."

The Open Curriculum in Kindergarten Education

Kindergarten education can emphasise a very informal curriculum in today's schools. The teacher then becomes a guide or stimulator. His/her job is to motivate, encourage, challenge, and secure pupil interest in learning. The informal classroom structure may emphasise the use of learning stations in the classroom. Each station is quite open ended in terms of what pupils may achieve.

A variety of kinds of materials abound at each station. Concrete (objects and items), semi-concrete (audio-visual materials), and abstract materials (library books) are located at each station. Pupils have considerable freedom in decision-making as to which tasks to pursue sequentially. The learner's own interests and purposes aid in deciding which learning opportunities to pursue. The following are examples of the kinds of stations contained in a classroom:

1. *A Library Book Centre:* Here pupils may listen to a story being read by the teacher in a stimulating manner. Illustrations are shown to learners in the book as the contains are read orally by the teacher or an aid. Selected objects on the table relate to content in the library books. Thus, a few model animals at this station relate directly to the content being read from the library books. The models are also discussed with pupils.
2. *A Drawing Centre:* Diverse art media are at this centre. The media include pencils, crayons, magic maker, coloured pencils, and watercolours. Creatively, the learner chooses what to portray as an art product on paper. Spontaneity and uniqueness of expression are desired in terms of processes emphasised in art work. Pupils may wish to tell of content in the finished art product. Sharing of ideas with other learners is to be encouraged.
3. *A Model Centre:* Models of animals, buildings, and people should be housed here. Learners may take the models to build diverse scenes. The models may also be discussed in terms of characteristics and traits. Pupils may secure additional ideas about each model by consulting picture books with large illustrations. Ideas secured should shared with other learners. Oral communication needs to be encouraged at each station.
4. *Role Playing Centre:* Toy dishes, plates, utensils, a kitchen sink, and refrigerator, among other items may well provide stimulating materials for pupils. Spontaneity of learners needs to be encouraged as they prepare and serve food to each other in a simulated setting. Quality of positive interactions is important in role playing activities.

Additional stations for the kindergarten pupil include:

(a) a reference materials station containing illustrated content for pupils;

(b) a costume station. Here, kindergartens may dress up in different costumes, such as in adult dresses, suits, slacks, shoes and hats;

(c) a construction station where pupils may enjoy making diverse objects. The materials utilised need to bear the understanding level of pupils. Necessary skills are possessed or can be developed by learners to construct and to make.

An open ended curriculum tends to emphasise existentialism, as a philosophy. Existentialists believe that:

1. each person needs to decide upon appropriate courses of action;
2. decisions and choices are to be made by the learner. The teacher is a stimulator and guide to assist pupils to learn.

A Subject Centred Curriculum

Selected kindergarten educators recommend a subject centred curriculum. A skills centred curriculum is then in evidence. In the area of reading, kindergarten pupils, when ready, would achieve the following skills in word recognition:

1. *Phonetic Analysis:* Her pupils would learn phoneme-grapheme relationships. Phonics skills would be selected by teachers for kindergartens to learn to associate sounds with symbols.
2. *Syllabication:* To identify new words, pupils divide words into syllables. Unknown words may become familiar with the identification of each syllable within a word.
3. *Picture Clues:* A pupil that does not recognise a word may identify the unknown with the use of pictures contained in a basal reader.
4. *Configuration Clues:* A basic sight vocabulary of words are developed by the learner. Mastering these words cuts down on reading errors made by pupils.

5. *Context Clues:* Kindergartens need to learn that a word pronounced must make sense with other words in sequential sentences.

Comprehension skills need to be emphasised as readiness of kindergarten pupils permits. These include reading to:

1. acquire facts;
2. secure sequential ideas;
3. obtain directions;
4. develop generalisations;
5. make predictions;
6. think critically.

A subject centred curriculum emphasises pupils attaining abstract, rather than concrete ideas. Pupils of kindergarten age with quality readiness experiences may achieve skills necessary in learning to read. A formal programme of reading instruction is then in evidence. A definite scope and sequence has been identified and is implemented. Scope and sequence in kindergarten becomes an inherent part of later grade levels in sequence.

A subject centred curriculum tends to minimise:

1. concrete and semi-concrete learning opportunities;
2. a hands on approach to learning;
3. the real world of experience.

Subject matter learned in mathematics could emphasise:

1. the operations of addition, and possible subtraction, for kindergarten pupils;
2. the commutative property of addition;
3. drill and practice pertaining to subject matter learned;
4. problem solving on the understanding level of pupils.

Textbooks, workbooks, and photocopied exercises could provide major learnings for pupils in the mathematics curriculum, when emphasising a subject centred curriculum.

Social studies and science units should have a predetermined scope and sequence for pupils. Definite subject mater objectives need to be in the offing for pupil attainment. Learning activities for kindergartners should assist pupils to achieve objectives. Evaluation procedures emphasise the degree to which pupils have achieved the subject centred goals. Cognitive objectives are predominate in a subject centred curriculum. Affective and psychomotor goals receive little or no attention in teaching-learning situations.

Measurement Driven Instruction

Measurement driven instruction (MDI) has received considerable attention in the educational literature. MDI emphasises the use of precise, measurable, objectives for pupil attainment. These specific ends have been predetermined for learners to attain. On the district level, instructional management systems (IMS) with its measurable stated objectives have been written for pupil achievement. Generally, the objectives have been identified several months to a year before their implementation in the classroom. State mandated objectives may also stress precise objectives for learner attainment.

Behaviourists with their emphasis upon MDI believe that whatever is taught to students can be measured. Through instruction, a pupil has or has not achieved an objective. It is then verifiable if an objective has been attained.

MDI has received emphasis on the kindergarten level of instruction. The emphasis upon instruction is toward the ends in MDI, not the learning activities, perse. Learning activities are important only, as they guide pupils toward goal attainment. What pupils are to learn is stated in the measurable objective. Evaluation is done strictly in terms of the measurably stated objective. Advocates of MDI align the learning activity with the objective. Validity and reliability are two concepts strongly emphasised when appraising pupil achievement in terms of objectives.

Educators who disagree with MDI believe the latter to:

1. emphasise excessively predetermined objectives for pupils to attain;

2. stress excessively that pupil achievement be measured. Internal interests, purposes, and goals of learners then are not important;
3. eliminate pupil involvement in selecting objectives, learning activities, and appraisal procedures;
4. minimise the spontaneity and interests possessed by students;
5. emphasise a teacher determined curriculum.

Conclusion

Three distinct philosophies of kindergarten education were discussed.

First of all, an activity centred curriculum was stressed. Here, pupils are actively involved in selecting goals, learning opportunities, and appraisal procedures. A variety of materials to learn from are readily apparent in a stimulating learning environment.

A second philosophy stressed the importance of pupils learning subject matter. Definite subject matter is prescribed for pupils to attain. The scope and sequence of the kindergarten curriculum has been prescribed for the young learner. Subject matter to be learned is strongly emphasised in the predetermined scope and sequence.

A third philosophy emphasises measurement driven instruction. Precise objectives are developed first in the kindergarten curriculum. The teacher then selects and aligns learning activities which guide kindergarten pupils to attain the objectives. Evaluation is emphasised only in terms of the measurably started objective(s). Ideally, the stimuli in the learning activity should not exceed what is contained in the measurably stated objectives. Emphasis is placed upon *measuring* observable outcomes of instruction.

Friedrich Wilhelm Froebel (1782-1852), labelled as the father of the kindergarten movement, advocated creativity as the major objective of education. Certainly, formalism was in evidence in Forebel's educational thinking. He stressed, for example, that a larger cube taken apart had to be put back together into a large cube, before learners could move on to a new learning opportunity. However, for his day in particular, Froebel was highly creative in stressing originality of experiences for pupils in using gifts, occupations, and mother play songs.

To synthesise diverse philosophies and beliefs in the kindergarten curriculum, the writer recommends that pupils have:

1. ample opportunities to choose interesting, sequential learning opportunities;
2. stimulating experiences which develop intrinsic motivation for learning;
3. opportunities to learn to read and write when readiness is in evidence;
4. sequential experiences which are meaningful in the arithmetic curriculum;
5. experiences broad in scope and appropriate in sequence pertaining to science, social studies, physical education, art, and music. A narrow curriculum of the so called basics or essentials is not adequate in modern society.

REFERENCES

Childhood Education, Published by the Association for Childhood Education International, has Articles Published Monthly on Kindergarten Education, 11141 Georgia Avenue, Suite 200, Wheaton, Maryland, 20902.

Cubberly, Ellwood P. *Public Education in the United States*. Cambridge, Massachusetts: The Riverside Press, 1947.

Eby, Frederick, *The Development of Modern Education*, Second Edition. Englewood Cliffs, New Jersey: Prentice-Hall, Inc., 1952.

Ediger, Marlow, *Elementary Education* (A Collection of Essay), Northeast Missouri State University, Kirksville, 1987.

Ediger, Marlow, *The Modern Curriculum* (A Collection of Essays), Northeast Missouri State University, Kirksville, 1986.

Fields, Marjorie V., and Dorris Lee. *Let's Begin Reading Right*. Columbus, Ohio: Merrill Publishing Company, 1987.

Hohmann, Mary, et. al. *Young Children in Action*. Upsilanti, Michigan: The High Scope Press, 1979.

Rhine, W. Ray (Editor), *Making Schools More Effective*, New York: Academic Press, 1981.

Additional Reading

Bhaskara Rao, Digumarti (1994). *Scientific Aptitude*. New Delhi: Ashish Publishing House. ISBN 81-7024-658-X.

Bhaskara Rao, Digumarti (1995). *Animal Kingdom*. New Delhi: Discovery Publishing House. ISBN 81-7141-274-2.

Bhaskara Rao, Digumarti (1995). *Batracology*. New Delhi: Discovery Publishing House. ISBN 81-7141-279-3.

Bhaskara Rao, Digumarti (1997). *Scientific Attitude*. New Delhi: Discovery Publishing House. ISBN 81-7141-381-1.

Bhaskara Rao, Digumarti (1996). *Scientific Attitude vis-à-vis Scientific Aptitude*. New Delhi: Discovery Publishing House. ISBN 81-7141-308-0.

Bhaskara Rao, Digumarti (2004). *Scientific Attitude, Scientific Aptitude and Achievement*. New Delhi: Discovery Publishing House. ISBN 81-7141-781-7.

Bhaskara Rao, Digumarti (2004). *Educational Administration*. New Delhi: Discovery Publishing House. ISBN 81-7141-842-2.

Bhaskara Rao, Digumarti, editor (1996). *Encyclopaedia of Education For All*, 5 volumes. New Delhi: APH Publishing Corporation. ISBN 81-7024-759-4 (set).

Vol. I *Education For All: The World Conference*. ISBN 81-7024-760-8.

Vol. II *Education For All: The EPA-9 Summit*. ISBN 81-7024-761-6.

Vol. III *Education For All: Quality Education For All*. ISBN 81-7024-762-6.

Vol. IV *Education For All: Planning and Monitoring*. ISBN 81-7024-763-4.

Vol. V *Education For All: The Indian Scenario*. ISBN 81-7024-764-0.

Bhaskara Rao, Digumarti, editor (1996). *Global Perceptions on Peace Education*, 3 volumes. New Delhi: Discovery Publishing House. ISBN 81-7141-319-6.

Bhaskara Rao, Digumarti, editor (1996). *National Policy on Education*, 2 volumes. New Delhi: Anmol Publications Pvt. Ltd. ISBN 81-7488-323-1.

Bhaskara Rao, Digumarti, editor (1997). *Care the Child*, 2 volumes. New Delhi: Discovery Publishing House. ISBN 81-7141-394-3.

Bhaskara Rao, Digumarti, editor (1997). *Education for the 21st Century*. New Delhi: Discovery Publishing House. ISBN 81-7141-389-7.

Bhaskara Rao, Digumarti, editor (1997). *Reflections on Scientific Attitude*. New Delhi: Discovery Publishing House. ISBN 81-7141-319-6.

Bhaskara Rao, Digumarti, editor (1997). *Success Story of a Primary Education Project*. New Delhi: APH Publishing Corporation. ISBN 81-7024-850-7.

Bhaskara Rao, Digumarti, editor (1997). *World Food Summit*. New Delhi: Discovery Publishing House. ISBN 81-7141-386-2.

Bhaskara Rao, Digumarti, editor (1998). *Adolescence Education*. New Delhi: Discovery Publishing House. ISBN 81-7141-432-X.

Bhaskara Rao, Digumarti, editor (1998). *Community and School Nutrition Education*. New Delhi: Discovery Publishing House. ISBN 81-7141-435-4.

Bhaskara Rao, Digumarti, editor (1998). *District Primary Education Programme*. New Delhi: Discovery Publishing House. ISBN 81-7141-396-X.

Bhaskara Rao, Digumarti, editor (1998). *Earth Summit*, 2 volumes. New Delhi: Discovery Publishing House. ISBN 81-7141-435-4.

Bhaskara Rao, Digumarti, editor (1998). *National Policy on Education: Towards an Enlightened and Humane Society*. New Delhi: Discovery Publishing House. ISBN 81-7141-426-5.

Bhaskara Rao, Digumarti, editor (1998). *Reforming School Education*. New Delhi: Discovery Publishing House. ISBN 81-7141-403-6.

Bhaskara Rao, Digumarti, editor (1998). *Teacher Education in India*. New Delhi: Discovery Publishing House. ISBN 81-7141-406-0.

Bhaskara Rao, Digumarti, editor (1998). *World Summit for Social Development*. New Delhi: Discovery Publishing House. ISBN 81-7141-420-6.

Bhaskara Rao, Digumarti, editor (2000). *Education For All: Achieving the Goal*, 3 volumes. New Delhi: APH Publishing Corporation. ISBN 81-7648-152-1 (set).

Vol. I *The Global Consensus*. ISBN 81-7648-155-6.

Vol. II *Mid-Decade Review Reports of Regional Seminars*. ISBN 81-7648-154-8.

Vol. III *Issues and Trends*. ISBN 81-7648-155-6.

Bhaskara Rao, Digumarti, editor (1999). *International Encyclopaedia of AIDS*, 11 volumes. New Delhi: Discovery Publishing House. ISBN 81-7141-522-6 (set).

Vol. 1 *Introduction to HIV/AIDS*. ISBN 81-7141-523-7.

Vol. 2 *HIV/AIDS-Issues and Challenges*, 2 parts. ISBN 81-7141-524-5.

Vol. 3 *HIV/AIDS-Socio Economic Realities*. ISBN 81-7141-524-3.

Vol. 4 *HIV/AIDS-Law Ethics and Human Rights*, 2 parts. ISBN 81-7141-526-1.

Vol. 5 *AIDS and NGOs*. ISBN 81-7141-527-X.

Vol. 6 *AIDS and Home Care*. ISBN 81-7141-528-8.

Vol. 7 *STD Case Management*. ISBN 81-7141-529-6.

Vol. 8 *HIV/AIDS Prevention and Care-Teaching Modules for Nurses and Midwives*. ISBN 81-7141-530-X.

Vol. 9 *HIV Prevention Education for Educational Institutions*. ISBN 81-7141-531-8.

Vol.10 *Instructional Modules for AIDS Education.* ISBN 81-7141-532-6.

Vol.11 *School Health Education to prevent AIDS and STD-A Package for Curriculum Planners.* ISBN 81-7141-533-4.

Bhaskara Rao, Digumarti, editor (2000). *International Encyclopaedia of Science and Technology Education,* 11 volumes. New Delhi: Discovery Publishing House. ISBN 81-7141-548-2 (set).

Vol. 1 *Science and Technology Education.* ISBN 81-7141-568-7.

Vol. 2 *Science Education in Developing Countries.* ISBN 81-7141-569-9.

Vol. 3 *Organizational Structure of Science.* ISBN 81-7141-570-9.

Vol. 4 *Science Education in Asia and the Pacific.* ISBN 81-7141-571-7

Vol. 5 *Science and Technology Education For All.* ISBN 81-7141-572-5.

Vol. 6 *Values, Ethics, Talent and Girls in Science and Technology Education.* ISBN 81-7141-573-3.

Vol. 7 *Popularization of Science and Technology Education.* ISBN 81-7141-574-1.

Vol. 8 *Science, Power and Society.* ISBN 81-7141-575-X.

Vol. 9 *Information Technology.* ISBN 81-7141-576-8.

Vol. 10 *Teacher Training in Science and Technology Education.* ISBN 81-7142-577-6.

Vol. 11 *Teacher Training in Science and Technology: A Curriculum Framework.* ISBN 81-7141-578-4.

Bhaskara Rao, Digumarti, editor (2001). *Distance Education in Different Countries.* New Delhi: APH Publishing Corporation. ISBN 81-7648-229-3.

Bhaskara Rao, Digumarti, editor (2001). *Decentralised Management of Education: Management of Education in Panchayati Raj and Municipal Bodies.* New Delhi: Discovery Publishing House. ISBN 81-7141-617-9.

Bhaskara Rao, Digumarti, editor (2001). *Electrochemistry for Environmental Protection*. New Delhi: Discovery Publishing House. ISBN 81-7141-619-5.

Bhaskara Rao, Digumarti, editor (2001). *Global Educational Studies*. New Delhi: Discovery Publishing House. ISBN 81-7141-616-0.

Bhaskara Rao, Digumarti, editor (2001). *Global Synthesis of Educational Assessment*. New Delhi: Discovery Publishing House. ISBN 81-7141-613-6.

Bhaskara Rao, Digumarti, editor (2000). *International Encyclopaedia of Human Rights*, 7 volumes in 13 parts. New Delhi: Discovery Publishing House. ISBN 81-7141-567-9 (set).

Vol. 1 *International Instruments of Human Rights*, 2 parts. ISBN 81-7141-569-4.

Vol. 2 *Regional Instruments of Human Rights*. ISBN 81-7141-604-7.

Vol. 3 *Human Rights and the United Nations*, 2 parts. ISBN 81-7141-605-5.

Vol. 4 *Fact Files of Human Rights*, 3 parts. ISBN 81-7141-606-3.

Vol. 5 *Study Stories of Human Rights*, 3 parts. ISBN 81-7141-607-3.

Vol. 6 *International Meetings on Human Rights*, 2 parts.ISBN 81-714-608-X.

Vol. 7 *Professional Training in Human Rights*. ISBN 81-7141-609-8.

Bhaskara Rao, Digumarti, editor (2001). *Jomtein Decade of Education*.. New Delhi: Discovery Publishing House. ISBN 81-7141-618-7.

Bhaskara Rao, Digumarti, editor (2001). *Nuclear Materials: Issues and Concerns*, 2 volumes. New Delhi: Discovery Publishing House. ISBN 81-7141-611-X.

Bhaskara Rao, Digumarti, editor (2001). *World Conference on Education for All*. New Delhi: APH Publishing Corporation. ISBN 81-7141-274-9.

Bhaskara Rao, Digumarti, editor (2001). *World Conference on Higher Education*. New Delhi: Discovery Publishing House. ISBN 81-7141-610-1.

Bhaskara Rao, Digumarti, editor (2001). *World Conference on Science*. New Delhi: Discovery Publishing House. ISBN 81-7141-612-8.

Bhaskara Rao, Digumarti, editor (2003). *Inspiring Experiences in Teacher Education*. New Delhi: Discovery Publishing House. ISBN 81-7141-656-X.

Bhaskara Rao, Digumarti, editor (2003). *International Studies in Education*, 3 volumes. New Delhi: Discovery Publishing House. ISBN 81-7141-647-0.

Bhaskara Rao, Digumarti, editor (2003). *Military Conversion: Impact on Science and Technology*. New Delhi: Discovery Publishing House. ISBN 81-7141-578-4.

Bhaskara Rao, Digumarti, editor (2003). *United Nations Millennium Summit*. New Delhi: Discovery Publishing House. ISBN 81-7141-632-2.

Bhaskara Rao, Digumarti, editor (2003). *World Assembly on Aging*. *New Delhi*: Discovery Publishing House. ISBN 81-7141-637-3.

Bhaskara Rao, Digumarti, editor (2003). *World Conference on Human Rights*. New Delhi: Discovery Publishing House. ISBN 81-7141-661-6.

Bhaskara Rao, Digumarti, editor (2003). *World Education Forum*. New Delhi: Discovery Publishing House. ISBN 81-7141-639-X.

Bhaskara Rao, Digumarti, editor (2003). *Education, Employment and Human Resource Development*. New Delhi: Discovery Publishing House. ISBN 81-7141-681-0.

Bhaskara Rao, Digumarti, editor (2003). *Successful Schooling*. New Delhi: Discovery Publishing House. ISBN 81-7141-677-2.

Bhaskara Rao, Digumarti, editor (2003). *European Education and Teachers*. New Delhi: Discovery Publishing House. ISBN 81-7141-702-7.

Bhaskara Rao, Digumarti, editor (2003). *Teachers in a Changing World*. New Delhi: Discovery Publishing House. ISBN 81-7141-694-2.

Bhaskara Rao, Digumarti, editor (2004). *International Encyclopaedia of Learning to Live Together*, 4 volumes. New Delhi: Discovery Publishing House. ISBN 81-7141-848-1.

Vol. 1 *International Conference on Learning to Live Together.*

Vol. 2 *Globalization and Living Together.*

Vol. 3 *Curriculum for Learning to Live Together.*

Vol. 4 *Science Education for the Contemporary Society.*

Bhaskara Rao, Digumarti, editor (2004). *International Guidelines on Open and Distance Teacher Education*. New Delhi: Discovery Publishing House. ISBN 81-7141-777-9.

Bhaskara Rao, Digumarti, editor (2004). *Adult Learning in the 21st Century*. New Delhi: Discovery Publishing House. ISBN 81-7141-797-3.

Bhaskara Rao, Digumarti, editor (2004). *Educational Practices: Research and Recommendations*. New Delhi: Discovery Publishing House. ISBN 81-7141-835-X.

Bhaskara Rao, Digumarti, editor (2004). *General Secondary Education In the 21st Century*. New Delhi: Discovery Publishing House. ISBN 81-7141-885-6.

Bhaskara Rao, Digumarti, editor (2004). *Reforming Secondary Education*. New Delhi: Discovery Publishing House. ISBN 81-7141-843-0.

Bhaskara Rao, Digumarti, editor (2004). *Human Rights Education*. New Delhi: Discovery Publishing House. ISBN 81-7141-882-1.

Bhaskara Rao, Digumarti, editor (2004). *United Nations Decade for Human Rights Education*. New Delhi: Discovery Publishing House. ISBN 81-7141-887-2.

Bhaskara Rao, Digumarti and B.S.V. Dutt, editors (2003). *Education: Programmes and Policies*. New Delhi: APH Publishing Corporation. ISBN 81-7648-470-9.

Bhaskara Rao, Digumarti, C.A.P. Swamy and B.S.V. Dutt (1997). *Self-Evaluation in Student Teaching*. New Delhi: Discovery Publishing House. ISBN 81-7141-374-9.

Bhaskara Rao, Digumarti and D. Naresh Kumar (2004). *School Teacher Effectiveness*. New Delhi: Discovery Publishing House. ISBN 81-7141-782-5.

Bhaskara Rao, Digumarti and D. Sridhar (2002). *Job Satisfaction of School Teachers*. New Delhi: Discovery Publishing House. ISBN 81-7141-652-7.

Bhaskara Rao, Digumarti, C. Sridevi and K. Vijaya (1995). *Achievement in Social Studies*. New Delhi: Discovery Publishing House. ISBN 81-7141-281-5.

Bhaskara Rao, Digumarti and Digumarti Pushpa Latha (1994). *Achievement in Biology*. New Delhi: Discovery Publishing House. ISBN 81-7141-264-5.

Bhaskara Rao, Digumarti and Digumarti Pushpa Latha (1995). *Achievement in English*. New Delhi: Discovery Publishing House. ISBN 81-7141-283-1.

Bhaskara Rao, Digumarti and Digumarti Pushpa Latha (1994). *Achievement in Science*. New Delhi: Discovery Publishing House. ISBN 81-7141-280-70.

Bhaskara Rao, Digumarti and Digumarti Pushpa Latha (1995). *Achievement in Mathematics*. New Delhi: Discovery Publishing House. ISBN 81-7141-278-5.

Bhaskara Rao, Digumarti and Digumarti Pushpa Latha (2004). *Education for Women*. New Delhi: Discovery Publishing House. ISBN 81-7141-873-2.

Bhaskara Rao, Digumarti and Digumarti Pushpa Latha, editors (1998). *International Encyclopaedia of Women*, 5 volumes. New Delhi: Discovery Publishing House. ISBN 81-7141-410-9 (set).

Vol. 1 *Status of World's Women*. ISBN 81-7141-494-X.

Vol. 2 *Women, Education and Empowerment*. ISBN 81-7141-498-1.

Vol. 3 *Women Challenges and Advancement*. ISBN 81-7141-497-4.

Vol. 4 *Women and Family Health*. ISBN 81-7141-497-4.

Vol. 5 *Women and International Action*. ISBN 81-7141-498-2.

Bhaskara Rao, Digumarti, Digumarti Pushpa Latha and Digumarthi Harshitha, editors (2001). *Biological Warfare*. New Delhi: Discovery Publishing House. ISBN 81-7141-597-0.

Bhaskara Rao, Digumarti, Digumarti Pushpa Latha and Digumarthi Harshitha, editors (2001). *Women as Educators*. New Delhi: Discovery Publishing House. ISBN 81-7141-602-0.

Bhaskara Rao, Digumarti and Digumarthi Harshitha (2004). *Adjustment of Adolescents*. New Delhi: APH Publishing House. ISBN 81-7648-836-8.

Bhaskara Rao, Digumarti and Digumarthi Harshitha, editors (2001). *Education in India*. New Delhi: APH Publishing House. ISBN 81-7648-207-2.

Bhaskara Rao, Digumarti, Digumarti Pushpa Latha and Digumarthi Harshitha, editors (2001). *Assessing Learning Achievement*. New Delhi: Discovery Publishing House. ISBN 81-7141-601-2.

Bhaskara Rao, Digumarti, Digumarti Pushpa Latha and Digumarthi Harshitha, editors (2001). *Energy Security*. New Delhi: Discovery Publishing House. ISBN 81-7141-598-9.

Bhaskara Rao, Digumarti, Digumarthi Harshitha and K.R.S. Sambasiva Rao, editors (1999). *Advanced Biotechnology*. New Delhi: Discovery Publishing House. ISBN 81-7141-516-4.

Bhaskara Rao, Digumarti and K.R.S.Sambasiva Rao, editors (1996). *Current Trends in Indian Education*. New Delhi: Discovery Publishing House. ISBN 81-7141-311-0.

Bhaskara Rao, Digumarti and D. Naresh Kumar (2004). *School Teacher Effectiveness*. New Delhi: Discovery Publishing House. ISBN 81-7141-782-5.

Bhaskara Rao, Digumarti and E. Sreekanth Babu (2004). *Educational Interests of School Students*. New Delhi: Discovery Publishing House. ISBN 81-7141-837-6.

Bhaskara Rao, Digumarti and K. Vijaya (1995). *A Text Book Evaluation*. Ambala Cantt: The Associated Publishers.

Bhaskara Rao, Digumarti and M.A. Fayaz (2004). *Problems of Primary School Drop-outs*. New Delhi: Discovery Publishing House. ISBN 81-7141-834-1.

Bhaskara Rao, Digumarti and N.V.M. Mohana Rao (2002). *Problems of Mentally Handicapped Children*. New Delhi: Discovery Publishing House. ISBN 81-7141-645-4.

Bhaskara Rao, Digumarti and S. Chandra Mohan (2002). *Sports Management*. New Delhi: APH Publishing House. ISBN 81-7648-467-9.

Bhaskara Rao, Digumarti and S.A. Khader (2004). *Problems of Private School Teachers*. New Delhi: Discovery Publishing House. ISBN 81-7141-838-4.

Bhaskara Rao, Digumarti and S.A. Khader (2004). *School Education in India*. New Delhi: Discovery Publishing House. ISBN 81-7141-849-X.

Bhaskara Rao, Digumarti and Sk. Johni Basha (2004). *Teachers' Population Education Awareness*. New Delhi: Discovery Publishing House. ISBN 81-7141-832-5.

Bhaskara Rao, Digumarti, V.V. Rao, V.V. Lakshmi and V.V. Krishna, editors (1999). *Status and Advancement of Women*. New Delhi: APH Publishing Corporation. ISBN 81-7648-169-6.

Babu, P.C., author and Digumarti Bhaskara Rao, editor (2004). *Flowers of Wisdom*. New Delhi: Discovery Publishing House. ISBN 81-7141-695-0.

Amala, P.A. and Anupam, P., authors and Digumarti Bhaskara Rao, editor (2004). *History of Education*. New Delhi: Discovery Publishing House. ISBN 81-7141-860-0.

Bhagya Lakshmi, L., author and Digumarti Bhaskara Rao, editor (2000). *Reading and Comprehension*. New Delhi: Discovery Publishing House. ISBN 81-7141-543-1.

Bhasha, S.A., author and Digumarti Bhaskara Rao, editor (2004). *Methods of Teaching Geography*. New Delhi: Discovery Publishing House. ISBN 81-7141-807-4.

Bhuvaneswara Lakshmi, Gadde, author and Digumarti Bhaskara Rao, editor (2000). *Attitude Towards Science*. New Delhi: Discovery Publishing House. ISBN 81-7141-541-6.

Bhuvaneswari Lakshmi, G., author and Digumarti Bhaskara Rao, editor (2004). *Methods of Teaching Life Science*. New Delhi: Discovery Publishing House. ISBN 81-7141-804-X.

Bhuvaneswari Lakshmi, G. and K. Subba Rao, authors and Digumarti Bhaskara Rao, editor (2004). *Methods of Teaching Biology*. New Delhi: Discovery Publishing House. ISBN 81-7141-914-3.

Chowdary, S.B.J.R. and Naga Raju authors and Digumarti Bhaskara Rao, editor (2004). *Mastery of Teaching Skills*. New Delhi: Discovery Publishing House. ISBN 81-7141-861-9.

Devraj, T.A.S., author and Digumarti Bhaskara Rao, editor (1997). *Trace Analysis of Uranium and Thorium*. New Delhi: Discovery Publishing House. ISBN 81-7141-375-7.

Durga Rani, K., author and Digumarti Bhaskara Rao, editor (2000). *Educational Aspirations and Scientific Attitudes*. New Delhi: Discovery Publishing House. ISBN 81-7141-555-5.

Dutt, B.S.V. and Digumarti Bhaskara Rao (2001). *Empowering Primary Teachers*. New Delhi: Discovery Publishing House. ISBN 81-7141-615-2.

Dutt, B.S.V., author and Digumarti Bhaskara Rao, editor (2004). *Comparative Education*. New Delhi: Discovery Publishing House. ISBN 81-7141-912-7.

Ediger, Marlow and Digumarti Bhaskara Rao (1996). *Science Curriculum*. New Delhi: Discovery Publishing House. ISBN 81-7141-321-8.

Ediger, Marlow and Digumarti Bhaskara Rao (2000). *Teaching Mathematics Successfully*. New Delhi: Discovery Publishing House. ISBN 81-7141-552-0.

Ediger, Marlow and Digumarti Bhaskara Rao (2001). *Teaching Science Successfully*. New Delhi: Discovery Publishing House. ISBN 81-7141-600-4.

Ediger, Marlow and Digumarti Bhaskara Rao (2001). *Teaching Social Studies Successfully*. New Delhi: Discovery Publishing House. ISBN 81-7141-596-2.

Ediger, Marlow and Digumarti Bhaskara Rao (2002). *Philosophy and Curriculum*. New Delhi: Discovery Publishing House. ISBN 81-7141-631-4.

Ediger, Marlow and Digumarti Bhaskara Rao (2002). *Improving School Administration*. New Delhi: Discovery Publishing House. ISBN 81-7141-633-0.

Ediger, Marlow and Digumarti Bhaskara Rao (2002). *Elementary Curriculum*. New Delhi: Discovery Publishing House. ISBN 81-7141-658-6.

Ediger, Marlow and Digumarti Bhaskara Rao (2003). *Language Arts Curriculum*. New Delhi: Discovery Publishing House. ISBN 81-7141-657-8.

Ediger, Marlow and Digumarti Bhaskara Rao (2003). *Psychology and Curriculum*. New Delhi: Discovery Publishing House. ISBN 81-7141-691-8.

Ediger, Marlow and Digumarti Bhaskara Rao (2003). *Teaching Language Arts Successfully*. New Delhi: Discovery Publishing House. ISBN 81-7141-678-0.

Ediger, Marlow and Digumarti Bhaskara Rao (2003). *School Curriculum and Administration*. New Delhi: Discovery Publishing House. ISBN 81-7141-709-4.

Ediger, Marlow and Digumarti Bhaskara Rao (2003). *Teaching Mathematics in Elementary Schools*. New Delhi: Discovery Publishing House. ISBN 81-7141-687-X.

Ediger, Marlow and Digumarti Bhaskara Rao (2003). Teaching Science in Elementary Schools. New Delhi: Discovery Publishing House. ISBN 81-7141-698-5.

Ediger, Marlow and Digumarti Bhaskara Rao (2003). *School Curriculum and Administration*. New Delhi: Discovery Publishing House. ISBN 81-7141-709-4.

Ediger, Marlow and Digumarti Bhaskara Rao (2003). *Elementary Curriculum Improvement*. New Delhi: Discovery Publishing House. ISBN 81-7141-740-X.

Ediger, Marlow and Digumarti Bhaskara Rao (2004). *School Organisation*. New Delhi: Discovery Publishing House. ISBN 81-7141-843-0.

Ediger, Marlow and Digumarti Bhaskara Rao (2004). *Relevancy in Elementary Curriculum*. New Delhi: Discovery Publishing House. ISBN 81-7141-845-9.

Ediger, Marlow, B.S.V. Dutt and Digumarti Bhaskara Rao (2003). *Teaching English Successfully*. New Delhi: Discovery Publishing House. ISBN 81-7141-707-8.

Elizabeth, M.E.S., author and Digumarti Bhaskara Rao, editor (2004). *Methods of Teaching English*. New Delhi: Discovery Publishing House. ISBN 81-7141-809-0.

Harshitha, D. author and Digumarti Bhaskara Rao, editor (2004). *Methods of Teaching Information Technology*. New Delhi: Discovery Publishing House. ISBN 81-7141-805-8.

Indira Devi, author and J. Prasanth Kumar and Digumarti Bhaskara Rao, editors (2004). *Values in Language Text Books*. New Delhi: APH Publishing Corporation. ISBN 81-7141-833-3.

Jalaja Kumari, C., author and Digumarti Bhaskara Rao, editor (2004). *Methods of Teaching Educational Technology*. New Delhi: Discovery Publishing House. ISBN 81-7141-810-4.

Jayasree, Kandi, author and Digumarti Bhaskara Rao, editor (1999). *Correlates of Socialisation*. New Delhi: Discovery Publishing House. ISBN 81-7141-517-2.

Jayasree, Kandi, author and Digumarti Bhaskara Rao, editor (2004). *Methods of Teaching Science*. New Delhi: Discovery Publishing House. ISBN 81-7141-801-5.

John Babu, Chikati, author and T.J.R. Prasad, G.M. Madhukar and Digumarti Bhaskara Rao, editors (1996). *Problem Solving in Mathematics*. New Delhi: APH Publishing Corporation. ISBN 81-7648-273-0.

Joseph Raju, B and G.A. Anitha, authors and Digumarti Bhaskara Rao, editor (2004). *Population Education*. New Delhi: Sonali Publications. ISBN 81-88836-31-3.

Lalitha, T., author and K.S. Prabhakaram, D.S.N. Sastry and Digumarti Bhaskara Rao, editors (2004). *Educational Philosophic Beliefs*. New Delhi: Discovery Publishing House. ISBN 81-7141-765-5.

Madhu Bala, Jampala, author and Digumarti Bhaskara Rao, editor (2004). *Adjustment Problems of Hearing Impaired*. New Delhi: Discovery Publishing House. ISBN 81-7141-831-7.

Madhu Bala, Jampala, author and Digumarti Bhaskara Rao, editor (2004). *Methods of Teaching Exceptional Children*. New Delhi: Discovery Publishing House. ISBN 81-7141-802-3.

Marja, Talvi and Digumarti Bhaskara Rao, editors (1996). *Educational Leadership and Social Changes*. New Delhi: Discovery Publishing House. ISBN 81-7141-320-X.

Nageswara Rao, S.and M. Srihari, authors and Digumarti Bhaskara Rao, editor (2004). *Guidance and Counselling*. New Delhi: Discovery Publishing House. ISBN 81-7141-840-6.

Nageswara Rao, S. and P. Sridhar, authors and Digumarti Bhaskara Rao, editor (2004). *Methods and Techniques of Teaching*. New Delhi: Sonali Publications. ISBN 81-88836-33-8.

Nirmala Jyothi, M., author and Digumarti Bhaskara Rao, editor (2003). *Non-detention System in School Education*. New Delhi: Discovery Publishing House. ISBN 81-7141-654-3.

Padma Tulasi, G., author and Digumarti Bhaskara Rao, editor (2004). *Methods of Teaching Elementary Science*. New Delhi: Discovery Publishing House. ISBN 81-7141-871-6.

Pala Prasada Rao, V., author and K. Nirupa Rani and Digumarti Bhaskara Rao, editors (2004). *Methods of Teaching Elementary Science*. New Delhi: Discovery Publishing House. ISBN 81-7141-871-6.

Prabhakaram, K.S., author and Digumarti Bhaskara Rao, editors (1998). *Concept Attainment Model in Mathematics Teaching*. New Delhi: Discovery Publishing House. ISBN 81-7141-424-9.

Prasanth Kumar, J., author and Digumarti Bhaskara Rao, editor (1998). *Effectiveness of Distance Education System*. New Delhi: Discovery Publishing House. ISBN 81-7141-437-0.

Prasanth Kumar, J., author and Digumarti Bhaskara Rao, editor (2004). *Methods of Teaching Civics*. New Delhi: Discovery Publishing House. ISBN 81-7141-806-6.

Prasanth Kumar, J., author and G. Sundara Rao and Digumarti Bhaskara Rao, editors (2000). *Open University Student Support Services*. New Delhi: Discovery Publishing House. ISBN 81-7141-550-4.

Raja Kumari, M.A. and D.R.S. Sundari, authors and Digumarti Bhaskara Rao, editor (2004). *Special Education*. New Delhi: Discovery Publishing House. ISBN 81-7141-846-5.

Raja Kumari, M.A. and D.R.S. Sundari, authors and Digumarti Bhaskara Rao, editor (2004). *Methods of Teaching Educational Psychology*. New Delhi: Discovery Publishing House. ISBN 81-7141-820-1.

Ramatulasamma, K., author and Digumarti Bhaskara Rao, editor (2002). *Job Satisfaction of Teacher Educators*. New Delhi: Discovery Publishing House. ISBN 81-7141-655-1.

Rama Krishnaiah, D., author and Digumarti Bhaskara Rao, editor (1998). *Job Satisfaction of College Teachers*. New Delhi: Discovery Publishing House. ISBN 81-7141-438-9.

Rama Kumar Ratnam, M.V., author and Digumarti Bhaskara Rao, editor (1998). *Dukkha: Suffering in Early Buddhism*. New Delhi: Discovery Publishing House. ISBN 81-7141-653-5.

Rama Krishna Prasad and P. Vide Sagar, authors and Digumarti Bhaskara Rao, editor (2004). *Methods of Teaching Physical Education*. New Delhi: Discovery Publishing House. ISBN 81-7141-868-6.

Rama Seshaiah, P. author and Digumarti Bhaskara Rao, editor (2004). *Methods of Teaching Home Science*. New Delhi: Discovery Publishing House. ISBN 81-7141-916-X.

Ramesh, Ganta and Digumarti Bhaskara Rao, editors (1998). *Environmental Education: Problems and Prospects*. New Delhi: Discovery Publishing House. ISBN 81-7141-423-0.

Ranga Rao, R., author and Digumarti Bhaskara Rao, editor (2004). *Methods of Teacher Teaching*. New Delhi: Discovery Publishing House. ISBN 81-7141-812-0.

Rathaiah, Lavu and Digumarti Bhaskara Rao, editors (1996), *International Innovations in Education*. New Delhi: Discovery Publishing House. ISBN 81-7141-359-5.

Rathaiah, Lavu and Digumarti Bhaskara Rao (1997). *Achievement Correlates*. New Delhi: Discovery Publishing House. ISBN 81-7141-385-4.

Ravi Krishna, M., author and Digumarti Bhaskara Rao, editor (2004). *Examination System*. New Delhi: Discovery Publishing House. ISBN 81-7141-824-4.

Ravi Kumar, M., author and Digumarti Bhaskara Rao, editor (2004). *Methods of Teaching Computer Science*. New Delhi: Discovery Publishing House. ISBN 81-7141-823-6.

Reddy, Sudhakar Y., author and Digumarti Bhaskara Rao, editor (2003). *Creativity in Adolescents*. New Delhi: Discovery Publishing House. ISBN 81-7141-659-4.

Reddy, M. S., author and Digumarti Bhaskara Rao, editor (2004). *Creativity in College Students*. New Delhi: Discovery Publishing House. ISBN 81-7141-697-7.

Rudramamba, B., author and Digumarti Bhaskara Rao, editor (2003). *Problems of Teaching*. New Delhi: APH Publishing Corporation. ISBN 81-7648-462-8.

Rudramamba, B. and V. Lakshmi Kumari, authors and Digumarti Bhaskara Rao, editor (2004). *Methods of Teaching Economics*. New Delhi: Discovery Publishing House. ISBN 81-7141-900-3.

Sanjeeva Rao, P.C., author and Digumarti Bhaskara Rao, editor (1996). *A Text Book of Geology*. New Delhi: Discovery Publishing House. ISBN 81-7141-313-7.

Satya Narayana, V., author and Digumarti Bhaskara Rao, editor (2001). *Physical Education, Social Attitudes and Leadership Qualities*. New Delhi: Discovery Publishing House. ISBN 81-7141-593-8.

Satya Narayana, P.V.V. and G. Krishna, authors and Digumarti Bhaskara Rao, editor (2004). *Curriculum Development and Management*. New Delhi: Discovery Publishing House. ISBN 81-7141-813-9.

Siva Lakshmi, G.V. and G.L. Subbaiah, authors and Digumarti Bhaskara Rao, editor (2004). *Methods of Teaching Environmental Science*. New Delhi: Discovery Publishing House. ISBN 81-7141-839-2.

Srinivas, M. and I. Prasada Rao, authors and Digumarti Bhaskara Rao, editor (2004). *Methods of Teaching History*. New Delhi: Discovery Publishing House. ISBN 81-7141-803-1.

Srinivasulu Reddy, M. and K.R.S. Sambasiva Rao, authors and Digumarti Bhaskara Rao, editor (1999). *A Text Book of Aquaculture*. New Delhi: Discovery Publishing House. ISBN 81-7141-482-6.

Srinivasa Rao, Mandalapu, author and Digumarti Bhaskara Rao, editor (2003). *Achievement Motivation and Achievement in Mathematics*. New Delhi: Discovery Publishing House. ISBN 81-7141-674-8.

Sunil Kumar, K. and K. Rama Krishana, authors and Digumarti Bhaskara Rao, editor (2004). *Methods of Teaching Chemistry*. New Delhi: Discovery Publishing House. ISBN 81-7141-913-5.

Sunita, E. and R. Sambasiva Rao, authors and Digumarti Bhaskara Rao, editor (2004). *Methods of Teaching Mathematics*. New Delhi: Discovery Publishing House. ISBN 81-7141-915-1.

Swarupa Rani, T. and J.R. Priyadarshini, authors and Digumarti Bhaskara Rao, editor (2004). *Educational Measurement and Evaluation*. New Delhi: Discovery Publishing House. ISBN 81-7141-859-7.

Vanaja, M., author and Digumarti Bhaskara Rao, editor (1999). *Inquiry Training Model*. New Delhi: Discovery Publishing House. ISBN 81-7141-515-6.

Vanaja, M., author and Digumarti Bhaskara Rao, editor (2004). *Methods of Teaching Physics*. New Delhi: Discovery Publishing House. ISBN 81-7141-867-8.

Valeri V. Koustiouk, author and Digumarti Bhaskara Rao, editor (2002). *A Text Book of Cryogenics*. New Delhi: Discovery Publishing House. ISBN 81-7141-642-X.

Vamsi Krishana, V., author and Digumarti Bhaskara Rao, editor (2004). *School Psychology*. New Delhi: Discovery Publishing House. ISBN 81-7141-880-5.

Veena Kumari, Balusu and Digumarti Bhaskara Rao (1996). *Operation Black Board*. New Delhi: APH Publishing Corporation. ISBN 81-7024-711-X.

Veena Kumari, B. author and Digumarti Bhaskara Rao, editor (2004). *Methods of Teaching Social Studies*. New Delhi: Discovery Publishing House. ISBN 81-7141-899-6.

Veena Kumari, Balusu, author and Digumarti Bhaskara Rao, editor (2000). *Psycho-Social Correlates of Achievement*. New Delhi: Discovery Publishing House. ISBN 81-7141-547-4.

Venkata Rao, P. and Digumarti Bhaskara Rao (1989). *A Text Book of Zoology-Junior Intermediate*. Guntur: Vignan Publishers.

Venkata Rao, P. and Digumarti Bhaskara Rao (1989). *A Text Book of Zoology-Senior Intermediate*. Guntur: Vignan Publishers.

Venkateswara Reddy, L. and Lakshmi Narayana, M., authors and Digumarti Bhaskara Rao, editor (2004). *Methods of Teaching Rural Sociology*. New Delhi: Discovery Publishing House. ISBN 81-7141-811-2.

Venkateswara Rao, V., author and Digumarti Bhaskara Rao, editor (2004). *Problems of Education*. New Delhi: Discovery Publishing House. ISBN 81-7141-841-4.

Venkateswara Rao, V., V. Vijaya Lakshmi and V. Vamsi Krishna, authors and Digumarti Bhaskara Rao, editor (2004). *Education For All*. New Delhi: Sonali Publications. ISBN 81-88836-30-3.

Venkateswara Rao, V., V. Vijaya Lakshmi and V. Vamsi Krishna, authors and Digumarti Bhaskara Rao, editor (2004). *Education in India*. New Delhi: Sonali Publications. ISBN 81-88836-858-9.

Venkateswara Reddy, L. and Lakshmi Narayana, M., authors and Digumarti Bhaskara Rao, editor (2004). *Education for Dalits*. New Delhi: Discovery Publishing House. ISBN 81-7141-872-4.

Venkateswarlu, K. and S.J. Basha, authors and Digumarti Bhaskara Rao, editor (2004). *Methods of Teaching Commerce*. New Delhi: Discovery Publishing House. ISBN 81-7141-808-2.

Venugopala Rao, K., author and Digumarti Bhaskara Rao, editor (2000). *Teacher Morale in Secondary Schools*. New Delhi: Discovery Publishing House. ISBN 81-7141-551-2.

Vidya, C., author and Digumarti Bhaskara Rao, editor (1996). *A Text Book of Nutrition*. New Delhi: Discovery Publishing House. ISBN 81-7141-309-9.

Vijaya Bharathi, D., author and Digumarti Bhaskara Rao, editor (2000). *Educational Philosophies of Swami Vivekananda and John Dewey*. New Delhi: APH Publishing House. ISBN 81-7648-309-9.

Vijaya Lakshmi, D., author and Digumarti Bhaskara Rao, editor (2004) *Basic Education*. New Delhi: Discovery Publishing House. ISBN 81-7141-881-3.

Books in Telugu Language

Bhaskara Rao, Digumarti (1986). *Dhrushya Sravana Bodhanapakaranalu (Audio Visual Teaching Aids)*. Guntur: Nagarjuna Publishers.

Bhaskara Rao, Digumarti (1993). *Jeevasashtra Bodhana (Teaching of Biology)*. Guntur: Nagarjuna Publishers.

Bhaskara Rao, Digumarti (1995). *Vignanasasthra Bodhana (Teaching of science)* Guntur: Nagarjuna Publishers.

Bhaskara Rao, Digumarti (1997). *Vidya Manovignana Seshtram (Educational Psychology)*. Guntur: Creative Press.

Bhaskara Rao, Digumarti (1998). *DSC Study Material*. Guntur: Nagarjuna Publishers.

Bhaskara Rao, Digumarti (1998). *Upadhyayudu Vidya. (Teacher and Education)* Guntur: Nagarjuna Publishers.

Bhaskara Rao, Digumarti (1998). *Vidya Drukpadalu (Perspectives of Education)*. Guntur: Nagarjuna Publishers.

Bhaskara Rao, Digumarti (1999). *EdCET Teaching Aptitude*. Guntur: Nagarjuna Publishers.

Bhaskara Rao, Digumarti (2001). *Bharata Samajamulo Upadyayudu Vidya (Teacher and Education in Emerging Indian Society)*. Guntur: Sri Nagarjuna Publishers.

Bhaskara Rao, Digumarti (2001). *Bhoutika Sastra Bodhana Paddathulu (Methods of Teaching Physical Science)*. Guntur: Sri Nagarjuna Publishers.

Bhaskara Rao, Digumarti (2001). *Jeeva Sastra Bodhana Padhathulu (Methods of Teaching Biology)*. Guntur: Sri Nagarjuna Publishers.

Bhaskara Rao, Digumarti (2001). *Vidya Manovignana Sastram (Educational Psychology)*. Guntur: Sri Nagarjuna Publishers.

Bhaskara Rao, Digumarti (2003). *Patasala Yajamanyam/Paripalana (School Management and Administration)*. Guntur: Sri Nagarjuna Publishers.

Gopala Krishna, G., A. Ramkrishna, K. Subba Rao and Bhaskara Rao, Digumarti (2004). *Jeevasashtra Bodhana Padhatulu (Methods of Teaching of Biological science)*. Guntur: Sri Nagarjuna Publishers.

Krishna Murthy, V., K.S. Sudheer Reddy and Digumarti Bhaskara Rao (2004). *Vidya Manovignana Sastra Adharalu (Foundations of Educational Psychology)*. Guntur: Sri Nagarjuna Publishers.

Lalini, V., V. Dayakara Reddy, M. Srihari and Digumarti Bhaskara Rao (2004). *Vidya Adharalu (Foundations of Education)*. Guntur: Sri Nagarjuna Publishers.

Subba Rao, K.P., P. Ayodhya and Digumarti Bhaskara Rao (2004). *Patasala Yajamanyam-Vidhya Vyavasthalu (School Management and Systems of Education)*. Guntur: Sri Nagarjuna Publishers.

Sudhakar, V., B. Ravindra Babu, D.S. Kumar and Digumarti Bhaskara Rao (2004). *Vidya Sanketika Sastram-Computer Vidya (Educational Technology and Computer Education)*. Guntur: Sri Nagarjuna Publishers.

Index

A

Abstract materials, 271
Achieve vital understandings, 1
Active engagement, 262
Activity movement, 97
Adequate recognition, 122
– yearly progress (AYP), 31
Adler, Dr. Mortimer, 48, 104
Administrator as an instructional leader, 1-7
  absences, 5
  absenteeism, 5
  administrators, 5
  drug abuse problems, 6
  high absentee rate, 4
  issues in instructional leadership, 1-3
  pregnant teenagers, 6
    girls, 5
  problems in teaching-learning situations, 4
  role of an instructional leader, 3-4
  tardiness, 5
Administrators, 1, 176
Adult education, 226
Advanced organisers, 119
Advocates of programmed learning, 231
Affective, 137
American National Reading Panel (NRP), 129
American society, 220
Analysing the goals of the national reading panel, 129
  attitudes towards reading, 133-134
  comprehension in reading, 132
  fluency in reading, 131
  phonemics in reading, 129-130
  phonics in reading instruction, 130
  quality reading, 131
  vocabulary development, 131
Analysis of teacher education online, 260-268
  advantages and disadvantages of online programmes, 260-264
  cost and convenience, 265
  courses, 265
  field work, 265
  kinds of communication, 263
    human interactions, 263
  major problem, 265
  multiple intelligence theory, 267
  preferred style of learning, 261
Annual yearly progress (AYP), 25, 175
Arithmetic, 81
Artifacts, 223
Attitudes, 1
Audio-visual materials, 26

Ausuble, 261

B

Bachelor of Science in Education (BSE), 260
Bacon, Francis, 50
Bacon, Roger, 51
Balance among cognitive, 137
Basics in the curriculum and moral development of learners, 81-85
basics arena, 82
methods of emphasising moral development, 83
modelling, 84
rewarding, 84
telling approach to moral development, 83
traditional approach, 83
values clarification approaches, 83

C

California Test Personality (CTP), 100
Cause and effect thinking skills, 107
CDs, 18, 111, 212, 223, 237
Certain amount of healthy tension and anxiety, 263
Challenging all students in the social studies, 209-216
adequate, 211
behaviourism, 215
challenge in the social studies, 209-214
constructivism, 215
emphasis, 213
human relations, 211
idealism, 214
intelligences, 211
methods of teaching, 213
philosophy of instruction, 214-216
social studies, 211
student portfolio, 212
Charter schools, 249
Chavez, Caesar, 91
Child Garden of Verse, 114
Child Left. Behind (NCLB) Act of 2001, 25
Church, 219
Civil war, 116
Classics in curriculum development, 102
Classroom discussion, 92, 236
– management, 172
– teacher, 26
Clear cut answers, 252
Clements, Andrew, 87
Coalition of essential schools, 69
Collection of desired poems, 238
Colonial America, 116
Columbine High School in Littleton, 33
Competition can be healthy, 250
Completing job application forms, 81
Comprehension, 133, 138
Computer, 18
– assistance, 91
– services, 26
Concept in teaching, 122
– learning, 185
– of administration, 1
Construction and art projects, 93
Contemporary education, 103
Content in the curriculum, 40-45
certainty of content to be learned, 40
content and programmed learning, 42
– – the learner, 44
– – – structure of knowledge, 42

humanistic objectives in education, 41
problem solving in the curriculum, 43
structure of knowledge, 43
Contestoga wagon, 98
Context clues, 198
Continuum, 229
Convenience factor, 260
Cooperative learning, 244-253
competition in the school curriculum, 247-253
discuss healthy competition, 250
guidelines, 250
journal articles, 244
questions, 246, 252
seemingly a learning style, 245
voucher system, 247
Cost of constructing new school, 149
Creative reading, 133
– teaching, 185
– thinking, 93, 124
Criteria for learning style, 267
Criterion referenced tests (CRT), 78, 167
Critical thinking, 93
Curriculum
district wide determination of the curriculum, 29-30
federal level, 31
individual differences, 32
intelligences, 32
meaning theory, 32
method of teaching, 31-33
personal needs of the student, 33-34
sequential library books, 28
state level in affecting instructional endeavours, 30
student centred views, 28-29
teacher centred plans of instruction, 29
Curriculum changes and improvement, 46-55
abstract learning for students, 48
career ladders, 53, 54
change in education, 52-55
classical humanism and the renaissance, 47-48
– humanists, 48
curriculum for upper class, 48
– revision, 49
issues, 52
liberal arts curriculum, 48
middle ages, 46-47
non-vocational pursuits, 48
reality in experiences, 49
reforms, 53
research needs, 54
scientific thinking and the renaissance, 50-52
– thinking, 51
social humanism and the renaissance, 49-50
– humanism, 49
statewide testing, 53
Curriculum development, 1
– emphasises pupils attaining abstract, 274
– to the learner versus adjusting the learner to the curriculum, 74-77
adjusting the curriculum to the learner, 74
– – student to the curriculum, 76-77
recommendations to improve the curriculum, 4, 28-34, 38, 55, 75, 77-79, 94, 120, 151, 162, 216

D

Daily discussions, 168
– newspaper, 88
Decision-making, 254-259
career ladder plans, 258
creative thinking, 257
critical thinking, 257
dogmatic, 259
education classroom need, 256
existentialist educators, 259
federal level, 254
for teaching, 69
numerous problems, 255
questions need, 258
school system, 258
state level, 257-258
system-wide level, 258-259
Development of tests, 25
– psychology, 3
Dewey, John, 50
Diagnose reasons for poor listening, 155
Diary entries, 223
Diorama, 91
Discovery, 190
Diverse manifestations, 181
Dominant psychology of education, 181
Drawing conclusions, 108
Drop Everything and Read (DEAR), 29, 132
Dunn, 266
DVD players, 11, 18, 111, 212, 219, 223

E

Ediger, 266
Education for all handicapped pupils, 254
Educational Alternatives Incorporated (EAI), 249
– intellectualism, 103
– psychology, 120
Educators, 247
Elementary and Secondary Education Act (ESEA), 31
Elitist, 146
Emphasise multiple languages, 168
Encourage careful listening, 155
Encyclopaedia entries, 223
Engage, 160
Engaging activities, 170
Enthusiasm, 136
Essay test, 92
Essentialist, 97
Estimate, 163
Evaluation and the psychology of learning, 231-233
diverse schools, 233
principals, 231
pupil achievement, 232
supervisors, 231
teachers, 231
teaching-learning situation, 232
Existentialists, 2
Experience charts, 143
Experimentalism, 2

F

Facial expressions, 240
Films, 111
Filmstrips, 111
Flexibility, 145
Framework of problem solving, 188
Free enterprise system, 248
Friendly letters, 81
Froebel. Friedrich Wilhelm, 269, 271, 276

G

Gagne, Robert, 185
Gestalt psychologists, 60
Globe skills laboratory, 206
Glossary, 132
Goals of education, 69
Good tutors, 25
Green, Jan, 87
Grouping, 89
Guidelines for teaching science, 192-199
  animals, 194
  biology, 192
  chemistry, 192
  consideration for implementation, 199
  current events in science, 197
  democracy in the classroom, 193
  encourages curiosity in learning, 194
  hands on approaches in science teaching, 194-196
  inservice education for science teachers, 196-197
  making connections in the science curriculum. 192
  observations. 196
  reading for facts, 198
  reading in science, 197-199
  science unit, 195
  students in the science curriculum. 199
  word recognition techniques, 198

H

Harmonising university, 265
Hawthorne. Nathaniel. 101
Health curriculum. 122
Heath. D.C.. 50
High expectations. 190
History, 106
Homogeneous and heterogeneous grouping in reading instruction, 143-146
  basal reader, 144
  criticisms of homogeneous grouping, 146
  equality, 145
  flexible plans of grouping, 143
  grouping homogeneously by classrooms, 144-146
  instruction, 145
  research, 146
  talented/gifted pupils, 146
Hunter, Madeline, 67, 68
Hutchins, Robert Maynard, 104

I

Idealism, 2
Illustrations, 111
Implementation, 150
IMS, 75, 181, 257
Increasing high school reading comprehension, 105-111
  life in society, 110
  understanding indepth what has been read, 105-110
Increasing listening comprehension, 154-160
  additional factor, 158
  ample background information, 157
  critical listening, 159
  directions, 155
  factors for being a good listener, 158-160
  improving listening behaviour. 154-157
  learning, 155
  listener, 160
  listening activity. 156

powerful factor in learning, 156
questions, 157
research results, 158
students need, 159
teacher needs, 156
Individual Education Plan (IEP), 254
Induction receive adequate attention, in teaching learning situation, 184
Ingredient in a good reading programme, 131
Instructional management systems (IMS), 3, 68, 71
Instructor of adult education, 228
Integrate computers and technology, 173
Internet, 188, 237
Issues in organising the curriculum, 57-61
correlated curriculum, 58
fused curriculum, 59
integrated curriculum, 60
separate subjects curriculum, 57

J

Jamestown colony, 218
Journal writing, 91
Junior high school, 149

K

Katz, Karen, 87
Kentucky, 248
Kilpatrick, William Heard, 98
Kind of activity for kindergarten pupils, 270
Kindergarten curriculum, 277
Klingele, William E., 150
Knowledge, 60, 217

L

Language Arts Handbook, 114
Leadership, 152
Learners, 149
Learning activities, 207, 213
– styles model of teaching, 266
– styles theory, 157
Lesson on the chalkboard, 105
Lessons, 29, 245
Library books, 188, 223
Logical curriculum, 206
– thing needs, 163
– thought, 107
Longfellow, Henry Wadsworth, 101

M

Magnet schools, 249
Magnetism and electricity, 195
Major curriculum, 209
– debates, 255
– goals, 145
– reason, 144
Manipulative materials, 25
Maslow, 262
Massachusetts May colony, 218
Materials of instruction, 25
Mathematics curriculum, 170-178
maths objectives, 174
multimedia approaches, 173
objectives of instruction, 174-178
phonic clues, 174
pupils products, 176
syllabication, 174
use of context clues, 174
– – picture clues, 174
Meaning theory, 157
Measurement driven instruction (MDI), 36-37, 275
Medieval, 159
Merit pay, 248
Michael of Montaigne, 49
Middle school, 148-152
additional reasons, 148

issues in the middle school, 149-153
middle school programme, 150
Mitchell, Lori, 87
Monk, Isabell, 87
Montaigne youth, 49
Motivation in reading, 139
Multiple intelligences theory, 199
Mural, 91
Musical, 211

N

National assessment of educational progress, 15
National Council for the Accreditation of Teacher Education (NCATE), 264
National Council Teachers of Mathematics (NCTM), 178
New Atlantis, 51
No Child Left Behind (NCLB), 31, 176
Law, 176, 187
Numerical results, 212

O

Objective, learning activities, and assessment, 15-19, 137
assessment procedures, 19
learning activities to achieve objectives, 17-18
state mandated objectives, 16
Occupations, 270
Old Order Amish, 88, 89
Online teacher education, 263
Oral communication activities, 116, 235
Organising the social studies curriculum, 205-208
logical social studies curriculum, 205-207
objectives, 207
psychological curriculum, 207
psychological social studies curriculum, 207-208

P

Parents, 4
Parks, Rosa, 87
Perceive purpose in reading, 122
Perceive purpose, 171
Philosophical conservatism, 103
Philosophy emphasises measurement driven instruction, 276
Philosophy of kindergarten education, 269-277
behaviourists, 275
comprehension skills, 274
definite materials, 270
history of kindergarten, 269-271
kinds of materials, 271
MDI believe, 275
open curriculum in kindergarten education, 271-273
additional stations for the kindergarten pupil, 272
drawing centre, 272
library book centre, 272
model centre, 272
role playing centre, 272
subject centred curriculum, 273-275
configuration clues, 273
context clues, 274
phonetic analysis, 273
picture clues, 273
syllabication, 273
Photocopied exercises, 274
Physical punishment, 269
Piaget. Jean. 3

Plan of curricular organisation, 57, 61
Plato, 102
Plethora of quality, 224
Plymouth Rock colony, 218
Poems, 114
Poham, James, 67, 68
Possess criteria for good listening, 160
Powerful factor in guiding students to achieve, 228
Predictions, 108
Principals, 7
Problem solving curriculum, 151
Problem solving, 93, 137, 185
Promoting oral communication experiences, 235-242
  choric reading, 238
  discussions in the classroom setting, 235-236
  informal debates, 241
  oral book reports, 236-237
  practicing debate, 242
  project methods of instruction, 236
  readers theater, 239-240
  reading poetry aloud, 237
  sharing of library books, 241
  story telling club, 240-241
  topics chosen, 242
Psychology in teaching mathematics, 180-186
  behaviourism in the mathematics curriculum, 180-182
  diagnosis in mathematics, 185-186
  humanism in the mathematics curriculum, 182-183
  objectives, 180
  psychology of education, 183
  realisation, 182
  sequential needs, 182
  structure of knowledge, 184
  teaching mathematics recommends, 183
Psychology of learning and adult education, 226-230
  adult learners, 227
  concepts, 227
  major means of ascertaining, 229
  precise objectives, 228
  psychology of instruction, 226-228
  specific psychologies of learning, 228-230
  teaching towards objectives, 228
Psychology of learning, 229, 232
Psychomotor level, 137, 138
Pupil achievement, 24, 177
Pupils with experience chart, 144

Q

Quality and quantity in the mathematics curriculum, 162-169
  affective objectives in mathematics, 164-165
  appraisal procedures in mathematics, 167-169
  cognitive objectives in mathematics, 162-164
  critical thinking, 163
  learning activities, 166
  – opportunities, 165
  – styles, 166
  motivation is a powerful factor, 166
  psychology of education, 166
  psychomotor objectives in mathematics, 165-166
  pupils, 166
  teacher needs, 166
  – observation, 167
  variety of appraisal procedures, 166

Quality deductive methods, 137
Quality in the multicultural curriculum
 excellence and equity, 86-93
 bodily/kinesthetic, 90
 book report, 91
 evaluation of achievement, 92
 intrapersonal, 90
 learning opportunities to achieve objectives, 87
 logical/mathematics, 90
 musical/rhythmical, 90
 port folio, 91
 verbal/linguistic, 90
 visual/space with art products, 90
Quality leadership, 2
Quality middle school, 149
Questions for discussion, 29

R

Read alouds for students, 112-117
 additional oral reading experiences, 117
 choral reading, 113
 formal dramatisations, 115
 oral book reports, 116
 reader theatre presentation, 113
 reading poetry aloud, 114
 round robin reading, 113
 singing activities, 116
Reading and recent educational philosophies, 94
 activity centred curricula, 97
 classics curriculum, 101
 essentials in the curriculum, 94
 feeling dimension in learning, 100
 grammar and writing, 95
 mathematics curriculum, 96
 measurement movement, 99
 oral communication, 95
 words, 95
Reading experiences, 87
Reading for a sequence of ideas, 106
Reading in health education, 119-128
 comprehension of subject matter, 123-128
 context clues, 123
 consonant, 123
 primary grade pupils, 123
 selected pupils, 123
 syllables, 123
 guidelines for teaching pupils, 121-122
 measurement and evaluation of pupil achievement, 127
 discussions, 127
 conferences, 127
 continuos teacher observation, 128
 essay tests, 127
 multiple choice tests, 127
 pupil written, 127
 problem solving, 125
 questions, 120
 reading to understand, 119
Reading level, 210
Reading programme, 28
Reading, 81, 110
Realism, 2
Recommendations for improving assessment procedures: written test, 24
Reconstruction time, 116
Reflective thinking, 125
Renaissance ara, 49
ROMs, 237
Rudeness, 8
Rule learning, 185

S

School administrator, 4, 7
School climate and learning, 8-14

additional harmful, 10
bullying, 12
classroom attitudes, 8
cowards, 10
egg the next person on persons, 10
evaluation to measures achievement, 12-14
materials of instruction, 11
negative behaviour, 9
problems inherent in democratic, 13
pupil lunch money, 9
put down, 10
school lunchroom, 12
stealing, 9
victim, 13
videos, 12
School curriculum, 51
– environment, 33
– professionals, 38
Science and social studies, 97
Science learning and the student, 187-191
attitudes, 188
criteria, 190
objective, 189
role of the science teacher, 189-191
science objectives and the learner, 187
Scientific, 211
Searson, 266
Self motivated student, 260
Semi-concrete, 271
Separate subjects, 58
Sequence of learning in the science curriculum, 201-204
Sequences and scope in the curriculum, 36-39
curriculum is teacher-student planning, 37
objective for learner attainment, 36
problem solving experience, 37
scope in the curriculum, 38
teaching strategy, 37
Shakespeare, William, 101
Sizer, 69
Skills, 1, 217
Skinner, B.F., 65, 68, 181
Slides, 111
Smith Mark Twain Elementary School in Brentwood, 14
Social studies curriculum, 208
Specific curriculum area, 61
SRA map, 206
Staff development of teachers, 3
State mandated objectives
administrators, 16
final set of objectives for reading, 16
teachers, 16
Statewide testing and the innovative mind, 20-27
African Americans, 2
average yearly progress (AYP), 21
characteristics of state mandated testing, 20-22
citizenship education, 24
community service, 23
drug abuse education, 23
fine art of music, 23
goals of instruction, 27
Hispanics, 21
innovations in the curriculum, 22
language students, 21
local efforts to improve the curriculum, 22
moral education, 23

multiage instruction, 22
multicultural instruction, 22
Native Americans, 21
ongoing experiences, 26
peer mediation, 23
perceive purpose in learning, 27
portfolio development, 22
quality criteria needed in instruction, 26
recommendations for improving assessment procedures, 24
social development, 23
Stevenson, Robert Louis, 114
Strengths, 171
Student achievement, 213
Student motivation in reading, 135-141
Students need develop breadth, 211
Subject curriculum, 58
Subject-centred versus an activity-centred curriculum, 62-64
activity-centred curriculum, 63
advantages, 62
synthesis of subject matter and action, 63
Successful reading, 139
Superintendents, 7
Sustained silent reading (SSR), 210
Syllabication, 198

T

Teacher aids, 25
Teacher education changes, 267
– self evaluation, 92
– student planning, 73, 76
– written tests, 224
Teachers emphasise structural ideas, 184
Teaching history in the classroom, 217-225
administered. 225
assessment of student achievement in history, 224-225
attitudes, 222
history emphasises, 216
immigrants, 218
knowledge objectives, 220
learning opportunities to achieve objectives, 223-224
mandated objectives, 221
methods of instruction, 223
philosophical beliefs, 219
selecting objectives in historical units of study, 220-222
semiconcrete, 223
subject matter objectives, 222
teacher of history needs, 224
technology, 219
Teaching versus an open ended approach, 65-73
Dewey, John and the curriculum, 71
Goodlad, John and curriculum development, 70
Herbart, Johann Friedrich and sequential steps in teaching, 68
hunter, Madeline and specific steps in teaching, 67
Poham, James and the use of behaviourally stated objectives, 66
Sizer, Theodore and curriculum development, 68
Skinner, B.F. and programmed learning, 65
Tyler, Ralph and curriculum development, 70
Teaching-learning situations, 2
Textbooks, 223, 237, 274
Thorndike, Edward Lee, 99

Tiedt, Iris M., 114
Torres, Leyla, 88
Trade books, 237
Traditional teacher education programmes, 262
Tried, 188
True, 188
Twain, Mark, 101

U

Unit titles, 221
Use of multimaterial approaches, 150
Use of phonics, 198
– – software, 91
Utilising the telephone directory, 81

V

Variety of activities, 90
– – evaluation devices, 190
Verbal intelligence, 172
Vermont school systems, 176
Video tapes, 111, 188, 237
Vygotsky research (1978), 261

W

Wanda Gag trade book, 113
Ways of assisting, 126
William, Chandler Bagley, 96
Word recognised, 124
Work books, 223, 274
World War I, 58, 59, 116
World War II, 59, 116
Writing, 81
Written books, 223
Wyeth, Sharon, 88